UNREPENTANT DAKOTA WOMAN

Unrepentant Dakota Woman

ANGELIQUE RENVILLE AND THE STRUGGLE FOR INDIGENOUS IDENTITY, 1845–1876

BY LINDA M. CLEMMONS

SOUTH DAKOTA HISTORICAL SOCIETY PRESS

Pierre

Library of Congress Cataloguing-in-Publication Data available upon request.

LCCN 2023941919 ISBN 9781941813485

Printed in the United States of America
Text and cover design by Richard Hendel

Cover: (front) Dakota doll, accession number 8447.33, Minnesota Historical Society; (back) Angelique Renville to Lucy Spooner, 8 June 1853, Stephen Riggs Papers, Box 3 folder 6, Courtesy Center for Western Studies, Augustana University, Sioux Falls, South Dakota.

The paper in this book meets the guidelines for permanence and durability of the Committee on Production Guidelines for Book Longevity of the Council on Library Resources.

Please visit our website at sdhspress.com

27 26 25 24 23 1 2 3 4 5 6

Contents

Angelique's World 1845–1876

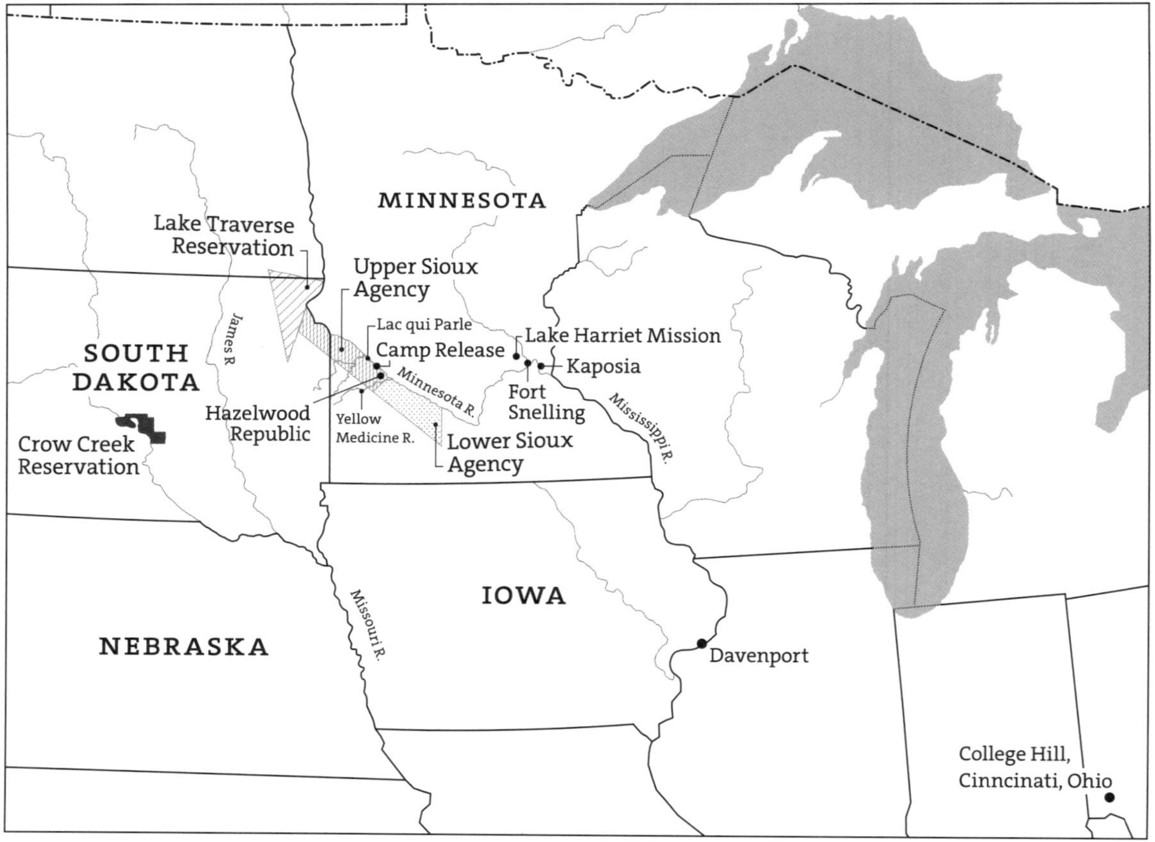

Selected Dakota Land Cessions, 1830–1858

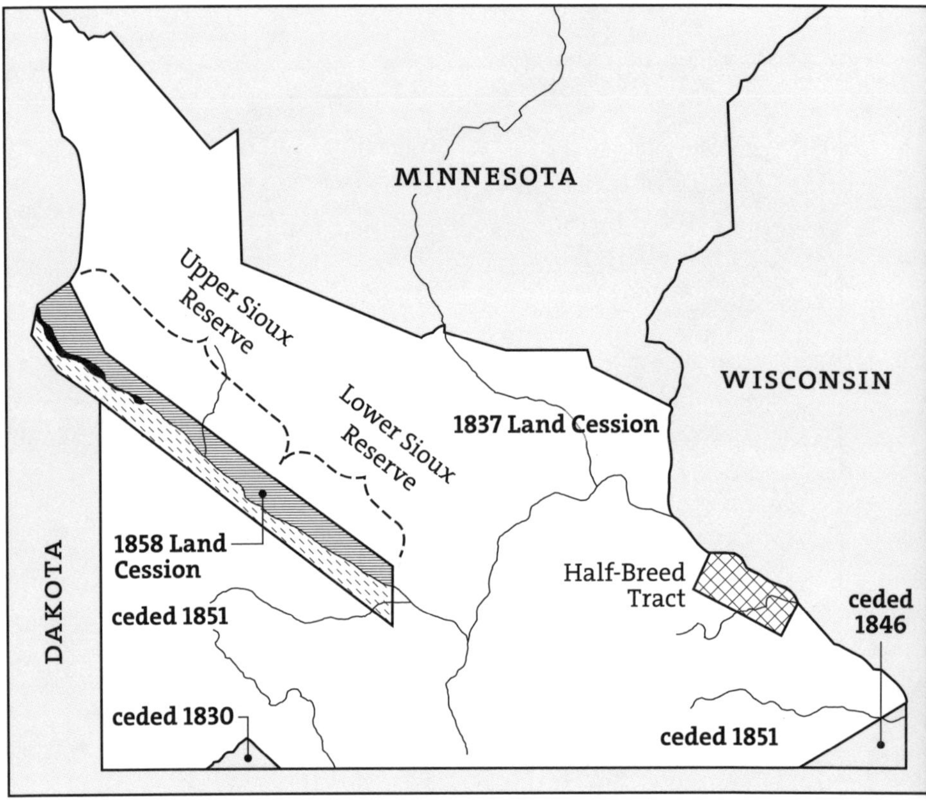

INTRODUCTION

Angelique E. Renville was born on 1 April 1845 in southwestern Minnesota and died of tuberculosis on 30 May 1876 on the newly created Lake Traverse Reservation, located in Dakota Territory (present day northeastern South Dakota and southeastern North Dakota).[1] Throughout her short life, Angelique navigated different cultural and religious frontiers. As a young girl, she resided with her Dakota relatives in various locations throughout Minnesota. From ages six to sixteen she lived with Stephen Riggs and his family, who were missionaries affiliated with the American Board of Commissioners for Foreign Missions (ABCFM), as their "adopted" daughter. At age sixteen, the missionaries sent her to Ohio for two years to attend a female seminary and then to work as an unpaid servant. After a brief return to Minnesota, she irrevocably broke ties with the Riggs family and settled in Dakota Territory with her Dakota husband and relatives. Despite the missionaries' best efforts to separate her from her family and Dakota heritage, Angelique remained close to her kin and culture throughout her life, especially her mother, sisters and brothers, and numerous other Renville cousins and Dakota relations.

While Angelique defined herself in relation to her extensive and close kin network, Stephen Riggs classified her entirely based on her acceptance of Christianity and "civilization." Riggs's changing use of her name over twenty years illustrates this singular focus. During Angelique's first years with his family, Riggs failed to state her name, age, or any other personally identifying information in his correspondence, even though she shared a classroom, workplace, and even a bedroom with his own wife and daughters.[2] Instead, his letters obliquely referenced a "half breed girl" who lived in his home. By not naming her, Riggs attempted to erase her family relations, Dakota identity, history, and language under the guise of saving her. Once Angelique joined the mission church, learned to read and write in English, and attended a female seminary in Ohio, however, Riggs publicized his adopted daughter's name and accomplishments at every opportunity. After Angelique chose to renounce the missionaries and move to Dakota Territory, Riggs's correspondence once again went silent about his one-time protégé as she reverted (in his mind) to "heathenism" and "savagery."

Of course, Angelique Renville was much more than just a reflection of the missionaries' priorities and a cautionary tale about the perils of "heathenism." Her story is important for what it reveals about the Dakotas, their conflicted relationship with Protestant missionaries, and especially one determined girl—and then woman—who lived through one of the most tumultuous times in Dakota history. At the time, according to archaeologist Janet Spector, missionaries, government officials, and settlers "wanted the Indians' furs, land, or cultural conversion, not their family histories."[3] Angelique and her Renville relatives are just a few among many Dakota people who deserve to have their stories told.

Angelique Renville's story, however, does not fall neatly into one linear, overarching narrative, nor does she speak to the experiences of all Dakotas or all Dakota women. Her mixed-ancestry heritage, as well as her extended and intimate interaction with Protestant missionaries, set her apart from many other, full-blood Dakota women. Likewise, her story does not fit the missionaries' didactic tale that began with so-called heathenism and savagery and ended with Christianity and domesticity. Instead, her biography had multiple twists and turns. At various points in her life she was strong, willful, and spirited, while at others she was compliant, deeply unhappy, and conflicted. The latter negative set of emotions directly related to many of her extensive interactions with ABCFM missionaries Stephen and Mary Riggs. Ultimately, Angelique Renville was a strong, independent, and unrepentant Dakota woman during a time when the land, culture, and religion of the Dakota Nation were under assault by missionaries, settlers, and United States Indian policy. She moved among different worlds in Minnesota, Ohio, and Dakota Territory, ultimately choosing her own path, family, and community, despite outside forces that attempted to choose for her. In this way, she illustrated the long-standing fluidity and flexibility of the Dakota Nation as a whole.[4]

Stephen Riggs and other ABCFM missionaries rarely focused on the stories of mixed-ancestry girls like Angelique Renville—or Dakota women in general—in their voluminous correspondence and writings. Even today, both popular and academic presses mainly publish biographies about American Indian men, overlooking the stories of Indigenous women. Author Elissa Washuta, a member of the Cowlitz Indian Tribe, scathingly criticizes popular American Indian biographies that mostly focus on "a dead chief from a plains nation . . . who suffered a violent death while at the peak of his power during a war that spanned at least two decades." In many of these biographies, "one Native American woman will appear. She won't be me. In the interest of historical accuracy, I'll call her a 'squaw.'"[5] As Washuta notes, popular biographies tend to focus on late nineteenth-century Plains warriors and leaders, to the neglect of most Native women, except perhaps Pocahontas or Sacagawea.[6] Folklorist Rayna Greene agrees, noting that most biographies show an "almost pathological attachment to Indian wars, horsemen of the Plains, and 'End of the Trail' chiefs, I suppose we should be grateful that anything at all has been written about Native American women."[7] Popular biographies, according to scholar Elizabeth Cook-Lynn, treat American Indian men and women as either heroes or villains, with Pocahontas, Sacagawea, Squanto, and Black Elk portrayed as exemplars of heroes, and Magua and Geronimo depicted as villains.[8]

In 1995, historian Nancy Shoemaker noted that schoolchildren could read biographies of Pocahontas or Sacagawea, but "pick up any [academic] book surveying American-Indian history . . . and there will be little mention of either specific [American Indian] women or of [Native] women in general."[9] Increasingly, however, academic presses are publishing biographies designed to address this imbalance. Recent biographies highlight the experiences of a diverse group of American Indians in terms of timeframe, geographic location, and social status.[10] While broadening their focus to include some prominent Native women, most academic biographies still primarily document the lives of American Indian men.[11] American Indian women who went about their daily lives raising children, harvesting and gathering food, and interacting with their kin remain largely unrecognized by biographers.

Likewise, historian Margaret Jacobs notes that much of the academic literature on western women "remains fixated on white women."[12] The story of the West, she explains, is often depicted as "a narrative of white women's trials and triumphs on 'the frontier.'"[13] Historian Antonia I. Castañeda also argues that "Euro-American individuals or groups, both male and female, remain the true subject of multicultural studies."[14] While the stories of white women are important to tell, they often exclude Native women. The stories of Native women of all classes, eras, and geographic regions help to contextualize and understand the dynamic nature of western encounters. Historian Catherine Denial contends that examining the accounts of Native women, who have often been "relegated to the fringes of the documentary record," allows historians to uncover a more intricate and complete story than popular histories tend to convey.[15]

Angelique Renville's story answers Denial's call to study American Indian women. Even though she never signed a treaty, participated in a battle, or held a prominent church or political position—or other Euro-American gendered notions of power—her life was important and had meaning for both Dakota and Minnesota society at the time. Moreover, her story is significant for students of history, as her life intersected with multiple historical issues related to Dakotas specifically, as well as American Indians in general, in the nineteenth century. Indeed, her experiences help to illuminate, as historian Clara Sue Kidwell notes, the facts about the historical climate and some of "the social, cultural, and historical forces that shape the lives of the individuals involved."[16] As such, Angelique Renville's life can help people understand historical events through a more inclusive and wider lens.[17]

Her story also provides insight into contrasting definitions of race and racial identity offered by government officials, Protestant missionaries, and Dakota families in nineteenth-century America. Prior to the nineteenth century, most Euro-American theorists followed Enlightenment thinking, which argued that American Indians were racially equal to Europeans. According to the "monogenetic theory," all peoples had the same origin and were fundamentally alike.[18] As one nineteenth-century Protestant missionary commented, "God has made all nations of one blood."[19]

This belief in inherent equality, however, did not include the idea that all societies were equal in the present day. Commentators argued that some peoples, including American Indians, had developed inferior cultures and religions over time. This belief led many people to see Indians as biologically equal but culturally and religiously inferior.[20] Two theories emerged as to why some cultures had supposedly degenerated over time. One theory held that a harsh environment and poor education had produced inferior cultures, while another argument described American Indians as representing a fallen society.[21] Even if tribes had declined over time, the monogenetic theory assumed that Indians could enter "civilized" society if they changed their environment, culture, and religion.[22]

The Enlightenment focus on the (potential) equality of American Indians sharply contrasted with the antebellum era's growing belief that some peoples were biologically inferior. Called polygenesis, this theory posited that different races had separate (and subordinate) biological origins. Thus, changing Indian culture would not allow them to fully participate in American society, as the problem was not environmental, but biological.[23] Because of the focus on biology, non-Natives (especially government officials in charge of Indian policy) increasingly defined "Indian-ness" by "blood" rather than by culture, religion, or kin relations. The idea that Indians could become "white" was replaced by the adage, "Once an Indian, always an Indian."[24]

Dakota families experienced both definitions of race placed on them by outsiders: government officials increasingly defined race as biologically immutable and divided Indians into categories based on blood, such as "full blood" and "half breed." Government officials expanded on these general terms by further categorizing individuals based on specific ratios of Dakota blood, written as fractions.[25] While ABCFM missionaries utilized the same racialized terminology as government officials, they generally adhered to older Enlightenment ideas that focused on "not race, but grace."[26] According to missionaries like Stephen and Mary Riggs, "blood" did not matter as much as culture, and especially not as much as religion. In other words, the missionaries offered vague promises of "equality," but only if American Indians renounced their cultural practices and religion.[27] Members of the Dakota Nation, however, frequently rejected outside definitions of race, instead adhering to a more flexible definition of membership in their communities, which focused on kinship and cultural identity.

Angelique Renville experienced each of these conflicting definitions of race: she was labeled as having "7/8 Dakota blood" on government lists, which made her a "mixed blood" by United States government standards. Although the missionaries also called her a "mixed blood" or "half breed," they hoped that through education she could become a "civilized" Christian, and—at least in theory—equal to themselves. Angelique herself, however, eventually rejected these assigned definitions of racial categorization, choosing her own identity not based on some arbitrary percentage of blood, but on cultural, religious, and especially kinship ties.

Angelique's story also provides insight into the conflicted relationship between American Indians and missionaries, especially their focus on educating young children. Decades before federal boarding schools, antebellum missionaries adopted—as the missionaries called it—Indian children into their families, hoping to Christianize and "civilize" them through education, church attendance, and work deemed appropriate for men or for women. Angelique's long interaction with the Riggs family illustrates the missionaries' intimate and controlling relationship with their adopted children. The missionaries attempted to regulate how she lived, spoke, dressed, studied, and worked. In the case of Angelique and her younger sister Agnes, Stephen Riggs even became their legal guardian. Historians including Margaret Jacobs, Katrina Jagodinsky, and Dawn Peterson have recently studied Indigenous children adopted into white families.[28] As Jacobs notes, historians generally encounter very few records of these adoptions; what they do find is almost always expressed entirely from the perspective of the white families who adopted the children.[29] Angelique's story adds to these groundbreaking works by providing a first-person account of a Dakota girl who was not only informally adopted into a mission family but who legally became their ward through the guardianship process. As Angelique's guardian, Stephen Riggs controlled her education, living arrangements, and most important, her land scrip, which he could legally use to promote her education and salvation. Despite a vast difference in power, both her mother Therese and ultimately Angelique herself challenged her adoption and guardianship in both subtle and open ways.

Angelique's experience also serves as a test case for the missionaries' assertion that American Indian children who had accepted "civilization" and Christianity could be fully integrated into American society. Angelique's story had a different ending. After spending years with the Riggs family, Angelique spoke fluent English, could read and write, had studied mathematics, geography, composition, singing, and all the domestic arts, and belonged to the mission church. In sum, she seemed to be the perfect success story for the missionaries to tout to the evangelical public. During her time at the Ohio Female College, however, Angelique's letters indicate that she lived in fear of her fellow students. At the same time, her missionary "sister," who attended the school with her, found acceptance as the president of her class and a star pupil. The only time Angelique received positive attention was when the other girls attempted to appropriate her "Indian stories" for their own writing assignments. She left the school after only a year. Historians have studied peer relations at Indian boarding schools, but what happened when Indian students had no friends? In Angelique's case, she was the only Indian in the school and was treated as an outsider and assumed to be incompetent and immature. In other words, she did not find acceptance in white society like the missionaries had promised.

Finally, Angelique's life cannot be separated from the momentous historical events she lived through, including the decline of the fur trade, a series of land cession treaties, the U.S.–Dakota War of 1862, and the Dakotas' exile from Minnesota. Angelique experienced many of these seminal events herself or had family members who did, including her sister Agnes who died while imprisoned at Fort Snelling in the months following the war. Throughout her short life, Angelique and her family experienced, as historian Margaret Jacobs commented, "the legacies of colonialism—trauma, pain, distrust, anger, denial, guilt."[30] However, as a member of a prominent mixed-ancestry family with members who rescued settlers during the 1862 U.S.–Dakota War and worked as scouts for the United States military after the war, Angelique's kin also would have angered other Dakotas, some of whom viewed them as traitors to their people.

While Angelique's life intersected with historical events and issues facing all Dakota families, it is important to stress that Angelique's story is not representative. As scholar Edward Valandra notes, biographies must challenge "the fallacious assumption that a particular Native autobiographic voice represents the whole of a Native nation (or nations)."[31] Angelique moved back and forth among different geographic and cultural frontiers. She embraced (or had thrust upon her) different identities throughout her life—that of a dutiful Dakota daughter, a quiet and submissive Christian girl, an unhappy student, and a Dakota wife and mother. At each point in her life, kin helped to ground and define her identity as a mixed-ancestry Dakota woman. These multiple identities did not always mesh seamlessly for either Angelique or the Dakota people in general, as both were increasingly pulled apart by missionaries, settlers, and government officials.

It was not an easy task to piece together all the different phases of Angelique's life; indeed, there are still gaps in her story. Traditionally, American Indian women like Angelique have been excluded from the written historical record. Euro-American observers did not think to write about Native women, and if they did, they frequently misrepresented their role in Native society. As Catherine Denial notes, most often Native women are "found only in documents created by men for quite different ends: trade narratives, wills, legal briefs, and military plans for imagined contingencies."[32] How, then, does one reconstruct the life of a person who left few, if any, documents? In response to this question, historian Annette Gordon-Reed argues, "Even an imperfect record can still be of some use."[33] The early years of Angelique's life (chapters 1 and 2) piece together her story, using an "imperfect record" consisting of mainly non-Native sources, including missionary correspondence, census records, newspaper articles, and government reports. These documents help to reconstruct her family's history and her daily routine with the missionaries but neglect to provide insight into Angelique's thoughts and feelings about her early years and education. Beginning in the 1860s, however, Angelique wrote letters in English to the missionaries, especially about her experience at the Ohio Female College, her time living with the Drake family in Ohio, her return to Minnesota, her relocation to Dakota Territory, and her fight for her land. These letters provide insight into her wide-ranging emotions about her schooling and her increasing tension with the missionaries. Transcripts of Angelique's remarkable letters appear in the appendix.

Although Angelique's letters provide a unique opportunity for historians to study the life of a Dakota woman, several issues made researching and writing about the Renville family challenging. Many of the written records do not use standardized spellings, including the surname "Renville." Multiple records (including land and census records and newspaper articles) use Rainville, Raineville, Reinville, Reineville, and Rinville, as well as numerous other permutations. Even Angelique's first name had several spellings, especially Angelic. Of course, the different spellings make finding information difficult; at times, I stumbled upon information that I would not have initially sought out due to an unconventional spelling. For consistency, I use the most common spelling, "Renville," unless appearing in a quotation. I also use "Angelique," as it is the way she generally signed her letters. Although it goes against standard editorial practice, I have chosen to not use *sic* to illustrate misspelling, brackets to add in words, or in any other way alter quotations from Angelique's letters. At a time when American Indian women's voices were often excluded from the written record, I wanted to make sure that Angelique spoke for herself, using her own words as she wrote them.

Another challenge arose over the names of multiple generations of the Renville family. Frequently, family members between and within generations shared the same English name. Most confusingly, multiple Renvilles were named Joseph, including Angelique's grandfather, father, and older brother. Her grandfather is identified in different sources by multiple names, including Joseph Sr., Joseph Jr., and Psincina, his Dakota name.[34] Her father is variously referred to as Joseph Jr., Joseph III, Joseph the Younger, Joseph Hrana, or just Hrana. For clarity, I use "Joseph Renville" or "Joseph Renville, Sr." when referencing her grandfather, and "Joseph Hrana Renville" or just "Joseph Hrana" when referencing her father.[35]

In addition to multiple "Josephs" across generations, Angelique also shared a name with her aunt (her father's sister), Angelique Winona Renville, who married Hypolite Dupuis—a prominent fur trader, justice of the peace, Dakota County's first treasurer, and manager of Henry Sibley's store. Through her ties to Dupuis, Angelique's aunt played a prominent role in Minnesota society. Thus, there are many more references to her aunt's life story; simply googling "Angelique Renville" can lead researchers down many paths, including erroneous ones. To make matters even more complicated, the missionaries frequently renamed Dakota students with monikers such as Robert, Moses, Mary, or Anna, sometimes in the process permanently erasing their Dakota names. Historians correctly stress the importance of using Dakota rather than English names in historical writing. Unfortunately, like many of the other Dakota students who boarded with the ABCFM missionaries, my research never revealed the Dakota names of Angelique, her mother, and most of her siblings.[36] As a result, I reluctantly used their English names, while at the same time acknowledging that this is an example of the pervasive influence of colonialism on the written historical record. Finally, I once again went against academic standards by referring to Angelique by her first name throughout the book instead of by her last name. This helps with clarity as I frequently discuss dozens of her Renville relatives throughout the book. More important, I also chose to use her first name to indicate the intimate nature of my rendition of her story.

Reconstructing Angelique's genealogical history using written documents also proved to be difficult and frustrating at times. Angelique's father, Joseph Hrana, was involved in several polygamous marriages. This made it challenging to sort out Angelique's family relations, especially her siblings and half-siblings. Census records, for example, replicated Euro-American marriage patterns, listing only one wife and set of children. This means that government records frequently excluded second or third wives and their children. Joseph Hrana also may have misled the missionaries and census workers about his wives and children due to the missionaries' condemnation of polygamy. Ultimately, however, Angelique probably did not perceive her family relations in this binary way; instead, she would have viewed all her siblings and half-siblings as her kin, regardless of "blood" and government census records. I have attempted to reconstruct Angelique's family history using flawed and deficient records, which means that her genealogy is inevitably incomplete.

Finally, I was, regrettably, unable to find an existing photograph of Angelique. I was briefly excited when Lucy Spooner Drake, with whom Angelique boarded in Ohio, mentioned in a letter that Angelique had sat for a portrait. Unfortunately, I was never able to track down this image; perhaps it is sitting in an archive or family home somewhere, or maybe it was simply lost over the last hundred-fifty-plus years. The only brief description I could find of Angelique was written by the missionary Martha Riggs, who described Angelique as a "dark-faced girl." Of course, this racialized description cannot be taken (literally) at face value. Martha was irate at Angelique at the time, and this comment may have been designed to chastise her for renouncing "civilization" and white society to side with the "uncivilized" and "dark" Indians.[37]

Despite the problems inherent in researching a nineteenth-century Dakota woman, I was able to piece together information covering the four main periods of Angelique's life—her early childhood, her time as an adopted missionary daughter, her two years in Ohio, and her marriage and relocation to Dakota Territory. Chapter 1 (1800–1850s) sets the stage for Angelique's story, focusing on her prominent fur trade family and the social and historical context of the era. Angelique was born into a time of great change for all Dakotas. Her early life intersected with the decline of the fur trade in Minnesota, land cessions beginning in the 1830s, and the arrival of Protestant missionaries in 1835. Chapter 2 (1851–1861) focuses on her years with the Riggs family as their adopted daughter. The entire Riggs family worked to raise Angelique to become a "civilized" and Christian woman. This chapter also references other Dakota children who boarded with the ABCFM missionaries, as they had many of the same experiences as Angelique. Chapter 3 (1861–1862) describes her time in Ohio, where she attended the Ohio Female College. Chapter 4 (1862–1863) discusses her continued residence in Ohio with Lucy Spooner Drake, a former missionary teacher. While Angelique was in Ohio, the U.S.–Dakota War broke out in 1862, ultimately taking the life of her sister, Agnes, and prompting her return to Minnesota. Chapter 5 (1863–1876) covers Angelique's renouncement of the ABCFM missionaries, her marriage to Wakaninape (Charles Crawford), her relocation to the Lake Traverse Reservation, and her increasingly strained relationship with the ABCFM missionaries and her conflicted view of Christianity. Chapter 6 returns to the same period (1863–1876) and examines her legal battle with Stephen Riggs over ending her guardianship and the sale of Angelique's and Agnes's lands. Within this chronology, several themes transpire across multiple chapters, including the contested nature of race in the nineteenth century; Angelique's tension with the missionaries, especially their use of her Dakota land scrip; and Angelique's conflicted relationship with Euro-American cultural norms and Christianity.

In many ways, Angelique's life was tragic. She was separated from her parents at a very young age and raised by ABCFM missionaries. Her father died in 1846, and her closest sister, Agnes, in 1863. Angelique died at the age of thirty-one from tuberculosis. She also lived through tragic life-changing events, including war, exile, and a missionary education intent on destroying all vestiges of her Dakota culture, religion, and language. Throughout all these tragic events, however, Angelique's letters show her to be a strong woman who ultimately made her own decisions. She also retained strong ties with her kin—especially her mother Therese—despite the missionaries' efforts to separate her from her Dakota relatives. When condemned by the missionaries for those choices, she fought back and refused to step down. In the years before her death, she even hired a lawyer to fight against the illegal sale of her and her sister's land. In a society that stripped women—especially American Indian women—of their rights, Angelique used skills she learned from the missionaries to fight for justice for herself and her family. I hope I have honored Angelique Renville's remarkable story.

::: 1 :::

ANGELIQUE AND THE RENVILLE FAMILY

1800–1850s

On 1 April 1845, Angelique E. Renville was born, most likely at Mde Iyedan (Lac qui Parle), a Wahpeton Dakota settlement of three villages located in southeastern Minnesota, about 150 miles west of present-day Minneapolis and St. Paul.[1] The location showcases a green valley, prairie bluffs, forests, rivers, streams, and lakes.[2] The French named the location "Lac qui Parle," or the "Lake that Talks," apparently believing they had accurately translated the Dakota name. However, Dakotas likely referred to the area by the less poetic but more practical and accurate name, "Lake that Connects," which illustrated the importance of the region as a crossroads for traders and other travelers.[3] At the time of Angelique's birth, about five hundred to seven hundred people lived in three Lac qui Parle villages, including a multicultural mix of Dakota, mixed-ancestry Dakota, and a small group of zealous Protestant missionaries affiliated with the American Board of Commissioners for Foreign Missions (ABCFM).[4] Throughout the nineteenth century, Lac qui Parle served as a central stopping and congregation point for Dakota hunters, fur traders, government officials, explorers, and both Roman Catholic and Protestant missionaries. Indeed, ABCFM missionary Thomas Williamson emphasized the hospitality of the region. "All strangers traveling through the country," he reported, "were welcome to a resting place and the best food it contained."[5]

Angelique grew up surrounded by numerous Dakota kin in this multicultural region. Her parents were Joseph Hrana Renville (Mdewakanton; born in 1809) and Therese Armatender (Sisseton; born in 1820).[6] Her father was married to three or more Dakota women at various points in his life, as polygamy was a significant but not universal part of Dakota marriage patterns.[7] Joseph Hrana's marriages to several wives makes it difficult to determine the mother of some of his children, at least based on written Euro-American documents.[8] Evidence is fairly consistent that Joseph Hrana and Therese married in 1838 or 1839 and had at least five children: Daniel (born in 1838), Angelique (1845), Agnes (1847), Thomas (1850), and William (1855 or 1856; died 1857). Less clear are the mothers of Angelique's other half-brothers and half-sisters from her father's relationships with Marie Oslasiche, Alphonsine Belgarde, and likely other Dakota wives. These siblings include Joseph (1828), Louise (1839), David (1840), Rosalie (1841), Marie (1846), and Julia (1848). One other son is listed as having died in 1839 at Lac qui Parle; his name and birthdate were not recorded.

Two government documents—the "1855 Half-Breed Affidavit" and the 1857 Minnesota Census—illustrate the problems that arise when attempting to compile an accurate genealogy of Angelique's family from Euro-American written sources. Although only separated by two years, these two documents offer conflicting information. In the "1855 Half-Breed Affidavit," collected for land allotment purposes, Joseph Hrana swore that he had "seven children now living," two of whom (Joseph and Rosalie) were from his marriage to an unnamed "full-blood" Mdewakanton woman. He affirmed that his five other children—Daniel, Angelique, Agnes, Thomas, and William—lived with him instead of their mother, "Terresia," whom he called a "full-blood" Sisseton. Renville's 1855 affidavit did not mention any of his other wives or children.[9]

The 1857 Minnesota census recorded an entirely different family configuration. The census did not list his wife (or wives) and only included Angelique, Daniel, Agnes, and Thomas. William passed away in 1857, which would explain his absence.[10] The document neglected to mention any of his other children or wives.[11] To add another twist, Joseph Hrana passed away in 1856, one year before the census was recorded. Other census records are equally misleading. For example, Minnesota's 1850 census lists Marie as his wife; his children included Joseph Jr., Louise, Daniel, Maria, and Julia.[12]

It is likely that some of the 1855 and 1857 documents' errors and discrepancies occurred due to Euro-American biases and failure to understand Dakota cultural and kinship practices. While numerical data is generally seen as objective, the census records and other statistics have historically reflected Euro-American social, political, and cultural values.[13] For example, the two documents' erasure of some of Joseph's wives and children likely stemmed from the fact that Euro-Americans tended to view polygamous marriages as illegitimate. Most existing state or federal documents list only one wife; thus, it is probable that Euro-Americans selectively documented parts of Joseph's family based on who they determined to be his "legitimate" wife at the time. As a result, the documents selectively ignored his other marriages and children.

Moreover, the documents took the Euro-American nuclear family —defined as a father, a mother, and their children—as the norm and attempted to force Dakota family relations into this model. Dakotas viewed kinship differently. Historian Colette Hyman observes that most Dakotas viewed their extended families as more important than their nuclear families.[14] Missionary Samuel Pond further explained that many "who are called by us uncles and aunts, are called by them fathers and mothers; so that many who are cousins are brothers and sisters with them, and some whom we call nephews and nieces they call sons and daughters."[15] Thus, the rotating—and restricted—composition of Angelique's family listed on the documents did not take into account Dakota marriage or kinship practices, which defined a family in a more expansive way.[16] Because of their inaccuracies and Euro-centric focus, historian and activist Nick Estes calls the census records and other government documents "symbolic instruments of colonial rule."[17] Whether these omissions occurred intentionally or through cultural misunderstanding, their effect on the historical record is undeniable.

Even though the census data and other documents effectually erased some of Angelique's family members, she lived the first years of her life surrounded by her mother, siblings, and numerous Renville kin. Angelique's grandfather, Joseph (Psincinca) Renville (born in 1779), was the son of a French fur trader and a Dakota mother. He grew up both in his mother's Dakota community of Kaposia and in French-Canadian fur trade society, perhaps spending time in Canada during his youth.[18] Renville parlayed his fur trade experience into key positions with the Hudson's Bay Company, the Columbia

Fur Company, and finally the American Fur Company.[19] He also had ties to Britain, as he had been a translator and a British officer in the War of 1812. Following that conflict, he cultivated relations with United States explorers and military and government officials, especially Lawrence Taliaferro, Indian Agent in Minnesota Territory from 1820 to 1839.

By the mid-1820s, Joseph Renville established his base at Lac qui Parle, constructing a fort and stockade for his trading business with the American Fur Company.[20] He lived at Lac qui Parle with his wife Tokanne (Mary Little Crow), who grew up in the Dakota village of Kaposia. The couple raised their nine children (five boys and four girls) to be part of fur-trading society, but the siblings also interacted with Dakota kin networks around Lac qui Parle and other parts of southern Minnesota.[21] Although itinerant Catholic priests baptized the Renville children, they had little daily contact with Christianity until the 1830s and participated in Dakota religious ceremonies and cultural traditions.[22]

Like the Renville family, a substantial population of those with mixed ancestry (Dakota and Euro-American heritage) lived in Minnesota by the early nineteenth century. Historian Bruce White estimates that as late as 1850 only about 16 percent of the population was non-Indian, while people of Euro-Indian heritage accounted for somewhere between 37 and 57 percent of the total.[23] While the mixed-ancestry population had ties to Euro-American society, fur trade historian Nicole St-Onge argues that mixed-ancestry Dakotas never created a self-aware "imagined community" as did other Métis communities in Canada and further west on the Plains.[24] In Minnesota, mixed-ancestry men and women followed different cultural patterns: some adopted American or Canadian identities, while others lived with their maternal Dakota relatives.[25] Even if the children eventually integrated into Euro-American society, ethnohistorian Mary K. Whelan argues that the fur trade often incorporated Dakota cultural practices, relied on kin ties, and utilized traditional subsistence and travel patterns.[26] Thus, according to historian Jane Lamm Carrol, Lac qui Parle, like other Dakota trading villages at the time, was a "multifaceted society" where Dakota peoples moved among Indian, mixed-ancestry, and white communities depending on their circumstances.[27]

Like other Minnesota mixed-ancestry families, the cultural practices of the Renvilles tended to be flexible and frequently combined aspects of both Dakota and Euro-American customs. For example, historians often point to Joseph Renville's use of a *tiyotipi*, or "soldier's lodge," as an example of his syncretic cultural practices. According to ethnohistorian Catherine Price, Dakota communities used the tiyotipi to maintain control on communal hunts. Before the hunt, the village council appointed *akicita* (soldiers, warriors, or enforcers of decisions) to the tiyotipi. Once the hunt began, these soldiers had extensive authority to punish a person if, for example, he went ahead of the hunting party and frightened the game. When the hunt ended, the tiyotipi was disbanded.[28] In 1830, Joseph Renville organized a soldier's lodge at Lac qui Parle; the soldiers were called "Tokadantee," or "Prairie Dogs."[29] His tiyotipi consisted of about fifty "soldiers" with whom he "confided various trusts, and occasionally sent them to distant points to transact his business."[30] Thus, Renville adapted the tiyotipi by using it for the fur trade instead of traditional communal hunts and making it a permanent rather than intermittent group.[31]

The Renville family also participated in traditional Dakota subsistence practices, including buffalo hunts, which usually occurred in the late spring, early summer, and again in the late fall. The hunts were often large communal affairs that brought together Dakotas with Lakotas, Yanktons, and Yanktonais from regions further west.[32] In 1840, ABCFM missionary Jonas Pettijohn reported that the entire Renville family, including Angelique's father Joseph Hrana, left on a buffalo hunt; they "found buffalo within 20 miles of here [Lac qui Parle]." "Young Joseph" came back to Lac qui Parle, but then left again to join another hunt.[33] Likewise, in 1843, several Renville siblings again participated in a buffalo hunt. The hunt went well, but Joseph Hrana said some "things" against "Marpi Wicaxta's son in law" that created friction within the community.[34]

Like their male relatives, the female members of the Renville family also possessed fluid identities, often alternating between the fur trade and Dakota societies.[35] In both communities, Dakota women played important social, economic, and religious roles.[36] Dakota women gathered vegetables, fruit, and wild rice, preserved buffalo meat, and grew corn, beans, and squash. They also prepared animal skins and made clothing and tipis from hides. They procured wood and water, and they made, transported, and erected their family's tipi.[37] In addition to their prominent contributions to their community's subsistence, Dakota women were known for their skill in handicrafts.[38]

Alongside their traditional duties, Dakota and mixed-heritage women played key roles in the fur trade. They frequently served as mediators, cultural brokers, and even negotiators.[39] Historian Susan Sleeper-Smith notes that when men were away from their villages, Native women often acted as surrogates for their husbands by accepting articles in trade, judging the quality of furs, and distributing gifts.[40] Dakota women also produced, sold, and purchased goods at the trading posts.[41] For example, in 1851, some Dakota women living near Mendota (near present-day Minneapolis/St. Paul) made moccasins during the winter, which they sold at St. Paul and used the proceeds to purchase "various articles necessary for their comfort."[42]

Certainly, Angelique would have been part of the fur trade culture through her Renville relatives, though it is likely that she lived with her mother Therese and her Dakota relatives for the first six years of her life. ABCFM missionary Mary Riggs wrote that this living pattern was common for mixed-ancestry children. "Having Indian mothers," she explained, "their early training is in most respects like that of Indian children."[43] Historian Jane Lamm Carroll confirmed Riggs's statement, noting that Dakota mothers who married Euro-American men often raised their young children and integrated them into their extensive kin networks.[44] For example, Jane Lamont, the daughter of Hanyetukihnayewn and Daniel Lamont, a Scottish trader, resided with her mother and Dakota relatives until the age of ten.[45] Likewise, Mary, the daughter of Anpetu Inajinwin and Lawrence Taliaferro, the Dakotas' agent, lived her formative years with her mother, grandmother, and Dakota relatives.[46] Lucy Prescott, also a mixed-ancestry Dakota, grew up surrounded by her Dakota mother's relatives.[47] Daybreak Woman spent the first half of her life with her Dakota mother and the other with her British Canadian father.[48] Mary Faribault learned traditional Dakota skills, like working hides and decorating moccasins, from her mother.[49] Pelagie Faribault often lived with her eight children in a different Dakota village from her fur-trader husband, a common situation for fur-trade marriages.[50]

Because they often lived with their Dakota relatives during their formative years, mixed-ancestry children like Angelique grew up enmeshed in Dakota culture, religion, and especially kinship obligations. Even before they could speak, Dakota children began to learn kinship terms and responsibilities; these lessons continued through childhood and into adolescence. Ella Deloria, the famed Dakota ethnologist, explained the importance of kinship: "Dakota life, stripped of accessories, was quite simple: One must obey kinship rules. One must be a good relative."[51] In addition to kinship obligations, children like Angelique learned to respect their elders, and to act with generosity, patience, and modesty.[52]

As young children grew older, they also learned proper gender roles from their elders. According to Dakota physician and cultural authority Charles Eastman, Dakota boys "imitated their fathers and grandfathers to the minutest detail."[53] Likewise, the "grandmother, not the mother, was regarded as the natural protector of the young maiden."[54]

Dakota boys learned to be warriors and hunters.[55] Young Dakota girls like Angelique helped their female relatives take care of the corn, gather berries, fruits, and vegetables, make maple sugar, and process the meats and hides from the communal hunts, whether for the fur trade or for their own consumption.[56] Female relatives would also have taught her to make shoes, clothing, and shelter, and how to care for young children.[57] Angelique and her friends likely played with dolls and small tipis to reinforce the lessons of their grandmother, mother, and aunts.[58] In addition to learning Dakota kinship responsibilities and gender roles, Mary Riggs noted that "mixed blood" children joined in "the feasts and the amusements of the Indians."[59] Thus, during the first six years of her life, Angelique would have learned Dakota cultural and religious practices and gender roles from her grandmother, her mother Therese, and other female kin.

At the same time Therese was instructing her children, however, traditional Dakota subsistence patterns, and especially the fur trade, increasingly came under assault. The crisis stemmed from a sharp decrease in the number of fur-bearing animals for hunting. By the early 1800s, the main animal hunted for fur in southwestern Minnesota was the muskrat, which yielded only a dime per pelt. By comparison, beaver skins—which were no longer found around Lac qui Parle—earned three dollars per pelt.[60] Likewise, the valuable buffalo increasingly ranged to the west of Lac qui Parle. By 1838, even muskrats declined, which rendered Joseph Renville Sr.'s trade "unprofitable."[61] At this point, the fur trade shifted from Minnesota and the other Great Lakes regions to areas further west.[62] By 1842, the American Fur Company had declared bankruptcy; by 1847 it had ceased trading. The remaining fur companies in the region switched to lumbering, banking, general merchandising, and land speculation.[63]

Older traders like Joseph Renville Sr. especially had difficulty coping with these challenging new conditions. By the mid-1830s, Renville's fur trade suffered from low prices and declining furs; he estimated that he lost between three and four thousand dollars, which was equal to about half his capital, over the past several years.[64] In 1843, agents of the American Fur Company "admonished [Renville] severely for the deficiency of his returns for several years past." Despite this reprimand, the company continued to furnish him with credit, leaving him to owe $4,200.[65] After he passed away intestate in 1846, Renville's probate records noted that he owed creditors "a considerable amount" and his "estate consists principally of indebtedness."[66] Renville's economic tribulations were common; according to ABCFM missionary Thomas Williamson, the decline of the fur trade left "some hundred families without means of getting food or clothing."[67] The only existing letter from Angelique's father Joseph Hrana described some of these shortages. He informed Henry Sibley, a prominent Minnesota fur trader, "We have no lead nor tobacco at Traverse."[68]

Joseph Hrana sought various other opportunities as the fur trade declined. Fluent in Dakota, French, and English, he worked as a translator for various government officials, Protestant missionaries, and explorers. In 1837, eight years before Angelique was born, Joseph Hrana interpreted for Stephen Riggs on his tour of Dakota Territory to evaluate mission opportunities among the Lakotas. Riggs praised Joseph Hrana for being "acknowledged on all hands to be the best interpreter for the Sioux language and probably understands it better than any other language." Although Riggs commended Joseph Hrana for his language skills, he also worried that he was not "a pious man" because he had not converted to Christianity.[69] In 1838, Joseph Hrana, his wife (probably Therese), and several of his children served as interpreters and guides for Joseph N. Nicollet and John C. Frémont, who explored eastern Dakota Territory for the United States government.[70] Like Riggs, Nicollet also appreciated Joseph Hrana's language skills, and described him as "a firm looking man of decided character."[71] Nicollet gave Joseph Hrana a horse and a double-barreled gun for his services.[72]

After Joseph Hrana returned from his travels, he unsuccessfully attempted to find employment with various fur traders. Following the death of his father in 1846, Joseph Hrana approached Henry Sibley and Martin McLeod (another prominent Minnesota fur trader) about taking over his father's station at Lac qui Parle. Sibley did not think highly of Joseph Hrana and "told him very frankly that [he was] not fit . . . to be in charge of so important a station."[73] In 1848, Sibley changed his mind, hiring Joseph for "the protection of the Indian trade during the season."[74] In 1849, Sibley and McLeod decided to employ him as a trader, but quickly regretted their decision. McLeod chastised Joseph Hrana for failing to "exert" himself and warned that his behavior would not be tolerated. "Depend on it," he lectured, "if there has been extravagance or misconduct on your part, the matter will be scrutinized to your great disadvantage hereafter. . . . You must exert yourself, and lose no time in so doing." He demanded that Joseph Hrana procure "100 fall robes," or he would not receive "more goods from me."[75] Due to his troubles with Sibley and McLeod, Joseph lived a periphrastic life through the 1840s and 1850s, moving to various locations across Minnesota, such as Kaposia, Lac qui Parle, and Fort Ridgley.[76] In 1856, Joseph Hrana moved one final time to the Hazelwood Mission on the Upper Reserve to live near his relatives and children who resided there, but he became increasingly ill with pulmonary consumption (tuberculosis). On 8 February 1856, Angelique's father died at the age of forty-seven.[77]

In addition to the loss of her father and the declining fur trade, Angelique's early years coincided with land cessions and removal. Beginning in the early 1800s, the United States negotiated treaties to obtain Dakota lands. In 1830, United States agents arrived at Prairie du Chien, located in present-day Wisconsin, ostensibly to broker a peace agreement among the Dakota, Sauk, and Ho-Chunk nations.[78] Once negotiations began, however, U.S. agents argued that peace could not come without land cessions. The resulting Treaty of Prairie du Chien stated that the Mdewakanton, Wahpekute, and Sisseton

Dakotas would "cede and relinquish to the United States forever, a Tract of Country twenty miles in width, from the Mississippi to the Demoine River."[79]

The land cessions continued—and accelerated—with the Treaties of 1837 and 1851. According to the Treaty of 1837, the Dakotas ceded lands between St. Croix and the Mississippi River to the United States.[80] In 1851, government agents pushed through the Treaties of Traverse des Sioux and Mendota. According to these two treaties, the Dakota Nation relinquished all their lands in Minnesota. In return for their lands, the government promised to establish a permanent reservation on the Upper Minnesota "extending for ten miles on either side of the river and from the western end of the cession down to the Yellow Medicine River."[81] During the ratification process, however, the U.S. Senate struck the reservation clause out of both treaties. Instead, senators inserted a new amendment that gave the president the power to decide where the Dakotas lived and how long they could reside in those places. In other words, the Senate took away the promised reservation without providing other permanent lands in return. Over the next several years, Dakota families relocated to the newly created Upper and Lower Sioux Agencies on their impermanent reservation. However, sometime soon they would be required to move again to an undetermined location.

Further trouble arose from the so-called "Traders' Paper," which negotiators surreptitiously added to the 1851 Treaty of Traverse des Sioux. This document bound the Upper Dakotas to give a substantial portion of the funds from the sale of their lands to traders, dozens of mixed-bloods—including members of the Renville family—and several other interests.[82] The estate of the elder Joseph Renville especially benefitted from the Traders' Paper, receiving a claim of $30,000 in back payment for his trade debts. His sons Joseph Hrana and Antoine received a lesser (but still substantial) payment of $17,540 held in trust for their late father's estate.[83] Joseph Hrana received an individual payment of $250; two of his brothers received around $1,000 for themselves and their families.[84] After payments to the traders like the Renvilles, the Sissetons and Wahpetons received about seven cents an acre; the Dakotas collectively ended up receiving as little as a penny an acre for their Minnesota lands.[85] Historian Catherine Denial summarized the cumulative effect of the Treaties of 1830,

1837, and 1851 as having "signaled the beginning of the end for established patterns of living among the region's native and mixed-blood inhabitants."[86]

As witnessed by the Traders' Paper, some mixed-ancestry traders like the Renvilles benefitted financially from the 1851 Treaty of Traverse des Sioux. Other earlier treaties had established a separate land base for mixed-ancestry Dakotas.[87] For example, the Treaty of 1830 created a 320,000-acre "Half-Breed Tract" located west of Lake Pepin on the border between Minnesota and Wisconsin. The president would assign up to 640 acres of these reserved lands to each "half breed" Dakota, whose status would be confirmed by an as yet undeveloped tribal roll.[88] Although the treaty established a "Half-Breed Tract" in 1830, the U.S. government did not actually allot any acres until 1854, which meant that the Lake Pepin Reserve remained officially unsettled for over twenty years. Government inaction aside, many mixed-ancestry Dakota men and women did not want to live apart from their Dakota relatives by pressing their claims.[89]

In 1854, speculators and squatters demanded that the government open the "Half-Breed Tract" for settlement. Congress bowed to this pressure and finally decided to allot the reserve. Technically, this could not be accomplished by a treaty since Congress did not recognize mixed-ancestry people as either Indians or as representing an independent nation. Henry M. Rice, a Minnesota delegate to the Senate, found a way around this restriction by suggesting that paper deeds, called "half-breed scrip," be issued to mixed-ancestry Dakotas for the value of their land.[90] Rice's resulting act authorized the president to issue scrip certificates, granting to "half breeds or mixed bloods of the Dakota or Sioux nation of Indians" up to "640 acres on unoccupied, unsurveyed lands not reserved by the federal government in exchange for relinquishing all rights in the half breed tract."[91] In other words, in exchange for their acres, eligible Dakotas could use their scrip to locate on "other unoccupied lands belonging to the Government."[92] In 1855 and 1856 commissioners traveled to Minnesota to collect affidavits verifying the "blood quantum"—an arbitrary measurement of Indian "blood"—of those eligible for allotments, including mixed-bloods from the original 1830 list, as well as their descendants.[93]

In the spring of 1857, the scrip finally arrived in Minnesota and was distributed at Wabasha, Red Wing, and other places near the Lake Pepin tract. Dakota men, women, and children who appeared on the 1855–1856 "Roll of Sioux Mixed-Bloods" would receive scrip in exchange for their acres on the "Half-Breed Tract." Although sale of the scrip was supposedly prohibited, land speculators worked around the restriction by creating a two-tiered system of power of attorney, which allowed them to "legally" purchase the "half-breed" allotments.[94] After the power of attorney was instituted, a market for the valuable scrip certificates sprang up in St. Paul. Scrip certificates could be bought for fifty to seventy-five cents per acre and resold for a substantial profit.[95] According to historian William Millikan, by the onset of the U.S.–Dakota War in 1862, approximately half of the scrip had been purchased from the original Dakota recipients.[96]

Members of the Renville family figured prominently in the 1855–1856 "Roll of Sioux Mixed-Bloods," created by government agents to determine who would receive scrip. Like other written Dakota records of the time, the roll is filled with confusing and contradictory information. For example, the roll listed Joseph Hrana as "3/4 blood, Mdewakanton"; his children Daniel, Angelique, and Agnes are recorded as "7/8 blood, Mdewakanton/Sisseton." Angelique's brothers Thomas and William are listed as "7/8 Sisseton" even though they had the same parents, and thus shared the same "blood" and "band" as their siblings.[97] The rest of Joseph Hrana's children are excluded from the list even though they had the same father. Moreover, in an 1837 register of "Mixed-blood Sioux," Joseph Hrana was listed as "quarter blood"; in the 1855 rolls, his "blood" had been increased to "three-quarters Sioux."[98]

As seen through the case of Angelique, her father, and her siblings, the commissioners' methods of establishing "blood" by conducting interviews and tracing genealogy were hardly scientific and could (and did) lead to incongruent, confusing, contradictory results. As with other documents, the "Roll of Sioux Mixed-Bloods" was influenced by Euro-American notions of marriage and lineage, which counted some offspring but not others. Men involved in polygamous marriage, like Joseph Hrana, did not have their second or third wives recorded, which in turn excluded several of his children from receiving scrip. Moreover, while "blood" was supposed to be biologically determined and thus immutable, the designations could change from one survey to the next, as evidenced when Joseph Renville was listed as "quarter blood" and then "three quarters blood" on different documents, or when brothers and sisters with the same parents were designated as having different "blood quantums" and tribal affiliations. For these reasons—and others—scholars Pauline Turner Strong and Barrike Van Winkle call "blood quantum" lists, like the "Roll of Sioux Mixed-Bloods," a "tragic absurdity."[99]

More important, the categorization of families based on blood likely contradicted how the Renvilles viewed themselves. During the fur trade years, their identity had been relatively fluid (although not always without contention), with children and adults moving in between Dakota and Euro-American society. Historian Jameson Sweet notes that prior to the nineteenth century, there was not a fixed racial hierarchy in the upper Midwest.[100] Likewise, historian Pekka Hämäläinen states that identity was not defined by blood for Dakotas, but by words, deeds, and family relationships.[101] In sum, Dakotas did not calculate identity on the basis of hereditary traits but by kinship.[102] Beginning with the Treaty of 1830, however, the United States government attempted to separate mixed-ancestry Dakotas from other Dakotas through distributions of land and money.[103] In this way, treaties legally divided Dakota families by "race" as defined by "blood," rather than by kinship ties or cultural affiliation, as traditionally practiced by Dakota families.[104] Certainly, many mixed-ancestry Dakotas did not accept this biological definition and continued to define family and kin in a more expansive and fluid way, but "blood" increasingly became part of federal Indian policy and was linked to treaty funds and separate land allotments. Indeed, the "half-breed tract" attempted to "de-Indianize" mixed-ancestry families.[105]

Angelique was ten years old when government agents distributed "half breed scrip" based on blood quantum. Unfortunately, the agents did not record how Angelique defined her own identity and place within Dakota society; for government purposes, she became a name and a number on a list: "Angelique, 7/8 Sisseton Dakota." This number meant, however, that Angelique and several of her siblings could each receive up to 640 acres of scrip (she and her siblings ultimately received 480 acres each) in return for giving up all their claims to the Lake Pepin Reserve. Because of her young age, she probably had few opinions about the rolls or the hypothetical lands she might receive at some future date. Even if she was unaware of its ramifications at the time, however, her inclusion on this list swept her up into nineteenth century debates over "blood," racial identity, and land. At least in the estimation of the United States government, Angelique was defined by an arbitrary determination of "blood" rather than her relationships, which was in turn linked to land cessions.[106]

At the same time government agents negotiated land cessions, Dakotas faced a different set of challenges from Protestant missionaries. In 1835, ten years before Angelique's birth, Protestant missionaries affiliated with the ABCFM (Presbyterian and Congregational) arrived in Minnesota with the goal of converting all Dakotas to Christianity. While other churches also sent missionaries to Minnesota, including the Roman Catholic and Episcopalian churches, the ABCFM had the largest and most sustained interaction with the Dakotas prior to the 1860s. The ABCFM's board informed potential missionaries that the Dakota were "in perishing need of that gospel . . . and they must embrace it or be lost."[107] Over the years, numerous missionaries attempted to carry out the board's mandate to bring "spiritual salvation and the best elements of the white man's civilization" to the Dakota Nation.[108]

From its headquarters in Boston, the ABCFM sent Thomas Williamson, Jedediah Stevens, Alexander Huggins, and their families to Minnesota to proselytize to Dakota people. These missionaries joined Samuel and Gideon Pond, brothers who had arrived in Minnesota in 1834 and established a mission by Eatonville, near Lake Calhoun in present-day Minneapolis.[109] After consulting with Agent Taliaferro, the Stevens family established a mission near Lake Harriet, also in present-day Minneapolis, about seven miles northwest of Fort Snelling. Thomas Williamson and Alexander Huggins, joined two years later by Stephen Riggs, opened a station at Lac qui Parle, which remained active until 1854.

From the two original stations, the ABCFM's Dakota mission eventually expanded to include eleven different stations throughout southern Minnesota. Over the next twenty-eight years, the ABCFM established a semi-permanent station near Fort Snelling (1841–1843) and more permanent stations at Traverse des Sioux (1843–1853), St. Peter's (1844–1847), Kaposia (1846–1852), Prairieville (1846–1853),

Oak Grove (1843–1853), Red Wing (1848–1854), Pajutazee/Yellow Medicine (1852–1862), and New Hope/Hazelwood (1854–1862). During the first half of the nineteenth century, the ABCFM appointed over twenty-five missionaries devoted to converting all Dakotas to Christianity.[110] Some of the more prominent members of the Dakota mission included the Hopkins (1843), Adams (1848), Aiton (1848), and Hancock (1849) families.

While Euro-American missionaries rotated in and out of the Dakota mission, Joseph Renville Sr. and his extensive family remained consistently involved in the ABCFM's flagship Lac qui Parle mission. Renville encouraged the missionaries to open a station at Lac qui Parle, then provided them with temporary homes, a place for their school, and provisions.[111] Thomas Williamson praised the elder Renville for aiding the missionaries "on our way and after our arrival" at Lac qui Parle.[112] Moreover, Renville served as the missionaries' main interpreter and helped to translate the Bible and other religious texts into the Dakota language.

Renville's kin also were some of the main (and at times the only) members of the Lac qui Parle church. In 1836, soon after Thomas Williamson arrived at Lac qui Parle, he "received Mr. Rainville to the communion of the church, and . . . his wife and some of his children."[113] In 1837, he "baptized the wife of Mr. Renville's oldest son [Joseph Hrana]."[114] Joseph Hrana soon took the lead singing at the mission church services.[115] In 1839, Thomas Williamson worried that if Joseph Renville Sr. left the church, he would undoubtedly "take many of the members with him as the most of them are his relatives and under his immediate influence.[116] In 1840, Williamson again fretted that the Renville family might relocate from Lac qui Parle due to the decline of the fur trade. "[I]f that family goes," Williamson worried, "it is probably much the larger part of our members will go also as most of them are near of kin to Mr. R[enville]'s family."[117] These fears were well-founded; the missionaries lamented that the Lac qui Parle church lost over half of its members after Joseph Renville Sr. passed away in March 1846.[118]

The Renville family also filled the Lac qui Parle school.[119] In 1843, Thomas Williamson enlisted two of Joseph Renville's daughters to teach "such females as they could at their fathers house promising to pay them at the same rate as is customary in the States i.e. 200 per quarter for the average number of scholars."[120] In 1844, the Renville sisters taught three male and twelve female students; these students had a higher average attendance rate than students of the other two missionary ABCFM teachers.[121] Williamson praised the sisters for their "superior talents for the government of a school."[122] Samuel Pond summarized the importance of the Renvilles to their school. All their efforts "to establish schools among the Sioux have hitherto failed," he explained, "with the exception of the school at Lac qui Parle, which owes its existence in a great measure to the influence of Mr. Renville."[123]

While Joseph Renville Sr. and his family supported the mission in many ways, they did not let the missionaries control them, nor did they always do what the missionaries demanded. In the end, the missionaries needed the Renville family more than the Renvilles needed the missionaries. Thus, when the missionaries acted disrespectfully, the Renvilles pushed back. In 1837, Joseph Renville Sr. asked Thomas Williamson to admit some of his relatives to the Lac qui Parle church. After examining the potential converts, Williamson decided that he could not receive the trader's relatives "because they gave to us no satisfactory evidence of a change of heart." Renville did not agree. He sent a message to the missionaries, informing them, "I have prepared these persons for admission to the church and if you do not admit them they will never attend your meeting again. . . . If you can do without me I can do without you." He followed through with his threat and stayed away from the missionaries for several months.[124] Renville punished the missionaries by taking away what they wanted most, which, of course, was converts.

The Renvilles also chose to ignore many of the missionaries' strict rules for church membership. In theory, the missionaries preached that an acceptance of Christianity was all or nothing; Christianity was founded on the complete abolition of "heathenism." Stephen Riggs lectured congregants that with regard to church membership, "There can be no compromise."[125] Despite Riggs's inflexible rhetoric, the missionaries tended to overlook it when the Renvilles refused to follow some of their rules. For example, Thomas Williamson lamented that he could never convince Joseph Renville Sr. that "when travelling," God required him to "rest in his tent during the Sabbath."[126]

The missionaries also chose to look the other way (at least most the time) when the Renvilles practiced a syncretic religion that combined Dakota, Catholic, and Protestant beliefs and ceremonies. Perhaps the best example of their fusion of spiritual beliefs is found in Mary Riggs's description of the burial of Joseph Hrana's son in 1839. In deference to Dakota beliefs, the Renville family generously distributed his belongings to community members and buried the child with some of his possessions, including his cradleboard and bed. They also wrapped the child's body first in white, then in scarlet, then in a "broadcloth *Shrenah*, or blanket." Before they buried the child, they wailed over the boy, in accordance with Dakota tradition, a practice that the missionaries condemned as "injurious to [their] health." The missionaries believed that "death should be greeted with equanimity" and that mourners should not wail or express excessive emotions. Rather, they should "share images of the happiness of their loved one in heaven, repent of their own sins, and draw closer to God."[127]

The Renvilles integrated Christian traditions into the funeral by burying the child instead of placing his body on a scaffold in a tree as Dakota cultural practices dictated.[128] While the missionaries commended the Renvilles for burying the body, they complained about the presence of certain Roman Catholic rituals, such as placing candles around the coffin during the visitation, which Mary Riggs could only surmise "was to enlighten purgatory." Indeed, Riggs complained that Catholic ceremonies "seemed to me less natural than those of the Indians."[129] Technically, the use of Dakota and Catholic practices should have merited a suspension from the church. While the missionaries condemned the Renvilles' syncretic funeral practices in private, no records indicate that the missionaries suspended any of the Renvilles from the church following the funeral.

While the missionaries excused several practices that should have warranted dismissal from their church, they drew the line at admitting men to their fold who were involved in polygamous marriages. Polygamy topped their (long) list of forbidden activities. Stephen Riggs called polygamy a "moral malaria" that demanded "neutralization."[130] Some Dakota men practiced sororal polygamy, wherein a man married two (or more) sisters.[131] There was some dispute among the missionaries about the prevalence of polygamy among Dakotas.

Stephen Riggs wrote that polygamy in Dakota culture was "quite a common thing."[132] Samuel Pond, however, reported that polygamy was the exception rather than the rule among the Dakotas. He calculated that perhaps "no more than one-twentieth had more than one wife at a time."[133] Thomas Williamson estimated that over half of the men he had met had polygamous marriages.[134] Numbers aside, most of the missionaries believed that even one polygamous marriage was too many.[135] ABCFM missionary Moses Adams called polygamy a "licentious and vile sin" and asserted that the "social relations of the Dakotas are rotten to the core with this vice."[136] Riggs linked polygamy with a litany of other sins, including infanticide, wars, and fighting.[137] The missionaries met as a group and resolved "that we will not receive a man having at the same time two wives to the communion of the church." However, they would receive the wives of those men without encouraging divorce.[138] The missionaries held Dakota women to different standards, as they were called "slaves" to men and thus were not responsible for the "sins" of their husbands.[139]

Joseph Hrana Renville was affected by the missionaries' strict anti-polygamy policy, as he had more than one wife for most of his adulthood. Indeed, several of the missionary letters note that Joseph Renville's "oldest son [was] an excommunicated member" for his polygamous relationships.[140] Another letter described Joseph Hrana as "impenitent."[141] An article in the *Minnesota Weekly Times* explained that he was originally a member of the church at Lac qui Parle, but "by Repudiating his wife and taking his late companion, he forfeited his Christian standing."[142] At the same time, however, the missionaries accepted his wife (likely, wives) into the church, illustrating the gender divide in their policy toward polygamy.

Perhaps Joseph Hrana believed that he could appease the missionaries, who often employed him as a translator, by legally divorcing one of his wives through the Minnesota state legislature. In February 1852, an article in *The Minnesotian* noted that Martin McLeod, Joseph's former fur trade employer and a close associate of the ABCFM missionaries, "introduced a Bill [into the state legislature] to divorce Joseph [Hrana] Renville" and his wife Yah-ho-pee.[143] In March 1852, the legislature took up Renville's divorce bill. The *Minnesota Pioneer* explained, "at every session of our Legislature, applications are made by white men, to be divorced from Indian wives." Perhaps not realizing that Joseph Hrana was of mixed ancestry, the article stated that "one of these cases [was] the application of Mr. Reinville [*sic*] for a divorce from Yah-ho-pee." According to the *Minnesota Pioneer*, Joseph Hrana had allegedly taken another wife and had "repudiated Yah-ho-pee." Several legislators then scoffed at his application to divorce Yah-ho-pee, stating that if they granted his request, it would encourage Joseph Hrana to petition for more divorces "as often as he gets tired of new wives." One legislator sarcastically suggested "that the petitioner be invited to remove to Utah, where polygamy is a virtue."[144] Interestingly, the article noted that "a clerical gentleman from Boston" attended the session and observed the "Reinville" divorce case. While the "clerical gentleman's" name is not given, he likely was an ABCFM missionary, as the board was headquartered in Boston. Moreover, it is curious that Martin McLeod, who introduced the bill for Renville's divorce, was a long-time acquaintance of both the ABCFM missionaries and Joseph Hrana.[145] Perhaps the ABCFM missionaries had influenced Joseph to apply for this divorce. If the missionaries had orchestrated the case, they were sorely disappointed. The *Minnesota Pioneer* published the result a week later: "Divorce of Joseph [Hrana] Reinville Lost."[146]

While the ABCFM missionaries went to great lengths to end Joseph Hrana's polygamous marriages, they could not change his status as a "half-breed." Both the missionaries and government agents stereotyped mixed-ancestry Dakotas as lazy and immoral. Lawrence Taliaferro, the Dakotas' agent, warned Samuel Pond that the "Half breeds" had "indolent habits and aversion to light labours," although he noted that these negative qualities could be countered by "flattering their vanity" and offering "small rewards."[147] Stephen Riggs echoed Taliaferro, proclaiming, "of all classes of men none were so inconstant as half-breeds."[148] Riggs also complained that "As a class the Dakota half breeds are not over stocked with energy, and spend a good deal of time in smoking. Many of them are not trust worthy."[149] ABCFM missionary Robert Hopkins described a "half-breed man" as "covered with a variety of black crimes . . . without friends or character—without occupation, and a confirmed drunkard."[150] Moreover, many mixed-ancestry Dakotas also had some familiarity with

Catholicism, or even considered themselves to be Catholic, which made them "bigoted and unprincipled Papists" and led them to "engage heartily in the work of opposing Protestant missionaries."[151]

The missionaries also believed that all Dakotas—mixed and full-blood alike—were easily influenced and would learn only the worst of Euro-American culture from white men who violated the Sabbath, drank alcohol, and participated in "illegal" marriages with Native women. "Whites in this region entirely neglect the means of grace making the Lords day a day of amusement or worldly business," Thomas Williamson complained, "and this with their licentiousness has a very pernicious influence on all the Indians."[152] When Indians and mixed-bloods viewed this bad behavior, they supposedly could not help but adopt it as their own. The missionaries believed that interaction with "such a class of men . . . tends not a little to increase the aversion to labour which is natural to savages."[153]

The missionaries also claimed that the fur trade had an "adverse influence" on their proselytizing.[154] They grumbled that the traders "desired not to make them [the Dakotas] agriculturalists" so that the men could hunt furs. This potentially affected church membership, as hunting took members away from church meetings and schools for extended times.[155] Fur companies allegedly wanted to halt "the general diffusion of intelligence among the Indians [because] it would diminish the profits of the fur trade, and the civilization of the Indians would effectively ruin that trade." In sum, the "powerful influence of this Company is and long had been exerted, either directly or indirectly, in favor of ignorance, barbarism and idolatry, and in opposition to education, civilization and Christianity."[156]

At the same time the missionaries harshly critiqued mixed-ancestry men and women and the fur trade, they also realized that they relied on these same people—especially Joseph Renville Sr. and his extensive family—to support their missionary work. As dependents of sorts, while they freely called fur traders "dishonest rascales" who turned Indians against "a comfortable livelihood by labor" in their private letters to the board, they attempted to keep their opinions from becoming public knowledge.[157] Gideon Pond wrote a scathing review of fur traders in a letter to the board, but the missionaries endeavored not to make this information public. Pond wrote, "The paragraph however which relates to the Fur Company is not intended for public eye. It is my opinion, and it is also the unanimous opinion of this mission that it is inexpedient that the paragraph named be printed or in any way made public."[158]

The missionaries also attempted to keep negative information about Joseph Renville Sr. out of the mission press. In private, they called Renville "vain" and "unrepentant" and criticized his "domineering disposition." They also internally disparaged his mixed-ancestry heritage and his ties to the fur trade. However, they publicly refrained from offering him negative feedback of any kind. If they crossed Renville, he would undoubtedly be offended and break off "friendly intercourse" with the missionaries.[159] Thomas Williamson explicitly warned the ABCFM not to have "anything appear in print" that was "in the smallest degree calculated to hurt Mr. R[enville]'s character or feelings."[160] Despite their personal feelings about Renville, they acknowledged his importance to their mission by making him a ruling elder in their church. As his fur trade business declined, the board even reluctantly agreed to pay Renville $200 for his work supporting the ABCFM.[161]

Learning to navigate their relationship with the ABCFM missionaries was just one challenge that the Renville family faced in the mid-nineteenth century. During this era, the Renville family, and all Dakotas across Minnesota, confronted a time of great economic and social transformation. Indeed, when Angelique was born, the world around her was quickly changing. Of course, Dakota life had never been static; her relatives had always adeptly adjusted to changes, including the arrival of Europeans, the development of the fur trade, and the ascendancy of the United States following the Revolutionary War.[162] However, change accelerated in the 1830s–1850s with the decline of the fur trade, the negotiation of a series of treaties which seized Dakota lands, and the arrival of Euro-American missionaries and settlers. Each of these competing groups wanted something from the Dakota people, be it their trade, their lands, or their souls.

Angelique's family stood at the crossroads of these historical events. Indeed, her father, Joseph Hrana, illustrated many of these changes. He straddled Dakota, French, and then American society and culture. He spoke Dakota, French, and English fluently, often serving as a translator for fur traders, explorers, and ABCFM missionaries. At the same time, he hunted bison and married multiple wives. He was courted by the ABCFM missionaries but was excommunicated due to his marriage practices. Like many other Dakotas, he moved his family around Minnesota searching for opportunities following the decline of the fur trade and the arrival of Euro-American settlers seeking Dakota lands. The United States treaties officially put him, a "half-breed," and his family members at odds—at least on paper—with full-blood Dakotas over treaty monies and lands.

For the first decade of her life, Angelique appears sporadically in written records, mainly linked with references to her father and other male Renville relatives. Of course, this is an artifact of written records that prioritized the activities of men over women; indeed, Angelique's mother Therese does not appear in written accounts until the 1850s. Like many other mixed-ancestry Dakota girls at the time, it is likely that Angelique lived much of her first six years with her mother and Dakota kin, though she also interacted with the fur trade community at Lac qui Parle overseen by her Renville relatives and had at least some early contact with ABCFM missionaries. From Angelique's birth in 1845 until 1851, she moved fluidly between Dakota and fur trade society, as her parents, grandparents, and great-grandparents had done before her.

Angelique's world irrevocably changed in 1851 when she was adopted by the ABCFM missionaries Stephen and Mary Riggs. Angelique left the home of her mother and her other female Dakota kin and went to reside at the Lac qui Parle mission with the Riggs family. She attended the mission church and school and learned English, literacy, and Euro-American gender roles. During Angelique's years at the Lac qui Parle mission, the Riggs family attempted to erase her previous six years of Dakota education and kinship ties. They would remake her into a model "civilized" and Christian girl.

::: 2 :::

ADOPTION AND SCHOOLING

1851–1861

In 1847, Angelique's six-year-old sister Rosalie Renville was sent to live with the Pettijohn family at the Lac qui Parle mission.[1] She remained only a few months until an aunt took her away to live with her in Mendota. In 1851, when Angelique also was six, her parents sent her to live with Stephen Riggs, his wife Mary, and their six (later, eight) children in their Lac qui Parle home. Unlike her older sister who only stayed a short time, Angelique ended up remaining with the Riggs family for over a decade, leaving only to reside with another mission family for one winter before returning to the Riggses' home. She was with the Riggs family when a fire burned down their home in 1854 and moved with them to a new mission station called Hazelwood on the newly created upper reservation. In 1855, the Riggs family also adopted Angelique's sister Agnes; Thomas joined his sisters in 1859, although he lived in the recently constructed Hazelwood boarding school.[2]

It is not known exactly why their parents sent Rosalie, then Angelique, and later Agnes and Thomas to live with the missionaries of the American Board of Commissioners for Foreign Missions (ABCFM). In doing so, however, they followed a common pattern for other mixed-ancestry Dakota children: around the age of ten, mixed-ancestry children—especially girls—often were sent away from their Dakota mothers and kin. Lucy Prescott, for example, lived with her Dakota relatives until the age of nine when she was enrolled at the ABCFM mission's boarding school at Lake Harriet. Likewise, around the age of ten, Jane Lamont went to reside with the Pond family. Nancy McClure lived with her Dakota grandmother until the age of eleven when she moved in with the Williamson family. Julia

Ann Laframboise was eight when she left her Dakota family.[3] While historians have noted that it was common for mixed-ancestry girls to move away from their Dakota mothers and kin, written sources generally omit why their families made this choice.

Like other mixed-ancestry families, Therese and Joseph Hrana Renville did not leave records explaining why they sent several of their children to live with the ABCFM missionaries. There are several plausible explanations. Perhaps they sent their children to live with the Riggs family because of the Renvilles' longstanding ties with the ABCFM. Angelique's grandfather had welcomed the missionaries to Lac qui Parle and played an instrumental role in the mission's church and school. Angelique's father had been a member of the Lac qui Parle church prior to his excommunication for polygamy; several of his wives also moved in and out of the church, although it is unclear if Therese was ever a member of an ABCFM church. Joseph Hrana had also worked as an interpreter for the missionaries as they traveled across Dakota Territory. At the request of their father, Joseph Hrana and his numerous siblings had learned to read and write in the Dakota language from the missionaries.

The Renvilles also may have used the missionaries as a temporary way to deal with personal and economic struggles. By the mid-nineteenth century, many Dakota families struggled to feed and care for their children as economic conditions worsened across Minnesota. For example, in 1850, Joseph Laframboise, a mixed-ancestry Dakota trader, lost his daughter Madeline to illness; his little girl Julienne was also "dangerously ill."[4] In 1854, his son Alexis "fractured his right hand with a pistol, and there is so little of it left, that the Doctor concluded to cut it at the joint. He suffers much."[5] Perhaps Laframboise did not have the resources to pay for medical care, as Stephen Riggs recorded that Alexis came to live at the Lac qui Parle mission around 1854 just after his accident.[6] Over the next few years, Laframboise sent four of his other children (Julia, John, William, and Justine) to live with Riggs. Angelique and her sister Agnes's residence with the Riggs family coincided with Joseph Renville's decline from tuberculosis. Fur trade parents, like the Laframboises and Renvilles, may have used the missionaries to care for some of their children while they dealt with multiple challenges

Finally, it is also possible that Joseph Hrana and Therese wanted their children to learn English and literacy to help them navigate Minnesota's quickly changing society. Since the early 1830s, Joseph Hrana had learned from his father the importance of literacy and becoming familiar with American cultural practices.[7] Likewise, records indicate that other Dakota parents sent their children to the missionaries for secular rather than religious reasons. In a letter to the missionaries, a Dakota man named Wamdiokiye asked that Gideon Pond take his son in, as Wamdiokiye was "anxious to have [his son] learn English."[8] Henok also "left his little son . . . to learn the English language and make a White man of himself."[9] Joseph Hancock, an ABCFM teacher, lamented that Dakota parents "wanted us to . . . teach their children to *read* and *write,* and *that only*."[10] Another Dakota man made an "application" to the missionaries to teach his two sons "in reading and arithmetic."[11] A missionary education could help Dakota children adapt and survive as Minnesota became a United States territory and then a state.

While some Dakota parents might have valued secular education, the missionaries believed that "civilization" was merely a means to promote a Christian end. Thomas Williamson explained that "the object of missions to heathen such as the Dakotas is first to make them a [C]hristian and second[d]ly a civilized people. The full benefits of civilization have never been enjoyed by any people without the gospel."[12] In practice, however, the missionaries promoted both "civilization" and Christianity once the children resided in their homes. Thus, the missionaries inserted themselves into every aspect of the children's lives in hopes of entirely erasing their Dakota cultural and religious identities; the missionaries dressed the children, cut their hair, told them to speak only in English while in their homes, taught them to read and write, enforced Euro-American gender roles, and interwove Christianity into most aspects of their education and everyday lives. The entire Riggs family worked to change Angelique so that she "might make of herself a good, true woman, and be of great benefit to her people."[13]

In many ways, the Riggses seemed to achieve their objectives with Angelique—at least while she lived with them—as she quietly did what the missionaries asked and, most importantly, joined the mission church. The missionaries' control over Angelique and the other boarders, however, was not absolute. During her time with the Riggs family, Angelique lived near or with her siblings, her mother, and various Renville relatives. In other words, she had access to a vast kin support system, much like she had during her first six years living with her mother and other Dakota relatives. Moreover, the missionaries realized that concerned relatives could take the boarders away—as had happened with Angelique's sister Rosalie—which forced them to make some accommodations throughout the children's residence in their homes.

Although Dakota kin remained tied to their children, the missionaries' boarding program distanced children from their known societies, roles, and identities. Most of the literature that highlights the trauma of boarding programs focuses on boarding schools established in the late nineteenth and early twentieth centuries. Historian Brenda Child explains that these boarding programs "suppress[ed] Indian cultures . . . while opening the door to alienation from land and the extension of everyday Anglo-American culture into the lives and souls of Indian people."[14] Historian and Dakota activist Waziyatawin states that educational programs "brought tremendous harm to the fabric of Dakota social, political, and economic life."[15] These comments about the tragic results of boarding schools equally apply to the missionaries' adoption programs; indeed, the missionaries' home programs can be seen as a much smaller precursor to the federal boarding schools. Both programs attempted to strip Indian children of their culture, religion, and language. Alfred Riggs, the son of Stephen Riggs, explicitly linked the home programs of his youth with the later boarding schools. Beginning in 1870, Alfred opened the Santee Normal Training School in Santee, Nebraska, which educated "hundreds of children and grandchildren" that his father had "reluctantly turned away as beyond his power to reach."[16] Alfred applied what he had learned from his family's small adoption program on a much larger scale, and his boarding school would finally realize his father's dream of providing "Christian training" for all the Dakota children his mission home could not accommodate.

Stephen Riggs and the other ABCFM missionaries, however, did not know at the time that a large Dakota boarding school would only be realized decades later. The first-generation of ABCFM missionaries worked tirelessly to establish their own boarding school. Beginning in the 1830s when they arrived in Minnesota, each of the missionaries—especially Stephen Riggs and Thomas Williamson—wrote letters to the ABCFM pleading for funds to establish a boarding school.[17] The governing board in Boston, however, refused to subsidize a boarding school for what they called the "savage" and "unknown" Dakotas of Minnesota. The ABCFM categorized this mission as experimental and refused to invest large sums of money until the program had shown potential.[18] For close to two decades the Dakotas' missionaries repeatedly requested funding in their annual reports and letters; they finally received authorization to construct a boarding school in 1856.[19] Even then, the boarding school remained small, underfunded, and disappointing to the missionaries.

Although the board members repeatedly denied funds for a Dakota boarding school, they did subsidize small day schools, mainly staffed by a rotating group of young female missionaries. At these schools, students received instruction during the day but returned to their families in their villages at night.[20] The missionaries complained that these day schools were inadequate. The children continued to speak Dakota and to participate in religious ceremonies, and many left the schools for months at a time to take part in traditional Dakota subsistence patterns. Samuel Pond grumbled that "owing to the absence of the Indians on hunting expeditions, or in making sugar, gathering rice and c., there is a considerable portion of the year in which we are unable to maintain in school at all."[21] Finally, day students frequently moved to different villages with their families "where there are no schools," which meant that they would "voluntarily withdraw" from the missionaries' instruction.[22]

As a halfway solution between the ineffective day schools and an expensive boarding school, missionaries decided to adopt Indian boys and girls into their families. Mary Huggins explained that these "adoptions" were "not really legal." Rather, they were "intended to give [Indian children] a Christian education."[23] Most of the boarders still attended the day schools with the other Dakota children but remained in the missionaries' homes after classes ended. This meant that these children would not participate in the seasonal rounds that separated students from the mission for long periods of time. Instead, they would receive intensive instruction in the English language and Euro-American gender roles—especially the girls—after school hours in the missionaries' homes. Thus, the intimate spaces of missionary homes became, as historian Margaret Jacobs puts it, "small theaters of colonialism."[24]

Living with the missionaries created a confusing dynamic for the children. On the one hand, the missionaries referred to them using the language of familial relationships and sentimentality: the children were their beloved "adopted Indian sons and daughters."[25] Mary Riggs fondly called a little Dakota girl "our adopted Anna." In another letter, she wrote that she "truly adopted [Anna] to my heart."[26] The Huggins family adopted a "lovely half breed girl" and "really loved little George," their adopted Dakota son.[27] Jane Williamson "seemed to love her [Dakota daughter] as if she were her own."[28] Mary Riggs professed to be heartbroken when one of the boarders returned to her Dakota family. When the little girl's mother took her away, Riggs "took her hand and pressed the lips of the adopted. I could not avoid weeping at the thought of her returning to her heathen home and habits."[29] Stephen Riggs reported that he had always cared for Angelique "as my own child."[30]

On the other hand, although the missionaries spoke of fondness and love for their adopted Indian children, these relationships clearly differed from standard parent-child bonds. Most obviously, most of the children, including Angelique, already had one or both biological parents. The missionaries, however, thought that they were better parents than any Dakota mother or father, as they could raise the children "properly." Historian Dawn Peterson argues that missionaries believed that Euro-Americans needed to impart their "superior" family structure, child-rearing practices, and land use patterns to "inferior" American Indians.[31]

Thus, the missionaries believed it was their duty to step in and take over for Indian parents, especially mothers, who "improperly" raised their children.[32] They viewed adopting an Indian child as an "act of rescue."[33] The missionaries did not see anything wrong with severing ties between Dakota mothers and their children; indeed, they felt the Dakotas should be grateful for the intervention. The Riggs family frequently reminded Angelique that her time with them was a "privilege" and an "opportunity."[34] Missionary daughter Mary Huggins Kerlinger wrote in her memoir that taking Dakota children into their families was one of the "best works the missionaries did."[35]

While the missionaries called the Dakota boarders their sons and daughters, they actually were part of an organized program that cost money. The boarders needed to be fed, housed, clothed, and educated. Unlike the later boardings schools that received federal financial support, the missionaries relied on private funding to pay for the children's needs. As their first source of funding, the missionaries often asked fathers associated with the fur trade or the U.S. government to clothe and board their mixed-ancestry children. Alexander Huggins reported, "The fathers of the half breed children find their clothing, and one man has paid something even in advance for the boarding of his two children [and] two others have promised to pay when they get able."[36] The father of another "Indian girl" furnished her "with a few dollars' worth of clothing."[37] Although these payments helped, the missionaries complained that the contributions were not enough to defray the costs. Thomas Williamson noted, "We have in our family two children of mixed blood whose parents give us something for keeping them but I think not quite so much as it costs besides the extra labour which they cause us."[38] Robert Hopkins reported a similar financial shortfall, writing that while the father of "two little Catholic Half-Breeds" said that he would clothe his children, "we do not much expect he will give us much of anything for boarding them, indeed I doubt whether he will be able to clothe them."[39]

If the parents could not afford to pay a stipend or provide clothing, the missionaries accepted contributions from donors who agreed to sponsor a Dakota child. Samuel Pond noted that his family "had a half breed girl fourteen years of age living in our family for about eight months.... She has made good improvement in learning since she has been with us, and her behavior is good. The expense of her board for this year will be paid by a gentleman in St. Louis."[40] Other donors from across the Midwest and East Coast sent boxes of used clothing, shoes, fabric and sewing supplies, and religious books for the children. The missionaries eagerly awaited the arrival of these charity boxes. In 1854, Selah Treat, the secretary of the ABCFM, informed the missionaries that "Mrs. A. H. Davis, of Amherst, has sent to the Missionary House a small box of articles (with $3 to pay the freight) for you and yours."[41] In 1858, Thomas Williamson noted that "Our friends at Ironton Ohio ... sent us two valuable boxes of clothing."[42] Mary Riggs gratefully received charity boxes from Christian friends in New England, Ohio, Indiana, and Illinois.[43]

These donations, however, were intermittent. For years, the missionaries asked the ABCFM to pay a yearly stipend for each adopted Dakota child. Moses Adams complained about the board's failure to fund the Dakota children he took into his family. "What the Committee will allow us or whether any thing for the maintainance [*sic*] of the Girl we have adopted in our family," he wrote, "we do not know."[44] In 1849, Thomas Williamson finally convinced the ABCFM to pay thirty-five dollars a year for each child boarded within a family. While this money was a start, and the sum was later raised to forty and then fifty dollars per child, it was hardly enough to "feed and clothe an Indian child."[45] Thus, the missionaries needed to supplement the small yearly sum with "clothing in donations and some provisions if . . . we hope to be able to keep these children without asking for more . . . from the Board."[46]

In 1856, documents listed Joseph Hrana Renville as the guardian of both Angelique and her younger sister Agnes, which made him (in theory) responsible for defraying their expenses at the Riggses' home.[47] Like most Dakota fathers, however, no records indicate that Renville paid for his daughters' care. In February 1857, Stephen Riggs found a new source of funding. Less than three weeks after Joseph Hrana passed away, Riggs signaled his intent "to act as guardian to the two little girls of J. Renville living in my family."[48] Riggs wrote to Martin McLeod, asking "what is the process of being appointed guardian in this Territory? Is it done by the court or Judge? . . . I shall be obligated to you for information on this point."[49] Riggs learned that the county probate judge could appoint a guardian for a minor under the age of fourteen whose father was deceased and whose mother was unmarried and deemed "incompetent."[50] In the 1850s, guardianships lasted until the age of twenty-one or until the marriage of "any female under guardianship." In 1863, the statute was amended to terminate guardianship for males at the age of twenty-one, and females at the age of eighteen or upon their marriage.[51] Once appointed, guardians had the legal right to sell their ward's real estate or other parts of their estate to pay for their maintenance and education.[52]

Stephen Riggs decided to apply for the guardianship of both Renville girls, arguing that their mother Therese was "incompetent" to care for two (although, illogically, not all) of her children. He explained that because Dakota parents were incapable of raising their children or following laws, it "became our duty as a great Christian nation to act towards them the part of guardian . . . bringing them under the controlling influences of a Christian civilization."[53] Riggs applied this general theory specifically to Angelique and Agnes. In a legal document found within Agnes Renville's probate records, Riggs justified his guardianship by claiming that the girls' Dakota relatives (especially their mother) were "without means of support, or education and totally disqualified to discharge the general duties of civilized life—they being of Dacotah and French blood (mixed)."[54] Riggs's justification followed nineteenth-century legal precedent, which considered "Indianness" itself to be grounds for terminating the rights of Dakota parents.[55]

In March 1857, Stephen Riggs filed paperwork with the probate court of Brown County for the legal guardianship of Angelique (aged thirteen) and Agnes (eleven). In his application, Riggs promised that he "shall and will faithfully in all things discharge the duty of Guardian to the said minors according to law."[56] Along with Thomas Williamson and Robert McCullough (a missionary friend), Riggs filed the required "Guardianship Bond" of $2,000, a type of insurance that supposedly protected wards from unscrupulous guardians.[57] In August 1857, Riggs believed that everything had been processed and declared himself "Guardian of Angelie and Agnes Renville infant heirs at law of Joseph Renville deceased."[58]

Once Stephen Riggs became the girls' guardian, he legally controlled their combined 960 acres of scrip. In June 1857, two months before the court had even declared the Renville sisters his wards, Riggs announced his intent "to attend to getting the scrip and locating them for our girls."[59] In his first act as guardian, Riggs carried out his plan, sending a colleague named Robert McCullough to claim his wards' "Sioux Half Breed Scrip." Riggs dutifully recorded McCullough's charges for retrieving their scrip—including "traveling expenses and time" ($20.24) and other expenses ($6.25)—in his ledger labeled "Account for Angelique Renville with S. R. Riggs, guardian." He kept a separate account for Agnes.[60] Riggs complained that, in total, it "cost me last summer upwards of $70 to locate the warrants of the two girls we have."[61] Once he had their scrip in hand, Riggs immediately informed the court that he planned to sell their "landed estate" because he "needed money to pay expenses of locating Half Breed Scrip on said land and also to pay Taxes on the same, and also to expend in the support and education of said wards."[62]

Riggs, however, had made a mistake. Although he believed the court had authorized his guardianship in August 1857, he learned four years later that he had failed to file all the correct paperwork. In an 1861 letter, John Rudolph, the probate judge for Brown County, remonstrated Riggs because "he never made an application to be appointed [guardian], nor . . . was appointed." Though Riggs had previously filed a "Guardian Bond," that too was done incorrectly, as the document contained only one instead of the two required signatures and was "defective in other respects." Judge Rudolph warned Riggs that "all proceedings should be strictly legal and according to the statutes" and asked him to forward the pertinent documents. Once Rudolph received these papers, he would then "perhaps be able to correct all the mistakes."[63] The judge explained that this legal paperwork was extremely important, as "real estate is in question," which made it even "more necessary that all proceedings should be strictly legal and according to the Statutes."[64] Of course, the "real estate" in question was the girls' scrip, which Riggs already had obtained in 1857 and had long planned to sell.

By 1861, Riggs successfully recompleted his guardianship paperwork and finally could attempt to sell some of the sisters' land to pay for their education and support. Riggs noted that Angelique owned "some prairie land, a part of which as her guardian I mean to use for her further education."[65] In another letter, Riggs again wrote about his plans for Angelique's scrip. As "her guardian," he stated, "I meant to sell another portion of her land last fall, and so support and educate her without drawing any thing more for her from the Board."[66] While the existing correspondence focused on Angelique's scrip, court documents show that he also hoped to sell Agnes's land. Despite his best efforts, it took Riggs another year to put their land on the market. During the delay, Riggs paid yearly taxes on the girls' acres, which amounted to around nineteen dollars for each of their 480 acres. Riggs dutifully paid the taxes but recorded the amount in his growing expense ledger. He also charged his wards six percent yearly interest on their accumulating debt.[67] This meant that the girls' debt to Riggs increased each year beginning in 1857, even though the court stated that he was not their official guardian until 1861.

It appears that Therese Renville attempted to challenge Stephen Riggs, who, with the support of the State of Minnesota, took away control of her daughters and their land. In 1858, just after Stephen Riggs claimed to have received guardianship of her daughters, Therese Renville gave a man named Mr. Robertson power of attorney "to obtain her own and her children's scrip and also her deceased husband's." Unfortunately, she was unsuccessful on all accounts. Robert McCullough, at Riggs's request, had already acquired the girls' scrip the previous year; Riggs continued to hold their scrip until he could officially begin to sell their acres. Therese also was told that she could not receive her husband's scrip because the pair had "never . . . been lawfully married." Instead, the scrip would go to "young Joseph," her husband's son from an earlier marriage.[68] Therese enlisted one "General Shields" to argue her case in Washington, D.C., but no records indicate that she was successful in getting her husband's or daughters' scrip returned to her.

It is not surprising that Therese failed on all fronts. Due to her supposed "incompetence," Therese lost the legal right to control her daughters' education, residence, and land. Instead, their new missionary "father" would "properly" raise her girls. To achieve this outcome, guardianship law gave Riggs the right to sell her daughters' scrip as he saw fit. Moreover, the courts and legislature in Minnesota deemed Dakota marriages to be invalid because couples did not marry according to Euro-American law, thus negating Therese's right to receive her husband's land after his death. Therese attempted to fight for herself and her daughters, but the Minnesota legal system stripped her of any rights due to her status as a Dakota woman.[69] This was just the first example of the long fight between Therese and Stephen Riggs over access to her daughters. As a young girl and a ward, Angelique could not challenge Riggs or his control of her land. However, she assuredly witnessed her mother's opposition, which she would replicate many years later when she came of age.

While Therese fought for her rights as a wife and mother, Angelique and Agnes settled into life with the Riggs family. They quickly became part of a larger community of Dakota children who boarded with various mission families. Thomas Williamson explained why the missionaries focused their efforts on Dakota children: "we should direct our principal attention to the children for their [*sic*] is little hope that those who have been born and grown to adult age heathens will ever be converted."[70] Because Dakota children were viewed as more malleable than adults, each of the mission families had at least one, and sometimes as many as six, Native children living with them. In 1850, there were two Dakota children living at the Lac qui Parle mission, one at Traverse des Sioux, and three at Kaposia.[71] By 1851, the total number had risen to fifteen children, including Angelique.[72] In 1852, Moses Adams reported that he had "five native children in our family at present; And, we expect to take Lydia Wakanmani again in a few days."[73] Mary Huggins Kerlinger, the daughter of Alexander Huggins, remembered that fourteen young Dakotas resided with her family at various times during her childhood.[74] In 1860, Stephen Riggs reported, "The whole number of Dakota children boarded in the mission families and Boarding schools, for a longer or shorter time, is *Sixty nine*, *twenty four* males and *forty five* females. Forty one of these are half breed."[75]

As Riggs noted, the typical Dakota boarder tended to be young, female, and of mixed ancestry. One of the most important selection criteria was age; the missionaries believed that younger children would be easier to convert. Boys and girls in their teens would struggle more to learn English or to give up ingrained gender roles. Stephen Riggs kept a notebook where he recorded the names and some information about each Dakota child taken into a missionary home or, after 1856, the boarding school. While he did not document the age of every child, those he recorded show that most of the children were under the age of twelve. The youngest boarder was "less than one year," and the oldest, twelve. The most common ages ranged from six to nine years old. The Renville children followed this pattern: Rosalie and Angelique were both six years old when they went to live with the missionaries, Agnes was eight, and Thomas was nine. The missionaries hoped that these young children would easily learn to read, write, and speak English, and most important, accept Christianity once separated from their families and community.

Gender mattered to the missionaries as well. They ideally wanted to convert Dakota males. According to historian Jacqueline Fear-Segal, the missionaries followed a patriarchal model of society that privileged male converts. Most of their early converts, however, were Dakota women.[76] This pattern was replicated with the Dakota boarders—the vast majority (almost two-to-one) were female. Of the students Stephen Riggs recorded, forty-five were girls, and twenty-four were boys. The numbers are even more skewed in terms of who lived in the missionaries' homes. The existing records show that only nine boys lived with the missionaries, while the other fifteen boys attended the boarding school.[77] Again, the Renville siblings exemplified this pattern. Although Joseph Hrana had more sons than daughters, the missionaries boarded three of his daughters but only one of his sons, and following the pattern of other boys, Thomas resided in the boarding school and not in a missionary home.

Because they had few male converts or boarders, the missionaries recalibrated their thinking to focus on the benefits that Dakota girls would bring to their cause. They argued that females would be useful "investments" by producing long-term social change within their villages. The young women would return to their communities and pass on their religious training to their sisters, husbands, and children. Mary Riggs explained to her mother why she took a little girl into her family: "I had hoped she might become a Christian and that by the training she would receive, she might become a blessed instrument in leading her Indian sisters to adopt habits that should raise them in this life from their deep degradation."[78] Martha Riggs hoped that after receiving "patient, careful, and prayerful training," Angelique would have the "capability" to help "her people."[79]

On the practical side, Dakota girls also would aid the missionary women with their never-ending domestic tasks. Missionary women, like other frontier women, performed a myriad of chores throughout the day. They cooked, cleaned, washed dishes and clothes, spun, wove, sewed, and knit, and planted small gardens. They also took care of their own large families. The Riggs and Huggins families both had eight children, Gideon Pond and Thomas Williamson each had ten children, and Samuel Pond had four. Dakota girls provided another set of hands to help with the women's daily tasks. Indeed, Martha Riggs, the daughter of Stephen and Mary Riggs, complained that when some of their female boarders left, "now we have to do our washing ourselves."[80]

Yet the missionary women also refuted the idea the Dakota girls lessened their workload and some argued that Dakota girls caused more work than male boarders. Martha Riggs explained that people perceived Indian girls as more helpful and less work than boys. She questioned this logic when her family took a Dakota girl they called Hope into their family. "I am half sorry mama did not take a boy instead of Hope, for every one thinks we ought to have plenty of time to do everything imaginable, because we have so many girls."[81] Mary Riggs agreed with her daughter's comment; although she put the little girls to work, "I never supposed an untrained Indian child of 8 or 9 years would be as much assistance as care and trouble. If she should remain with us and become a child of Jesus, we shall be repaid a thousand-fold, for all our anxious and worrisome hours."[82] Mary and Martha appear to have begrudgingly supported the little girls in their homes: female boarders had great potential to convert other family members, but they required supervision and training, which took the missionary women away from their household tasks.

In addition to the missionaries' focus on age and gender, they also made sure to mention the "blood" of each child who boarded in their homes. The majority of boarders can be identified in the mission records as having mixed-ancestry, which usually meant a French, English, or American father.[83] For example, Moses Adams, who worked at the Lac qui Parle Mission, informed the ABCFM that since his family's arrival, "we have taken four children into our family—two boys and two girls—the boys and one of the girls are about 12 or 14 years old and the other is about seven. They are mixed blood perhaps more French than Dakota. Their parents engage to let them remain with us."[84] Likewise, Mary Riggs wrote, "I have been very much occupied this winter. In addition to our own family who are all at home excepting Martha, we have two children with us this season. One of them is a Dakota, and the other is of mixed descent."[85] Samuel Pond noted the "blood" and cultural affiliation of a little Dakota boy who lived with his family. The boy was "A half breed who has always lived with the Indians until last year."[86] Of course, the Renville siblings came from a prominent mixed-ancestry family.

Although the missionaries always mentioned a child's "blood" status, they did not think that biology was destiny, nor that "blood" was immutable. Instead, they focused on the supposed cultural and religious deficiencies of the mixed-ancestry children. Mary Riggs informed her sister that "mixed blood" girls "if possible are more useless and idle than Indian girls and their brothers are still more lazy and proud."[87] However, the missionaries argued that through secular and religious education, Dakota and mixed-ancestry children could become "white." Stephen Riggs explained, "If they cease to be Indians and become white people, as we have reason to hope they will by means of proper efforts, the tribes will disappear but it will be by becoming merged in the great American people. And who will not rejoice in that?"[88] Riggs even proposed "to make a new dictionary meaning of the word white so that it shall include all mixed bloods of Indian descent and civilized Indians."[89]

The missionaries hoped that Angelique would illustrate this wondrous transformation. Martha Riggs described Angelique as a "little dark-faced girl" when she first arrived at the Riggses' home.[90] The goal was to convert Angelique to "white," as they claimed to have done with other mixed-ancestry boarders like Nancy McClure, the stepdaughter of Antoine Renville, Joseph Hrana's brother. From age eight until sixteen, McClure boarded with several missionary families. After her time with the missionaries, she described herself as "more white than Indian in my tastes and sympathies" and became a member of the Presbyterian Church. Frank Blackwell Mayer, a painter who visited Lac qui Parle and other Dakota villages in Minnesota, met Nancy McClure on the day of her wedding to another mixed-ancestry Dakota man. Mayer wrote that while McClure "possesses Indian features," they had been "softened into the more delicate contour of the Caucasian."[91] Stephen Riggs described McClure as strikingly "ladylike in her appearance."[92]

While the missionaries believed that the transformation from the "dark-faced" Angelique to the "Caucasian" and "ladylike" Nancy McClure was possible, they were under no illusions that the process would be quick or easy. Indeed, it would take years to accomplish. The missionaries worried, however, because most Dakota children stayed only a few weeks or months before being taken back by their kin. Moses Adams explained that the missionaries had "great difficulty heretofore in attempts to raise native children in the families of the missionaries. If we succeed in keeping this full-blooded Sioux in our family until she is of age it will be an exception, for every similar attempt has failed heretofore."[93] Evidence shows that Adams was correct to be skeptical. As previously mentioned, Rosalie Renville only remained a short time with the Riggs family before her aunt claimed custody. Stephen Riggs also lamented that a Dakota man "gave us a little girl about 9 or 10 years old and said she should stay with us for four years. She was a remarkably promising child and would soon have been of considerable assistance to Mrs. Riggs, who became very much attached to her; but at the end of three months . . . her mother took her home."[94] A girl the missionaries named Anna only remained three months, while Eliza Widokawin stayed "about a year."[95]

While many of the boarding children left after a few weeks or months, Angelique lived with the missionaries for over ten years. Due to her extended stay with the Riggs family, Angelique—and several other boarders including her sister Agnes and Julia Laframboise—had the weight of the missionaries' expectations on her young shoulders. She would be the shining example of how their hard work and sacrifices would lead her to "civilization" and Christianization. In turn, Angelique was expected to spread Christianity and the values of domesticity to her Dakota kin and eventually to her own children. Angelique's missionary "friends had great hope of and for her."[96]

In order to achieve Angelique's transformation, the missionaries began the process of "civilizing" Angelique and the rest of their new charges the minute they walked through their door. Like the late nineteenth century federal boarding schools, the missionaries first changed all aspects of the children's appearances. The missionaries described the Dakota children as dirty and ill-cared for. Mary Riggs informed her mother that "Anna which is her English name of the little girl who is now with us came on Friday in as tattered and dirty condition as you can easily imagine."[97] Because they were "filthy, ragged, and degraded" when they arrived at her home, Mary Riggs immediately began "the scrubbing and combing process. The latter of course included the destruction of countless vermin! and must be faithfully attended to for a long time."[98]

Following their scrubbing, the new boarders received Euro-American clothing. The missionaries described their Dakota apparel as physical markers of their poverty and "savagery." Mary Riggs complained that "a great many of [Dakota children] have poor ragged and dirty clothes, and most all of them the latter, and some of the little boys wear no clothing or very little."[99] Like his wife, Stephen Riggs derisively commented on the Dakota's "different stages of undress" which reflected their character: they were "all lazy, stolid, dirty."[100] Riggs also referred to their clothing as "uncouth."[101] The missionary women replaced the children's "savage" clothing with "garment[s] of civilization" taken from charity boxes donated by patrons or clothing that older Dakota boarders had made in sewing class.[102] Immediately after Wamdiokioya's daughter entered her home, Mary Riggs "washed and dressed her up."[103] Mary Riggs also gave another adopted Dakota girl "new dresses . . . in Isantankay (American) fashion."[104] As a final step in their physical transformation, the boys, and occasionally the girls, had their hair cut. Stephen Riggs reported that the missionaries "cut off [Simon, Lorenzo, and Henok's] hair and dressed them up as white men."[105] In 1855, when they arrived at Hazelwood, Agnes Renville and four other Dakota girls "had their hair cut off short."[106]

Many of the children also received altered or new names. For the most part, mixed-ancestry Dakota children who had Euro-American names kept their birth names, although the missionaries frequently standardized the spelling; for example, "Angelic" became "Angelique," which is the way that she usually signed her letters. Mixed-ancestry children with French names were occasionally Anglified, so Marguerite Renville became Margaret Renville. Occasionally, Angelique signed her letters as "Angie," a more Anglified version of her French name.[107] Children with Dakota names were given new English names that had no relationship to their given names. These names were not chosen by the children or their parents but had significance for the missionaries. Some boarders were named after donors, such as Susan Ellison Washdaiyodankewin, who was named after Susan Ellison (and the Ellison family in general), who "rendered valuable aid to the mission."[108] Anpetnakitoninwin, or Dawning Day Woman, was renamed Isabella Burgess after an Ohio woman who bequeathed $500 to the Dakota mission.[109]

Some boarders also were named after the female missionaries. Lydia Wakanmani was named after Lydia Huggins; Fanny Huggins Hapan, after Fanny Huggins; and Eliza Widokawin after Eliza Huggins. These girls received their first (and occasionally middle) names from a missionary woman, while their father's Dakota name became their last name.[110] This contradicted Dakota naming practices, which did not include last names. It also symbolically devalued their Dakota mothers and wrote Euro-American patriarchal gender assumptions onto the children's names.[111] Although more common for girls, some Dakota boys also received missionary names, including a Dakota boy called "Thomas Lawrence" after Stephen Riggs's son. This undoubtedly created confusion, as both Thomas Lawrences lived in the Riggses' home at the same time.[112] Besides sowing confusion, as historian Taylor Spence argues, the missionaries' naming practices disregarded gender, did not translate into the named individual's own language, and failed to reflect American Indian kinship relations.[113] Even the missionary daughters sometimes realized the absurdity of the naming process. Martha Riggs commented that her "mamma" was going "to inflict some such name as Emma on the poor [Dakota] child" who came to board with them.[114]

After the children were dressed and renamed, they undoubtedly would have become familiar with their new residences. All the missionary homes were extremely small and cramped, especially for large families. In 1852, Stephen Riggs noted that with Angelique and "our own six children and Miss Lucy Spooner [a young teacher] who is with us, they make as large a family as our house will accommodate."[115] Because of the lack of space, the Dakota children did not have their own bedrooms. Rather, they shared rooms with other Dakota boarders, the missionary sons and daughters, and even their teachers. In the Pettijohn home at Lac qui Parle, Nancy McClure shared a room with Rosalie Renville for the short time she remained in their home. Two other Dakota girls named Caroline and Julia also shared a room at the Pettijohn home. Later, when Nancy moved in with the Huggins family, she lived in an attic room with Mary, the Huggins daughter.[116] Stephen Riggs reported that his sons Alfred and Thomas lived with "Joseph Latour, a half breed boy, [in] . . . a room up stairs."[117] Angelique shared a room with Martha Riggs and Lucy Spooner, a young teacher. It appears that Martha received the new furniture while Angelique made do with older furnishings. In one of the first letters she wrote at the age of nine, after three years living with the missionaries, Angelique informed "dear miss Spooner" that "I sleep in the same place. miss Riggs got the new bed. . . . Angelique.[118]

After moving into the mission homes, the children began attending school in the mornings. Missionary teachers divided the children into different classes based on age and ability. Younger boarders attended the day schools with other Dakota children who still lived with their families. These day school classes were mostly taught by missionary wives and their older daughters or young women from back east who rotated in and out of the mission every two years.[119] By 1851, when six-year-old Angelique would have started at the day school, the missionaries had developed a set curriculum after close to fifteen years of trial and error. This curriculum focused almost exclusively on teaching literacy, as the ability to read the Bible would purportedly hasten the children's conversions.[120]

Surprisingly, given the missionaries' focus on teaching literacy to promote conversion, students first learned to read in the Dakota language rather than in English. This decision served the missionaries' larger goal of achieving quick conversions. Over the years, the missionaries realized that teaching literacy in English was a difficult, gradual process because students needed to first learn an entirely new language.[121] Because speed was of the essence, missionaries taught students to read in Dakota to eliminate the time needed to learn English. Alfred Riggs summarized the importance of teaching in Dakota: "It has been our belief that to reach the people at large you must get to them through their own language.[122]

To teach literacy in Dakota, the missionaries needed to translate the Dakota's oral language into a written one. In the mid-1830s, Samuel and Gideon Pond created the "Pond alphabet," which was based on the Roman alphabet. They first linked all vowels in the Dakota language—and most consonant sounds—with a corresponding letter in the English alphabet. Many Dakota sounds were unknown in English and did not correspond to any letter, and because oral Dakota did not use the letters *c*, *f*, *g*, *j*, *r*, *v*, and *x*, the Pond brothers assigned these letters to unique Dakota sounds. For instance, they used *c*, *j*, and *x* to represent *ch*, *zh*, and *sh*, respectively.[123] Using the Pond system, the missionaries translated the Bible, hundreds of hymns, and other religious texts into Dakota.[124]

In the classroom, the younger children learned their "ABCs" using the Pond alphabet printed in elementary readers like *Dakota ABC Wowapi*. Martha Riggs reported that "Mary and Agnes get a book every day in school, put their head behind it and sing A.B.C.D."[125] Once the children learned the alphabet, they moved on to easy Dakota readers, such as the *Model First Reader—Wayawa Tokaheya,* which taught vocabulary using pictures. After learning basic reading skills and vocabulary, the children were instructed to "read a few verses in the Dakota Bible every afternoon—the more advanced ones read a chapter once or twice a week." Only when they were "able to read with ease in the Dakota Bible" did they begin to learn to "read and spell in English."[126] The teachers advocated that scholars who "learned to read Dakota before commencing English, learn to read English with great readiness."[127]

While the teachers focused almost entirely on literacy, they did introduce "practical mathematics," although they did not have much success except among those children who boarded with the missionaries.[128] The students also practiced singing and gender-specific projects, such as sewing for the girls. Angelique's 1852 "examination," after one year with the Riggses, illustrates the mission school's curriculum for the younger children. During her examination, she read, spoke a Bible verse, did some sums on the blackboard, and sang hymns and "America" in Dakota. The school walls also displayed Angelique's "patchwork" sewing project with her name in it.[129]

If students like Angelique remained in the mission school and mastered literacy, basic mathematics, and finally English, they progressed to more advanced studies. These children would be moved from the Dakota day school into classes with the missionaries' own children. In practice, only those Dakota children who boarded with the missionaries progressed enough to take higher level classes, as they needed a strong academic foundation and fluency in English. For example, in 1854, Miss Spooner's higher level school consisted of the Riggs children, two Dakota children who boarded with the Riggs family (one of whom was Angelique), another Dakota girl who had spent two years with another mission family, and three Dakota day-scholars, all of whom had previously lived with mission families.[130] Likewise, in 1855, Mr. Aiton taught a group of students in English class which consisted "of ten, viz. our own five children and Miss. Pettijohn's niece and our four boarding scholars."[131]

Once she moved into the higher-level class, Angelique studied arithmetic, grammar, spelling, geography, and history with the missionary children. She also wrote compositions and even published books of poetry and essays.[132] Classes were frequent but relatively short. Martha Riggs explained, "We have school half a day every day but Saturday in the afternoon."[133] All of the students also had singing and music lessons, which took place separately from their academic coursework. Martha Riggs reported that her older sister Isabella "teaches singing school. She has five scholars Smith [Williamson], Martha [Williamson], Huldah [?], Anna [Renville], and Angelique [Renville]."[134] In 1859, Anna Jane Riggs wrote that she and Angelique were taking music lessons.[135]

As one of the most important parts of their education, the boarders participated in extensive religious studies. During school hours, the children read passages from the Bible, first in the Dakota language, and as they progressed, in English. They also attended numerous Sabbath schools and other Bible study meetings during weeknights and twice on Sunday. Stephen Riggs noted, "Our Sabbath School . . . is made up chiefly of the children of our Boarding School and those of my own family."[136] Martha Riggs confirmed that "all the [boarding] girls come to meeting."[137] In 1855, Angelique attended Mr. Hunter's Sabbath School with several missionary children.[138]

The missionaries wanted to promote the children's educational and spiritual transformations by putting them on display for vistors. The year after Angelique arrived at Lac qui Parle, Stephen Riggs reported that he held an "examination and exhibition of our schools. Quite a number of specators were present. Misses Spooner's classes in English appeared very well. They were examined in spelling, reading, arithmetic and geography; and sung and performed various tunes and airs both in English and Dakota to the great gratification of the audience."[139] Although Angelique was probably too young to participate in this exhibition, in 1855 she took part in a Thanksgiving program for twenty-nine visitors, during which "the children sang 'A.B.C.' and then . . . all joined hands and going round the table sung 'Children go to and fro!' . . . Angelique was the oldest [at the age of ten], hand in hand."[140]

The Dakota boarders did not demonstrate sweeping, sewing, or farming for the visitors. Domestic "classes," however, played an outsized role in their missionary education. Indeed, household training —especially for the girls—frequently superceded literacy, math, and geography. After the day-students went home, the boarders received vocational instruction specific to their gender. In practice, this meant that they worked in the missionaries' homes and fields. Through this work, the missionaries hoped the children would internalize Euro-American gender roles to replace the ones they had learned from their kin during their early years. The missionaries denigrated their previous gender roles, characterizing Dakota men as lazy and the women as slaves to their husbands.[141] The secretary of the ABCFM, David Greene, wrote a letter to Abel Itewawinehangan chastising all Dakota men for their treatment of women. "When will you learn to do the hard work—cut the wood, plant the fields, gather the crops, and carry the burdens, instead of making the women do it all?" he lectured. "It is not generous and kind for your people to make the women work so hard. The missionaries do not do it. We do not do so here. Let them cook food, take care of the house and the children, make clothes, and c. That is enough for them; and let the men do the work outdoors."[142] The missionaries attempted to put Greene's demands into practice; they would teach the boys "to cut wood, and 'make corn', and the girls to sew, knit, spin, and weave, duties so essential to civilization."[143]

Because of the boarders' gender imbalance in the mission homes, the entire Riggs family focused primarily on educating "their girls" in the "arts and duties of true womanhood."[144] This training was so important that the girls "on an average spent at least as much time in learning to spin sew knit and c. as in learning to read and write."[145] The missionary women assigned chores to even the youngest girls. Mary Riggs wrote that "our little girl . . . wipes dishes picks up chips and sweeps some."[146] The girls also learned to sew from a young age. In 1855, at the age of ten, Angelique made a dress almost by herself.[147] In 1856, Angelique worked on "the edge for a pair of pantelets."[148] While the younger girls performed small domestic chores and learned to sew, the older girls assumed more responsibilities around the home. Nancy McClure, who boarded with three different missionary families over the years, described her days at the mission. "At these missions we girls [learned] how to sew, knit, and, as we grew older, to spin, weave, cook, and do all kinds of housework."

Several historians have criticized this domestic education for not being educational at all. Rather, the missionaries used the children as unpaid labor.[149] Certainly, the missionaries' homes and large number of children required extensive labor, especially for women.[150] Someone had to do this work, and quite often it fell to the older boarding students. In 1858, when Martha Riggs left for the Western Female Seminary, Anna Jane Riggs, Angelique, and Agnes performed "all the work" within the mission home.[151] In 1859, after Anna Jane also left for school, Stephen Riggs commented, "Only one of the girls [Angelique] is large enough to do a great deal; she is over sixteen [she was actually fourteen]—in fact a young woman in size, and without her [the missionaries] could not have gotten along this winter."[152] The missionaries never would have considered paying Angelique or Agnes for their work. They argued that domestic education directly contributed to the girls' civilization and salvation; this training would allow them to marry well (meaning a white husband) and become part of Euro-American society. The missionaries also couched the children's service in terms of familial bonds rather than that of worker to employer. Mary Riggs stated that Julia Laframboise "took a daughter's share in the love and labor of the household."[153] After the other missionary daughters left for school, Martha Riggs noted, "that it seemed but right that Angelique, having enjoyed the privileges of the home, should lend a helping hand when it was needed."[154] The question of unpaid labor again brings into sharp relief the conflicted relationship between the missionary "parents" and their adopted Dakota children.[155]

The boarders' relationship with the missionary children was equally problematic. The lives of both the Dakota and missionary children became entangled as they sewed, cleaned, and washed clothing together; attended school and worshipped in the same classes; and shared tight living quarters, including bedrooms. Did the missionary children treat the Dakota boarders as inferior? As servants? As friends? As peers? At different times and different levels, the answer appears to have been all of the above.

Like their parents, the missionary children claimed to have forged strong bonds and friendships with some boarders. Mary Huggins remembered that Julia Laframboise had lived in their household for over five years, and Huggins "loved her like a sister."[156] In Martha Riggs's letters, she always listed a mixed group of Dakota and missionary children and described their activities in school, work, and play. Indeed, given the missionaries' naming practices, it is sometimes hard to distinguish the Dakotas from the missionary children.

At times, they collectively acted like any other group of young children and played together. In 1855, Martha Riggs reported that during a late spring snow, "Isabella and I with the rest of the children went sliding on a pond that is near the house. Mr. Hunter had a pair of skates but the ice was too soft to skate as well."[157] The girls also frequently visited neighbors together. In August 1860, Martha and Angelique "walked to Dr. Ws Monday afternoon to see Nannie who was quite unwell."[158] A few months later, Nannie, Martha, and Angelique "went down to Mrs. John B.'s to sew for her."[159] In March 1860, Anna Jane Riggs noted, "We girls that is Angelique Agnes and I, went over to Mrs. John B. Renville's to sew for her last week. We went rather early in the morning and staid till evening. Sophia Renville was there also."[160] Dakota girls like Angelique, Agnes, and Sophia were folded into the daily lives of the missionary children; they lived in such close proximity to each other that their lives could not help but become intertwined.

Intertwined, however, did not mean equal. Missionary parents raised their children to view the Dakota boarders as culturally and religiously inferior, albeit capable of salvation. Mary Huggins explained that she "never thought of the Indians as an inferior being. . . . They were however for me divided into two classes. The Christian and the heathen."[161] Because the Dakota children were "heathens," Mary Huggins and other missionary children believed that their parents' cause was righteous and that the boarding program was a privilege for the Dakota children.

Indeed, the missionary children actively participated in their parents' war against heathenism. For instance, they took it upon themselves to help convert the Dakota boarders. The missionary children staged informal prayer meetings, encouraged the boarders to read the Bible, and rebuked any statements or actions that countered Christian beliefs. In a letter to a fellow missionary, Nancy Jane Williamson related how she walked with Mary, a boarder who lived with her family, to see her brother's grave. When they approached the grave, Mary commented that her brother's soul had escaped through a hole. Nancy quickly told Mary that her belief was nothing more than superstition and she "hope[d] she w[ould] learn better after awhile."[162] Nancy Jane Williamson and Eliza and Mary Huggins also worked to convert Victoria L'Ange and Julia Laframboise. The two missionary girls felt they "had a responsibility to Victoria and Julia so we took them into our prayers. Although there were only four of us . . . [w]e had little prayer meetings every Sunday afternoon and . . . [we] felt great spiritual exaltation."[163] Like Victoria, Julia, and other Dakota boarders, Angelique Renville's acceptance into the Riggs family was predicated on her continued adherence to Christianity and Euro-American cultural norms.

The missionary children, like their parents, measured the success of their Dakota students in three ways: whether they could read and write, how well they spoke English, and most important, if they had joined the mission church. The missionaries claimed that the Dakota children who boarded with them fared better on all three of these standards and counted these children as some of their only "success" stories. In general, Thomas Williamson stated that their day-students learned little, so "there is little encouragement here to attempt teaching any except such as are boarded for that purpose."[164]

Regarding literacy, the missionaries claimed that Dakota boarders learned to read at a faster rate than other students. At Oak Grove, Gideon Pond mentioned that he had not taught any Dakotas to read, except Miss Titus, "who is a half-breed and has lived in our family since she was a small girl." Likewise, at Traverse des Sioux the missionaries did not "have not a single Dakota reader except perhaps, three or four who . . . have lived a considerable time in one of the mission families at that place."[165]

The missionaries especially touted the English skills of those children who came to them at very young ages. Thomas Williamson boasted that when Henok came to live with his family, he "did not speak, or appear to know a word of English, and had made but little progress in learning to read Dakota. He now reads both English and Dakota fluently." He also "speaks and read[s] [English] so well that a stranger would hardly suspect that it was not his mother tongue."[166] Another young Dakota boy, Moses Thunder Lawrence Pettijohn, lived with the Pettijohn family from the age of two. Jonas and Fanny Pettijohn reported that after a few years at the mission he did not speak any Dakota.[167] Younger children learned to speak English as their primary language, and older children spoke passable English after only a short time with the missionaries. The Williamson family took an eleven-year-old boy into their family who did not speak any English.

They informed the ABCFM that after living with them, the boy "now reads both English and Dakota fluently; and though his knowledge of the former is not so extensive as it would have been, if he had always used it, he speaks it and reads it so well that a stranger could scarcely suspect that it was not his mother tongue."[168]

Most important, the missionaries boasted that the Dakota boarders had higher rates of religious conversion than any other section of the Dakota population.[169] The available church membership records support this assertion. A Dakota girl who resided with the Williamson family for a short time later became a member of the Yellow Medicine church. The missionaries attributed the woman's conversion to "her early teaching [as] manifested by her greater familiarity with Bible truth and readiness to answer questions."[170] Another girl who joined the church had "lived in . . . [a mission family] for two or three year past; and we think she gives sufficient evidence of having passed from death unto life to justify us in admitting her to the fellowship of the church."[171] The missionaries reported other conversions, including that of Jane Lamont, who professed her belief in Christianity after living with the Samuel Pond family.[172] Sophia Renville and Lorenzo Lawrence also joined the church after extended interaction with mission families.[173] Julia Laframboise joined the church in 1852.[174] In 1861, both Angelique (age sixteen) and her sister Agnes (age fourteen) were received into the Hazelwood church after having "for years been members of the Riggs family."[175]

The supposed successes of the boarding program, however, were belied by the fact that Dakota boarders and their parents resisted and challenged the missionary program in many ways. The missionaries wanted to completely separate Dakota parents from their children. In reality, Dakota parents and other kin continued to play active roles in their children's lives even though they lived in mission homes. Because of Dakota parents' "interference," Stephen Riggs confessed that "the difficulties of getting scholars and keeping them have proved more than I anticipated."[176]

Dakota parents removed their children from the missionaries for various reasons, especially if they were unhappy, homesick, or ill. One little Dakota girl, for example, experienced difficulties coming to terms with living apart from her family. Every time she saw her grandmother at a Sunday church meeting, she "began to cry.

She cries whenever she sees any of her relations."[177] The missionaries noted that her parents took her away before she learned to speak much English.[178] Another little girl became ill and died while under the missionaries' care. Her grieving parents immediately removed their other children who also lived with the missionaries "and openly [disavowed] all sympathy with Missionaries or favor for education."[179]

Missionary classroom practices also angered Dakota children and their parents. Children like Angelique who had been raised by their Dakota relatives had learned by role-playing and exploration. In contrast, missionary teachers followed a Euro-American model of education where teachers expected their students to sit quietly at their desks for long periods of time. They also expected students to arrive on time, remain the entire school session, and perform their given lessons in an orderly and timely fashion. As was common at the time, teachers taught by rote, which did not allow for creativity.[180] Many Dakota children did not take to these methods. Martha Riggs reported that students in "Aunt" Ruth's class refused to sit still and made her "almost crazy."[181] Teacher Eliza Huggins also complained that she found it "very difficult to keep the children quiet and studious during study hours."[182]

When the children would not sit still, several of the teachers turned to corporal punishment, which again conflicted with Dakota childrearing practices. Dakota parents rarely spoke harshly to their children or disciplined them with physical force, relying instead on verbal suggestions or illustrations to correct their behavior.[183] Stephen Riggs commented on how the two competing philosophies of discipline created friction. "We find it [teaching the children] difficult work," he wrote. "Dakota parents are very sensitive about the way in which their children are taken care of. . . . [I]f they are naughty and we correct them, it makes quite a buzz in the community."[184] Aunt Ruth especially had "pretty scriptural notions in regard to the use of the rod, which are not quite popular among these native americans."[185] Several parents immediately pulled their children from school after Aunt Ruth whipped them. Carrie Ironheart's parents visited her after spending the winter further north. After Carrie told them about her treatment, her parents "took her away, alledging[*sic*] as the reason that we whipped her." The missionaries, however, defended Aunt

Ruth, stating that "This was . . . untrue. Carrie was a good girl, though not very apt to learn."[186]

Clearly, Dakota parents knew what was happening at the schools and intervened when they decided that the missonaries had crossed the line. This illustrates the larger point that the boarding childen were not entirely separated from their kin as generally happened in the late nineteenth-century Indian boarding schools. The Carlisle Indian Industrial School (established in 1879 in Pennsylvania), for example, was built far from most reservations, which by design made it difficult for students to run away or for parents to have a say in their children's daily treatment. The ABCFM mission stations, however, were established near Dakota villages so that the missionaries could preach to potential converts. When the Riggs family lived at Hazelwood, Martha Riggs reported "some of the [I]ndians live very near. . . . The village is about a mile and a half from our house."[187]

Because their children lived within walking distance, Dakota parents and other kin could visit the boarders. One Dakota mother brought dried bison meat to her sons while they lived in the Hazelwood Boarding School.[188] Jane Lamont's mother attended Bible study meetings—even though she had no desire to convert—so she could see her daughter. Gideon Pond did not stop her visits, but worried about Lamont's mother's influence because she "belongs to the Indian medicine dance and last Sunday was dressing a deerskin."[189] Thomas Williamson noted that another Dakota boarder saw her parents daily. While some of the missionaries worried about this interaction, Thomas Williamson believed that contact with their kin made the boarders "contented and happy in [their] new [mission] home."[190]

In addition to visits from their kin, many of the boarders also went home to their villages for short or extended periods. In 1855, Julia Laframboise returned to her father's home to care for ill relatives.[191] Victor Renville spent part of four winters living with the Williamson family, but remained "at home the rest of the time to assist his father on the farm or accompany him on a buffalo hunt."[192] The missionaries did not stop Victor's visits, but lamented that "he would have made progress but for visits home."[193]

Like the parents of other boarders, Joseph Hrana and Therese Renville lived close to their daughters and son at both the Lac qui Parle and Hazelwood missions. In the mid-1850s, Therese lived with her husband and other Renville kin near the Lac qui Parle mission. When the Riggs family relocated to the new Hazelwood mission, Joseph Hrana and Therese followed so they could continue to see Angelique, Agnes, and Thomas. After Joseph Hrana's death and Stephen Riggs's subsequent guardianship of her daughters, Therese chose to remain a constant presence in her children's lives.[194] In 1859, she resided about half a mile from the Hazelwood mission in a nearby Dakota encampment.[195] In 1860, Therese moved into a small, sixteen-by-eighteen-foot government brick home near the Hazelwood mission. Stephen Riggs declared her new home "miserable," as it was finished "in such a way as not to be comfortable."[196]

Even though Therese's lodging was poor, the proximity of her home to Hazelwood allowed her to visit her children. She often walked to the Riggs home with food for her children. She also took her children several times to participate in traditional Dakota subsistence and religious activities. In spring 1858, Therese and her daughters left Hazelwood for a week to participate in a bison hunt with their numerous Renville relatives.[197] Her children also visited her several times. In August 1860, when Therese fell ill, Angelique and Agnes rushed to their mother's home and stayed with her until she got "considerably better . . . though [still] quite weak."[198]

During these years, the Riggs family did not leave any records about how they felt about Therese's presence in her children's lives. Likewise, Therese could not write her side of the story. Clearly, however, Therese remained an active presence in her children's lives. Perhaps the missionaries tolerated her visits because she did not appear to have challenged Riggs's ultimate authority over her children. Angelique, Agnes, and Thomas continued to live in the Riggses' home and to attend the mission church and school. Of course, Stephen Riggs remained the girls' legal guardian and controlled their scrip. Therese, and later Angelique, learned that co-existence with the missionaries was possible, but only if they deferred to the missionaries, kept any criticisms to themselves, and remained committed to "civilization" and Christianity.

Moreover, it is likely that Therese witnessed several incidents over the years that taught her the consequences of overtly challenging the boarding program. In 1858, for example, a seven-year-old girl named Mary Cloud lived at the Hazelwood Boarding School.[199] Two years later, Stephen Riggs reported that Mary Cloud's mother took "her away under false pretenses" and attempted to move with her "up north," presumably far away from the missionaries.[200] Riggs sent missionary Hugh Cunningham and Michel Renville to bring Mary Cloud back. They failed, as Cunningham and Renville refused "to force her away from her mother." A few days later, the missionaries sent John Other Day (another Dakota man), who "brought her back *by force*." Anna Jane Riggs reported that "Mr. Otherday just jerked her away from her mother, and put her in the sleigh, and came away." Mary's mother was so upset after Other Day took her daughter that she attempted to hang herself. News that Cloud's mother had died reached her and the missionaries. Mary and her relatives mourned, while the missionaries dug a grave, constructed a coffin, and went to retrieve the body. Fortunately, Mary Cloud's mother was found alive and brought back to Hazelwood. Despite her mother's obvious distress, Mary Cloud continued to live with the missionaries. Riggs, in an understatement, admitted it was a "sad case."[201] Therese, from her residence near the Riggs home, would have witnessed the traumatic separation of Anna and her mother and learned the consequences of challenging the status quo.

Perhaps Therese counseled her children not to run away after the Mary Cloud incident. Other Dakota boarders, however, successfully fled from the mission. Robert Hopkins noted that four boarders ran away from his home "because the customs of [their] Indian relatives were more congenial to their taste."[202] Anna Jane Riggs wrote about a similar incident involving two Dakota girls who lived with her family. The girls' mother asked Stephen Riggs to let them return home. According to Anna Jane Riggs, "papa was not willing and so in the afternoon the girls slipped out of the house and were gone."[203] Mary Riggs reported that another young Dakota girl "stayed only a month, and then ran away."[204] Likewise, Lorenzo Lawrence, another boarder, "while at school cried for his mother. He ran away from school to a camp across the Mississippi River."[205]

Even those boarders who did not run away to their villages often had the support of their young relatives at the missions themselves. Siblings, cousins, and other kin tended to board together at the same mission station. One of the best examples was the Renville family. Agnes lived with Angelique at the Riggses' home and Thomas resided at the boarding school. The Renville siblings also had numerous other kin who floated in and out of the mission as boarders, including an aunt (Margaret Renville) and several cousins (Sophia, Anna, Victor, and Mary Alice Renville). Other families also sent multiple siblings and cousins to live with the missionaries, including the Laframboise siblings (Julia, Alexis, William, John, and Justine). Again, unlike the late nineteenth-century boarding schools, Dakota children who lived with the missionaries were never fully separated from their kin and communities, no matter how pernicious an influence the missionaries might judge those ties to be. The missionaries understood that they were responsible for what happened to the children within their homes.

The proximity of Dakota parents like Therese to their children could be a double-edged sword, however. Therese could visit her children, bring them food, and even take them away for a few days on a buffalo hunt, but this closeness also allowed the missionaries to insert themselves into the most intimate of family affairs to pursue their own goals. For example, because Therese and Joseph Hrana lived within walking distance of the mission, Stephen Riggs was able to bring Angelique and Agnes to visit their father just before his death from tuberculosis on 8 February 1856. Riggs, however, viewed the family reunion more as an opportunity to teach the girls about the importance of Christianity than as a family tragedy.

Mary Riggs described Angelique's emotions on the day of her father's death. "She feels tenderly sad. Her mother is quite overcome with grief. Poor woman! It is said she fainted from sorrow and exhaustion." Despite Angelique's sadness, Riggs "[had] hope that he has exchanged the sorrows and toils of earth for a happier land, but God only knows whether his profession were sincere or not." Indeed, Joseph Hrana, who had once been part of the mission church but had been excommunicated years earlier for polygamy, reportedly "renewed his profession of faith in the Redeemer" just before his death.[206] By securing Joseph Hrana's reacceptance of Christianity, Riggs hoped to show the dying man's daughters that he had truly repented and had "gone to be a participant in the duties and joys of God's family above."[207]

According to Stephen Riggs, once Angelique and Agnes arrived at Joseph Hrana's death bed, he told his daughters that he recognized them and that he was "going up to-day." Riggs also reported that Joseph "empathically" said that the "Savior [was] near." A short time later, "he was gone." Immediately after he "peacefully, calmly fell asleep," his kin "commenced a long, loud and bitter wailing." For years, missionaries like Riggs had tried to get Dakota families to halt their "savage" wailing following a death, and this was no exception. Indeed, Stephen and Mary Riggs had spoken against the Renville's family wailing at the death of Joseph's young son in 1839. Continuing his almost twenty-year crusade against wailing and other vestiges of "heathenism," Riggs kneeled "and commenced praying in a very low voice." After a minute, Riggs claimed to have silenced the mourners, "save for one old man, who was singing to the departed one."[208]

Neither Angelique nor Agnes recorded their thoughts about their father's death. It is not known if they wailed with their Dakota relatives or if they deferred to Riggs, who stood next to them acting as their "father" even though their father, mother, and other kin also were in the room. The description of the scene comes from the pen of Stephen Riggs, who recorded it as a morality tale illustrating the clash between "savagery and civilization" and "heathenism and Christianity," with Christianity winning out in the end. Riggs, it seems, did not realize that his story did not quite conclude as planned, as the old man remained, continuing to sing in Dakota and outlasting Riggs's prayers. Certainly, the lesson that Riggs wanted to impart to the girls was that Dakota religion was a thing of the past. They needed to continue to accept the church's teachings, just like their father supposedly had on his deathbed.

Although the girls were "tenderly sad" at their father's passing, Riggs led Angelique and Agnes away from their mother and relatives to continue their education at the Hazelwood mission. Joseph Hrana's death also allowed Riggs to petition the Minnesota court for legal guardianship of Angelique and Agnes. Although Therese lost custody of Angelique and Agnes and failed to safeguard their scrip, she continued to visit with Angelique, Agnes, and Thomas over the next several years, even as they remained with the Riggs family. The Renville siblings also had contact with their immediate and extended Dakota kin. In 1861, however, these connections were further challenged (but not broken) when Stephen Riggs sent Angelique away to a female seminary in Ohio. He paid for her travels and education by finally realizing his longstanding plan to sell a portion of her scrip.

::: 3 :::

THE OHIO FEMALE COLLEGE

Fall 1861–Spring 1862

After close to a decade living in missionary homes and attending the mission school and church, Angelique Renville and another mixed-ancestry boarder named Julia Laframboise had advanced farther in their studies than most other Dakota students. The missionaries proudly declared both girls ready to move on to higher education at a female seminary with several of the missionary daughters. In 1857, Martha Riggs reported that "Julia LaFramboise is staying with us now and is studying diligently to prepare herself for entering at Oxford [the Western Female Seminary in Oxford, Ohio] a year from next fall. . . . The next candidates besides myself and Julia will be Anna [Jane Riggs] and Angelique and perhaps Martha Williamson."[1] Mary Riggs also hoped that Julia and Angelique would continue their studies, although she was less optimistic than her daughter Martha about their success. "We include on our lists for 'the Great Western', our adopted daughters," she wrote, "but it is uncertain whether they [will] graduate or not. I think Julia Laframboise intends to go through the course and I hope she may. She appears well, so that with all our discouragements we have some encouragements. I do not mean that her personal appearance is particularly pleasing, but she seems teachable—conscientious and studious."[2] Despite Mary Riggs's conflicted evaluation of Julia, in September 1858, she left for Ohio with Isabella Riggs to attend the Western Female Seminary, becoming the school's first "foreign student."[3]

In 1861, Eliza Huggins, a teacher of the advanced class at the Hazelwood mission, also considered Angelique ready for further studies. "Angelique Renville, a young lady of sixteen years, who had been in this school from the beginning . . . was our oldest and most advanced scholar," Huggins reported. "She had gone through the common school Geography and the History of the United States—had commenced English Grammar and had nearly completed Arithmetic. Her deportment in school was orderly, respectful and lady-like."[4] In September 1861, Angelique followed in Julia Laframboise's footsteps and left Minnesota with Martha Riggs, not for the Western Female Seminary as originally intended, but for the Ohio Female College. The change in plans occurred because the main building of the Western Female Seminary burned down in winter 1860, leading the girls to enroll at another Ohio school.

Right before she left for Ohio, Angelique signed Mary Huggins's autograph book: "Blessed are they that do His commandments that they may have right to the tree of life and may enter in through the gates into the city Your friend, Angelique Renville."[5] In her entry, Angelique wrote fluently in English, demonstrated her knowledge of Christianity and the Bible, and was part of the mission community who filled Mary's book with inspirational sayings that paraphrased scripture. Indeed, most people casually flipping through the autograph book would not have known that Angelique was a Dakota girl. Thus, these short sentences encapsulate a missionary "success" story—they had supposedly erased her early years with her mother and Dakota kin and turned her into a "good true woman."[6] Angelique's "progress" allowed the missionaries to further test their longheld belief that grace superceded race and that "civilization" counted more than "Indian blood."[7] The missionaries deemed her ready to take the next step and become fully integrated into the larger American society.

As Angelique readied herself for her trip east, Mary Riggs lectured her that she should "be very industrious, and economical, of time and all other talents committed to her" at her new school.[8] Riggs's optimistic view that Angelique had the talent and work ethic (of course instilled by the missionaries) to succeed in a female seminary soon butted up against the reality that other non-missionaries did not hold the same views about American Indians. The missionaries' ideas about race, which stressed acceptance into American society if Angelique changed her culture and religion, did not translate to the Ohio Female College. Instead, the students and staff often treated Angelique as inferior. Indeed, the missionaries—and even their children like Martha—often struggled to adhere to their own ideals about the abilities and equality of "civilized" and Christian American Indians. Despite her years living with the Riggs family, Angelique struggled socially, academically, and likely with depression, punctuated by fleeting moments of levity with her roommate Martha Riggs and on trips during school breaks. This certainly was not what Angelique or the missionaries had hoped for when she left Minnesota.

When Angelique, Julia, and the missionary daughters left Minnesota to attend a female seminary, they joined hundreds of other middle- and upper-class American women who left their homes to further their education. Following the Revolutionary War, female seminaries sprang up across the United States, offering higher education and domestic instruction for well-off Euro-American women. Many of these seminaries provided courses that mirrored those offered at male colleges.[9] For example, Ipswich Female Seminary in Ipswich, Massachusetts, run by Zilpa P. Grant and Mary Lyon, provided rigorous courses for its students, including math, history, theology, philosophy, and religion.[10] Mount Holyoke, one of the most influential female seminaries of the era, offered Latin, moral philosophy, history, geography, and many of the sciences.[11] While some of the female seminaries taught sewing, needlepoint, dancing, drawing, and etiquette, others like Ipswich and Mount Holyoke deemphasized these "ornamental" subjects.[12] Even those schools that promised academic rigor, however, did not challenge gender roles of the era that stressed marriage and motherhood for women. Rather, seminaries would prepare women to better fill these important roles; mothers needed to receive a rigorous education to properly raise and educate their future children.[13]

The schools also provided a strong religious education.[14] Many of the seminaries had ties to evangelical Protestantism, especially the Presbyterian, Congregational, and Methodist churches. Mary Lyon, for example, founded Mount Holyoke as a religious institution with links to the Congregational church.[15] The Presbyterian church supported the Western Female Seminary. At both schools, students attended church services on Sundays and read and studied the Bible throughout the week.[16] In addition to religious instruction, these female seminaries explicitly promoted missionary work for women, especially with the ABCFM, a Congregational and Presbyterian organization.[17] Mount Holyoke teachers hung ABCFM maps in the common rooms, encouraged their students to pray for their missionary sisters abroad, circulated a journal extolling the exploits of female missionaries, and established religious study groups devoted to the mission cause.[18] They also held "monthly concerts" where students read missionary letters aloud or listened to speakers.[19] By the late nineteenth century, one-fifth of all women affiliated with the ABCFM had attended Mount Holyoke. Many other ABCFM female missionaries had attended similar institutions.[20] In general, missionary women tended to be some of the most highly educated women of the antebellum era.[21]

Many of the women associated with the Dakota mission illustrate the importance of seminaries as training and recruiting grounds for female missionaries. Mary Riggs, for example, "was a pupil of Mary Lyon, when she taught at Buckland, and afterward of Miss Grant at Ipswich."[22] While at the Ipswich Female Seminary, Riggs reported that she took demanding courses, including algebra, ecclesiastical history, natural theology, philosophy of natural history, and religion.[23] She also trained to be a teacher and strengthened her "missionary spirit."[24] Shortly after Mary's graduation, she married Stephen Riggs, almost sight unseen, in order to become a missionary among the Dakota people. At seminaries like Ipswich, women received a rigorous secular education and learned about the importance of religious self-sacrifice and missionary work. When their own daughters came of age, mothers like Mary Riggs hoped to send them to one of the religiously affiliated female seminaries. They extended their support of female seminaries to the few long-term American Indian boarders, like Angelique and Julia, who showed academic promise.

While hundreds of female seminaries existed throughout the United States in the first half of the nineteenth century, Mary Riggs and other Minnesota missionary women favored the Western Female Seminary in Oxford, Ohio, for their daughters. Four main reasons led them to consider the "Great Western" to be the perfect school for their children. First, the Western Female Seminary, like its sister school at Mount Holyoke, offered a rigorous, high-quality, four-year education that was equivalent to a college degree. Students studied astronomy, geology, biology, physiology, botany, physics, Latin, English, and history.[25] The school deemphasized "ornamental" courses, such as music and needlepoint, as well as domestic classes, though students performed several hours of domestic labor each day to keep tuition costs low. Martha Riggs, for example, reportedly cooked for the sick (which she described as "tiresome and not very pleasant") and mopped the school.[26] Another missionary daughter made the early morning fires, rang the first bells, and woke the other girls for their early domestic work.[27]

Second, in addition to a rigorous curriculum, the Western Female Seminary had an explicitly religious purpose that appealed to the Dakota missionaries. Students attended church services at the Second Presbyterian Church in Oxford on Sunday mornings, studied their Bibles on Sunday afternoons, and attended other church services at Western on Sundays and Thursdays.[28] Like Mount Holyoke, the school also promoted missionary work, eventually sending many of its graduates to proselytize at missions around the world.[29] Third, many of the missionaries previously lived in Ohio, which meant that their daughters could visit relatives during breaks without having to make the long and expensive trip back to Minnesota. Finally, the school was affordable for the cash-strapped missionaries. The daughters of clergy and missionaries paid $60 a year for board and tuition, while other students paid $2.50 a week.[30] According to education historian Margaret Nash, the Western Female Seminary prided itself on providing its female students with rigorous academic and religious training at an affordable price.[31]

Isabella Riggs attended the Western Female Seminary (1856–1858; 1861), as did her sister Martha (1858–1860), Nancy Williamson (1856–1860), and Julia Laframboise (1858).[32] Although the curriculum typically lasted four years, the girls (with the exception of Nancy Williamson) took longer to graduate, as they needed to take turns going to school to save money. For example, Isabella spent two years at the Western Female Seminary but returned to Minnesota before graduating to give Martha a turn to attend in 1858. After living in Minnesota for one year, Isabella asked her parents if she could resume her studies in Ohio. Her siblings took precedence, however, and she was not allowed to complete her senior year until 1861.[33]

The Riggs and Williamson families evaluated the Western Female Seminary positively and planned to continue rotating their daughters, along with Angelique Renville, into the school. But in January 1860, while Martha Riggs was in attendance, the main building burned down. Although the Western Female Seminary promised to quickly reopen in a new building, Martha chose to complete her spring term at the Ohio Female College, located about forty miles south in College Hill, a neighborhood of Cincinnati.

After her spring term at the Ohio Female College, Martha decided to take time off and return to Minnesota for the summer. When she arrived home, she "found all the girls have grown very much—Agnes is as tall as I am—while Anna Jane and Angelique are taller."[34] Martha always intended to return to the Western Female Seminary in the fall, but, while she was in Minnesota, F. Y. Vail, an agent for the Ohio Female College, sent Stephen and Mary Riggs a letter asking the Riggs family to enroll their daughters, including Angelique, in his school.[35]

As the Riggs family weighed their options, they compared the two Ohio seminaries. Though the Western Female Seminary had reopened, it did not have a permanent building. The Ohio Female College had a beautiful campus with multiple buildings and lush grounds. The College was also larger than the Western Female Seminary; in the 1850s the Seminary had fifty-two students and ten faculty, while the College had over two hundred students and eighteen faculty.[36] Finally, the College catered to a more affluent population. Despite the differences in size and income, both schools pledged to offer its students a rigorous education. Students at the Ohio Female College took challenging courses, including chemistry, philosophy, geography, astronomy, English literature, anatomy, and physiology.[37] Historian Leonard Sweet argued that Oxford Female College was one of the few seminaries that achieved equal status with male colleges at the time. Its students used many of the same textbooks, received the same course work, and required four years for graduation like comparable male schools.[38]

The Ohio Female College also promised that its students would receive a "true Christian female education" which would "bless the family, our country, and the world."[39] Religious instruction included "short morning lectures, connected with the daily reading of the Bible, singing and prayer in the chapel, and a weekly exercise in the systematic study of the Scriptures."[40] This religious education would help to create "a powerful auxiliary to the enlargement and extension of Christ's kingdom."[41] Although the school's promotional materials promised a heavy dose of religion and evangelism, in practice its curriculum and ethos focused less on religion and missionary work than the Western Female Seminary. After switching to the Ohio Female College, Martha Riggs complained to her brother Alfred that she was horrified to find that "there are only fourteen or fifteen professing Christians. A sad thing is it not?"[42]

While Martha questioned the Ohio Female College's commitment to religious instruction, she lauded its strict academic standards for admission. Applicants to the Ohio Female College needed to show they had "a good knowledge of English Grammar, Modern Geography, Written and Mental Arithmetic as well as the History of the United States."[43] They also were required to send letters attesting to their educational background and character.[44] As corroborated by Angelique's admission, her missionary teachers had successfully argued that she met the school's standards. Indeed, Eliza Huggins's 1860 evaluation of Angelique may have been submitted to illustrate her preparedness for further education. As stated in the introduction, Huggins attested to the fact that Angelique had studied geography, the history of the United States, English grammar, and arithmetic. She promised that Angelique's demeanor was "orderly, respectful and lady-like."[45]

While Eliza Huggins served as Angelique's public advocate, in private, some of the missionaries—especially Martha Riggs—expressed skeptism about Angelique's abililities. In the fall of 1860, when plans were under way to send Angelique to Ohio, Martha wrote to her brother Alfred, "I'm very much afraid Angelique won't be ready by next fall, though she seems to be enthusiastic enough as regards to it."[46] Martha also questioned Angelique's plan to bring her brother Daniel with her to school. Martha again informed Alfred, "Angelique is quite interested in the idea of going to school another year. She lays most magnificent plans about it—Daniel is going too she says. I imagine myself escorting him around—It would be too funny."[47] Despite the missionaries' efforts to separate Angelique from her family, she kept extensive contact with her mother, siblings, and other kin while living at the Lac qui Parle and Hazelwood missions. She assuredly wanted her brother Daniel to accompany her to Ohio to provide support, as she had never been completely separated from her family. Martha's comment, however, indicates that she believed Daniel would not fit in and would be an embarrassment to her in Ohio.

Martha's worries about Daniel's comportment in "civilized" society are a bit perplexing, given his extensive interaction with the ABCFM mission throughout his life. Although he did not board with the Riggs family like his sisters and brother Thomas, Daniel learned to read and write at the Kaposia mission school.[48] Moreover, it appears that between 1852 and 1855, Daniel lived in Galesburg, Illinois, with his uncle John B. Renville. While in Galesburg, Daniel and John may have attended Knox College or boarded with a Presbyterian family to study English.[49] During their time in Illinois, both attended the Galesburg Presbyterian Church.[50] By 1856, Daniel and John had returned to Minnesota. John brought Mary Butler, a white woman, back with him from Galesburg; the two married and worked together as missionaries to Dakota families for the rest of their lives.

Whatever the reason for Martha's critical evaluation of Daniel, it is not surprising that she—and the rest of the Riggs family—supported sending Angelique to school in Ohio to remove her from the "negative" influence of her kin. Perhaps most important, she would no longer be able to see Therese, who still lived within walking distance of the Hazelwood Mission. Once she was separated from her family, the College would complete Angelique's transformation from "savagery" to "civilization," which the Riggs family had begun a decade earlier.[51]

Although Angelique's time with the missionaries had supposedly prepared her for higher education, she faced many challenges at the Ohio Female College. She certainly would have been out of her element at a large school that catered to wealthy Euro-American daughters of the Midwest. Perhaps the Western Female Seminary, with its focus on evangelical religion and missionary work, its smaller number of students, and its mission to educate less affluent pupils would have been a better fit. Angelique had spent ten years in a sheltered religious community that stressed the importance of Christianity and austerity, both central components of the Western Female Seminary's ethos. She also had been taught the importance of giving up all aspects of her Dakota identity, which again fit into the "Great Western's" focus on missionary work.

Angelique may have had trouble no matter which school she attended. In Ohio, Angelique was thrown into a world vastly different from her own. She took unfamiliar courses in a second language while learning to navigate city life. Although Martha Riggs also came from the same sheltered environment, there was one main difference: she was not an Indian and looked and acted—albeit with more religious fervor—like the other girls. In contrast, Angelique was the only American Indian girl attending the school. As a Dakota woman who still had ties to her relatives and community (despite the missionaries' best efforts), Angelique was an outsider who would struggle relating to the administrators, teachers, and especially her peers.

Angelique's socioeconomic status also set her (and Martha, for that matter) apart from the other students. Most of the students who attended the Ohio Female College came from wealthy families. Indeed, the College was cost-prohibitive for all but the most affluent. In 1862, tuition cost $200 per year (approximately $5,500 in present-day dollars), $140 more than the Western Female Seminary. The exorbitant rates covered "board in the College household . . . light, heat, washing . . . maternal care, and tuition."[52] Uniformed servants waited on the students and "staff included cooks, laundresses, and maids."[53] Despite the College's hefty overall cost, the school charged extra for ornamental courses, including languages, music, drawing, painting, and needle work.[54] For example, tuition for German and French cost between sixteen and twenty-four dollars per year; music (depending on whether the student added vocal exercises) cost at least fifty dollars; drawing classes started at twenty-five dollars.[55] The missionaries also needed to pay for their daughters to travel between Minnesota and Ohio. In 1860, Stephen Riggs thought it would cost fifty dollars to get Martha home from school, while Mary Riggs offered a lower but still high estimate of thirty-five.[56] Martha Riggs commented that all of the "add-ons" made the Ohio Female College "the worst place I ever was in for making folks spend money."[57]

Total expenses made the College far too expensive for a missionary budget. Stephen Riggs never made more than $500 a year for his family of ten.[58] Riggs lamented that "a third of the whole family allowance would not suffice to pay the expenses of one [family member], at the most economical of our colleges or schools."[59] Despite their tight budget, both Stephen and Mary Riggs valued quality education—for both their sons and daughters—and vowed to put all their children through school. They used various strategies to achieve this goal, often sending only one or two children to school at a time. For example, in order to allow Martha and Angelique to attend one year, Isabella and Anna Jane ended up staying in Minnesota.[60] The missionaries also received donations to help support their children's education. For instance, "Mrs. Blaisdell and the other Christian friends of the Second Presbyterian Church of Cincinnati" helped to pay Isabella Riggs's tuition at the Western Female Seminary.[61]

In winter 1860, following the fire at the Western Female Seminary, the Ohio Female College offered Martha reduced tuition. Later, when Martha returned to Minnesota, F. Y. Vail, the college's agent, offered to refund all the money that she had paid in the spring. In addition to the tuition refund, Vail promised to enroll Anna Jane Riggs "for $50 a year—or for $75 including music," as her father had previously offered Vail advice which "had been so much service to him that he [felt] as if he ought to educate pa's daughters for nothing."[62] Stephen Riggs must have determined that price was affordable, especially with Martha's tuition refund, as he sent Anna Jane to the Ohio Female College in fall 1860.

Martha worried, however, about the atmosphere of the Ohio Female College on her impressionable sister, having experienced it herself for one semester after the fire. She was "sorry Anna would not have gone to Oxford—for the first year at least—she is so young. I fear she will be lead astray more easily than she would have been at the good old Western."[63] Martha reported a litany of problems she faced during her one semester at the new school. The College did not "have one quarter as many rules [as the Western Female Seminary], and those we do have are not nearly so strictly enforced."[64] Many of the girls were not professing Christians; they also had "never known any privation . . . and complain daily about food and other things which are so much better than our home ever sees."[65] With regard to her courses, she complained that none of her lessons at the Ohio Female College equaled the courses she had taken at her previous school.[66] She even called the president of the school "an abominable teacher."[67] For all these reasons, Martha worried that Anna Jane would "fall into temptation" at the College "more than she might in some other place," but took comfort in the fact that "god can care for her there."[68]

Despite Martha's worries, Anna Jane survived her year at the Ohio Female College. Her success likely contributed to the Riggses' decision to send Martha and Angelique to the school in 1861. Perhaps more important, however, was the school's offer of continued reduced or (likely) free tuition for the girls. The College promised to support pastors and missionaries by reducing their daughters' tuition by 25 percent.[69] The school would further reduce tuition bills for "Western Ministers" who had devoted "their lives [to] the pastoral and missionary service," had large families "with six to eight children to support and educate," and made less than $300 to $500 a year.[70] For these daughters, tuition would be reduced by 50 percent, or waived entirely.

The latter scenario appears to have been the case for the Riggs family. After promising to pay the entire tuition of the missionary daughters, the Ohio Female College's catalogue provided a lengthy example of a missionary who received this subsidy:

> The missionary is amongst our aborigines, and, having grown grey in a most laborious missionary service of more than twenty-five years, with a family of eight children to support and educate with the small salary of a missionary, found himself unable alone to educate his daughters for the missionary work. I need not say that we esteemed it a high privilege, as well as a duty, to extend the requisite aid to three of the daughters of this beloved missionary—young ladies of high intellectual powers, devoted piety, thirsting for knowledge—and two of them now making happy and honorable progress in study—being salt in the Institution, and intending to return as laborers to their father's missionary field.[71]

The passage concluded by stating that the College received the girls "without expense."[72] Although Stephen Riggs is not mentioned by name in the paragraph, there is little doubt as to his identity: he had worked with the Dakotas for twenty-five years and had eight children. The passage, however, is a bit unclear about who received the aid. Certainly, Anna Jane and Martha received reduced or free tuition, but was Angelique the third daughter? In 1862, the year of the catalogue's publication, the two girls at the school were Angelique and Martha, so the catalogue implies that both received free tuition.

Nonetheless, Riggs dutifully recorded in his guardianship ledger that he paid $100 for Angelique's yearly tuition at the College. He also recorded other expenses related to her education in Ohio on her steadily growing account. He listed $28.27 for "Angelique's outfit on sending her to school," $24.50 for her travel expenses to Ohio, $37.50 for incidental expenses, and $8 additional spending money during her year at the College. In addition to her school expenses, he continued to pay the yearly taxes on her land. In all, by the time she left for Ohio, Angelique owed Riggs $290.73. This included his running list of expenses since 1857, six percent interest added in each year, and her new school expenses.[73]

Since becoming her guardian, Riggs had always planned to sell Angelique's lands. While he had been unsuccessful in the late 1850s, in 1861 he vowed to finally sell 120 acres (called a "quarter section") to pay her accumulated debt and new school expenses in Ohio. He justified his decision to sell her land in a letter to the ABCFM's leadership. After sending Angelique to Ohio, "she has not been counted as one of our scholars here, and I have not drawn for her support from the treasury of the Board. She is now in her eighteenth year [she was actually sixteen and seventeen when she attended the school]—owns some prairie land, a part of which as her guardian I mean to use for her further education."[74] In this same letter, he also signaled his intent to sell a quarter section of Agnes's land even though she did not attend a female seminary at this time.

Although Minnesota guardianship law allowed Riggs to sell his wards' land, he was required to follow set procedures. First, he needed to obtain a license to sell from the county court. On 26 July 1861, he filed his petition with the Brown County probate court, writing, "the said Guardian needs money to pay expenses of locating Half Breed Scrip and said lands and also to pay taxes on the same, and also to expend in the support and education of said wards."[75] He applied to sell one quarter section each of Angelique's and Agnes's land. Second, the court required that he "serve notice" on "the next of kin of the ward[s], and all persons interested in the estate, to appear before the court . . . to show cause why a license should not be granted for the sale of such estate."[76] In September 1861, the court served notice to Therese Renville, requiring that she appear before the probate judge on 9 September "to show cause why the petition of said guardian for license to sell a portion of the estates of said wards shall not be granted." No existing documents indicate whether Therese appeared before the court. In the 1850s, she had attempted, and failed, to keep Riggs from gaining control of her daughters' scrip. She would have been at a similar disadvantage if she had attended the hearing. She did not speak (or at least was not fluent in) English, was not literate, had already been deemed "incompetent" by the court to raise her daughters, and had to contend with a prominent missionary guardian who promised to use the money to support her daughters' "civilization" and Christianization—a goal strongly supported by the federal and state governments at the time. If Therese did testify against the sale, the court ignored her wishes, as Riggs was granted a license to sell 120 acres of each of the daughters' land.

After obtaining the license, Riggs next was required to advertise the land sale in a local newspaper and post three fliers around the town where the auction would take place. He did so, noting when and where the land would be sold to the highest bidder. On 2 October 1861, Riggs auctioned off Angelique's land for $1.25 an acre ($150 total) to none other than F. Y. Vail, the Ohio Female College's agent.[77] No one bid on Agnes's land, so he withdrew it from sale. As he waited for the paperwork from the sale of Angelique's land to clear, Riggs dutifully recorded in his "guardians account" that Angelique owed him $20.65 for selling "120 acres of land at guardian's sale." He also recorded $1.75 for a patent (the document that transferred the title) and deed on the land sale.

It took another year to finalize the sale. In January 1862, Riggs was informed that he had failed to properly complete the process for the sale. The registrar of the Henderson, Minnesota, Land Office returned the patent on Angelique's land, as "the Scrip has not been Received."[78] Later, Riggs ran into further trouble because he needed to pay the 1861 taxes on Angelique's land prior to its sale. In spring 1862, Riggs charged his friend J. W. Holtsclaw with completing the sale. Holtsclaw encountered still more problems, informing Riggs that he could not "get the patent and deed recorded as you directed. They could not be recorded till the tax was paid."[79] Holtsclaw paid the tax and asked Riggs to reimburse him. Finally, on 10 March 1862, Holtsclaw confirmed the sale of 120 acres of Angelique's land.

Despite the completion of the sale, Riggs complained he cleared only "a little over $100 after the expenses of Probate sale and the taxes for last year were deducted."[80] According to Riggs's guardianship account, the land sale only covered part of the debt that Angelique had accrued over the years. After the sale of her land, Riggs recorded that she still owed him $140.73.[81] Despite the low return on her land, Riggs patted himself on the back for taking "care of Angelique as my own child" and giving her "the means of improvement."[82]

The conclusion to Angelique's land sale story gets a bit murkier. As noted, Riggs sold the land to F. Y. Vail of the Ohio Female College.[83] This was not the only time Riggs sold (or attempted to sell) his wards' scrip to a female seminary to pay for their education. In June 1862, Riggs wrote a letter to the Rockford Female Seminary asking if he could use Dakota scrip to pay for "the board and tuition of two Dakota girls under [his] care."[84] Of course, the two Dakota girls were Angelique Renville and Julia Laframboise. The Rockford trustees questioned Riggs's plan, asking how much the girls' land was worth and if they would need to pay taxes on the land. After both girls experienced trouble in Ohio (as will be discussed), Riggs wanted to find another seminary where he could use their scrip to pay for their tuition.

There is no indication that the sale of Angelique's land to Vail or the potential sale of scrip to the Rockford Female Seminary broke any laws at the time. Nonetheless, Riggs's and Vail's use of Angelique's scrip calls into question whether they truly had her best interests at heart. After expenses, Stephen Riggs cleared $122.40 ($100 for her acres and $22.40 for him to sell her lands). He then recorded that he sent $100 to College Hill for Angelique's tuition.[85] But if Vail himself had promised to cover Angelique's and Martha's tuition in that year's school catalogue, why did Riggs record that he sent $100 in cash to the College? Moreover, it appears suspect that Vail corresponded extensively with Riggs about the College and its reduced tuition, and then was able to purchase Angelique's land—at a considerably reduced price. According to a historical survey by the U.S. Department of Agriculture, in 1860, counties where the "Half-Breed Tract" was located were worth between $6 and $9 per acre, whereas Vail paid $1.25 per acre.[86]

Due to a lack of documentation, whether there were any backchannel dealings between Riggs and Vail is pure speculation. Still, it is clear that Riggs never asked Angelique if she wanted to sell her scrip, nor did he ever consult with her on how she wanted to use the proceeds. Moreover, while Minnesota law gave Therese the opportunity to speak against the sale of her daughter's land, it is unclear if she testified. Of course, this was perfectly legal at the time. Minnesota law gave Riggs complete control over his ward's estate, as long as he filed the correct paperwork and followed the required procedures. Going forward, Riggs planned to sell more of Angelique's land (and her sister's) before Angelique turned eighteen and her guardianship would end. He wrote, "I think it best to sell . . . the remainder—get her out of debt and give her the means of improvement. . . . I have no doubt that when she comes of age she will be better satisfied with this course than to have had all the 480 acres of land kept to pay taxes on."[87] Despite these assertions, at some level Riggs may have worried that Angelique would not approve or make the same choices and thus hastened to sell her remaining scrip before she became of age.

With the sale of her scrip in the background, Angelique and Martha set out for Ohio. In the 1860s, it took about two weeks to travel from the Hazelwood Mission to the Ohio Female College. The missionaries frequently journeyed east to visit friends and relatives and to conduct missionary business. As such, Martha and Angelique likely would have gone at least part of the way with Stephen Riggs, Thomas Williamson, or one of their many associates. On previous trips, the Riggses had used multiple forms of transportation, including boats, wagons, a steamer, and the railroad.[88] At various points along the way, they stopped and visited with missionary friends and supporters. For example, when Martha Riggs returned from the Ohio Female College in 1860, she spent several days in Chicago visiting her brother Alfred, who attended the Chicago Theological Seminary, and stopped at other ABCFM mission sites in Minnesota. When her sister Anna Jane traveled to Ohio in fall 1860, her father took her to La Crosse, after which various missionary friends took over, shepherding her to various points across the across the Midwest until she reached Ohio.[89]

Although Martha and Angelique did not write about their entire trip east, it must have taken longer than anticipated or they left Minnesota late, as they arrived in the first week of October 1861, about a month after the school term began. On one leg of their trip, they took a train from Michigan City to Indianapolis, arriving at their destination at 4:15 in the morning. When they arrived in Indianapolis, a missionary friend named Mr. Jackson was supposed to meet them at the station, but Martha reported that their contact was late and the girls "waited in the depot until it grew light." Finally, Mr. Jackson arrived and took them to his home, where "Angelique and I have been making ourselves useful." The girls remained with Mr. Jackson in Indianapolis longer than planned due to Martha's sore eyes.[90] They finally left Indiana and arrived safely on campus "without any disasters having happened to us."[91]

On arrival, Angelique likely would have been impressed with the campus and its main buildings, especially when compared with the Riggses' small mission home. The college certainly promoted its setting and buildings at least in part to justify its exorbitant tuition. The 1862 *Thirteenth Annual Catalogue and Prospectus* promised that the Ohio Female College was located on "one of the most beautiful and healthful positions in all the Western States."[92] Its campus contained twenty-three acres of land "beautifully diversified with hills, groves, ravines, rivulets, and native fountains," which afforded "ample space for promenades and gymnastic sports."[93] Students could wander through the institution's extensive gardens, greenhouse, shrubbery, and fruit orchard.[94] The school even had an "artificial lake," although Anna Jane Riggs remarked, "It is so small that it looks just like a mud puddle."[95] Anna Jane might not live in a lavish home in Minnesota, but she certainly came from a state with many impressive lakes.

As befitting a school for the affluent, the Ohio Female College had been "built on a grand scale."[96] The college had eight structures which offered "superior accommodations for chapel exercises, lectures, recitations, instructions in music, drawing, [and] painting."[97] The main building had cost nearly $100,000 to build, rose three stories, and contained "ninety-seven apartments, seventy-seven closets, and ten spacious halls."[98] The structure also had a kitchen, a dining hall, classrooms, dorm rooms, and common areas for dances and lectures. Its founders guaranteed the school was safe for its students; perhaps referencing the recent fire at the Western Female Seminary, the Ohio Female College promised, "This model structure is heated by steam generated in boilers situated two hundred feet in the rear, so as to avoid all danger from fire and explosion."[99] The school also touted the health benefits of the main building; the air in the dormitory rooms was "ventilated by valves and flues in such a manner as to remove all the air from the rooms every thirty minutes, and replace it by pure air drawn from the upper atmosphere by means of a tower and subterranean passage." This system allowed the air in the rooms to always be "kept pure, and suitable for respiration and the renovation of the blood."[100] While the students had "pure air," the school's catalogue neglected to mention that they did not always have heat. Angelique complained that her dorm room was "so cold I can hardly write."[101] Due to its high construction and operational costs, the Ohio Female College found itself in continual financial trouble and became insolvent in 1867.[102]

Part of the college's financial problems assuredly stemmed from declining enrollment. In 1850, the Ohio Female College had around two hundred students; this number had fallen to approximately one hundred by 1860. Martha Riggs commented on the low number of students when she arrived, noting that "instead of the buildings being full to overflowing, there are quite a number of vacant rooms even now."[103] The school, however, held that its student body seemed to be rebounding. Angelique wrote, "Miss Allison says that this school is fuller then it ever was since she has been here. Last tirm there was only ninty that boarded in the College but now there is about a hundred two or three."[104]

Students who attended the College participated in three terms: a sixteen-week fall session and two twelve-week spring sessions. Each session consisted of a new group of classes followed by examinations. The results of the exams "determine[d] the advancement of the pupil to the next stage of the course or the admission to a degree."[105] The students had winter, spring, and summer breaks between the three sessions. The school charged those who remained over breaks additional fees, so most students travelled home as they came primarily from Ohio and Indiana. Because of the long distance home, and the need to economize, Martha and Angelique visited family friends or relatives in Ohio during their breaks.[106]

Throughout her time at the College, Angelique wrote letters back to the Riggs family. These letters finally allow historians to hear from Angelique in her own words, instead of seeing her thoughts and feelings filtered through the pens of missionaries and other non-Dakota voices. Of course, these letters have their own biases. Angelique knew that the Riggs family expected her to be grateful for her time there, which may have led her to censor, or at least temper, some of her commentary. Despite these limitations, her letters provide insight into her life in Ohio, her schoolwork, and most telling, her struggles throughout her time at the College.

Aside from her discussion of school topics, Angelique's letters illustrate that she saw herself as part of the Riggs family; after all, she had resided with them for ten years, and they called her their adopted "daughter" or "sister." Angelique's letters echoed this same language, referring to the Riggs siblings as her own. She closed a letter to Alfred Riggs stating, "I am your Aff[ectionate] sister Angie Renville."[107] Like most children, Angelique wrote the Riggs family about her time at the school; in return, she requested news from home. She began one letter noting that she was happy to finally "hear from home for we had not had a letter fore four or five weeks."[108] In another letter, she asked if "Thomas [Riggs] got the letter written to me yet I am looking for it."[109] She also expressed that she missed the Riggs family, especially baby Mary Cornelia Octavia Riggs (called Cornelia), who had been born in February 1859. Many of Angelique's letters closed with, "A kiss for baby and a love for all the rest."[110] Another letter asked Mary Riggs to "Give a kiss to baby for me and tell her that Angie wants to see her very badly. . . . Give my love to all folks."[111] Mary noted that Cornelia missed Angelique as well, writing, "Cornelia remembers you still. Often when she wakes in the morning she says 'tell me about Martha and Angelique and Alfred' sometimes varying the order by placing you or Angelique first on the list."[112] While Angelique missed the Riggs family, she also wanted news about her Dakota family in Minnesota, asking in one letter, "Is my mother well and all the other folks?"[113]

The many struggles Angelique faced at school heightened her homesickness. Her academic problems began immediately on her arrival at the Ohio Female College. Administrators examined each new student to determine which "attainments she may have already made, and her place in the course of study is assigned to her in accordance with such examination."[114] Based on these tests, teachers divided students into either a four-year Collegiate Course or a two-year Preparatory Stage. Administrators further subdivided students into levels within those two broad designations.

After testing the students, administrators placed Angelique far below Martha in her class assignment. Martha was assigned to the highest level of the Collegiate Course: "Fourth Year—Senior Class." Martha's senior curriculum included philosophy, "Evidences of Christianity," Higher Rhetoric, English Literature, Logic, Aesthetics, Ethics, and Guizot's *History of Civilization*.[115] These courses represented the culmination of her studies, and she would receive her degree at the end of the school year. Administrators, however, placed Angelique into the lower, two-year Preparatory Course. Unlike the Western Female Seminary which required students to be at least fifteen years old, the Ohio Female College took girls as young as twelve.[116] This meant that Angelique, who had been taught with missionary children her own age at Hazelwood, was grouped with much younger students in the lower course—ages twelve to her sixteen and then seventeen.

Although the school catalogue stated that Angelique's cohort would study written arithmetic, introduction to algebra, ancient and Biblical geography, and botany, Martha reported that Angelique's schedule consisted of "History, Arithmetic, and Music." It is uncertain why her course load was much less than advertised and whether the other girls in her group faced the same discrepancy between the promised classes and their actual schedules. Perhaps due to her lower placement, Angelique fought to take Latin, like Martha. Lucy Spooner Drake, a missionary colleague who lived close to the College and kept close tabs on both girls, stated, "Angelique's great desire seems to be to study Latin." But the missionaries (and the school administrators) questioned her decision and suggested that she spend her time reviewing basic course materials. Lucy Drake and Mary Riggs, however, left the decision whether Angelique would study Latin to Martha, as she "would know best what she [is] capable of doing and what is best for her."[117] It appears that Martha supported Angelique's choice, and Mary Riggs half-heartedly endorsed the plan. "Although we should not have selected Latin for her," Mary wrote, "if she has a strong desire to study it, and can have the necessary books and opportunity free of expense, we shall not object."[118]

Perhaps because she chose to take Latin herself—even if Martha had ultimately given the approval—Angelique reported that Latin was her favorite class. She informed Stephen Riggs that "I am studying lattin I like it very much so far."[119] In another letter, Alfred Riggs asked Angelique "which of my studies I liked the best." She wrote back that she liked "latin the best I think I will like it still more when we get in the reader. Miss Hendrick is my teacher in latin I think she is the best latin teacher here."[120] Interestingly, Martha told Alfred that Angelique's favorite class was music, as she was "getting along pretty well in her music, better than in anything else I think."[121] Though Martha was often asked to speak for Angelique, her music response illustrates that she could give inaccurate answers based on her own assumptions about Angelique's abilities. It seems she did not ask Angelique what she thought about her subjects.

Martha's response to Alfred also implied that Angelique struggled in many of her classes, which was, unfortunately, correct. For some unknown reason, she had three different teachers in music. Each time she was assigned a new teacher, she had to relearn concepts already covered. She reported, "My music teacher is changed for the third time and when I am changed I have to practice just what I have been." Her most recent music teacher "would think I was not singing when I was doing my best." Angelique tried to put a positive spin on her rotating and critical music teachers, noting, "I have to do more myself so I expect I will learn more in the singing line."[122]

Angelique also struggled to write her compositions, as she often could not "think of anything to write."[123] Because of her difficulties, completing a composition was a proud achievement. In one letter, she informed Stephen Riggs, "This is Saturday morning, and I have just got my composition done fr which I am very glad."[124] Even when she successfully finished a composition, Lucy Drake and Angelique's teachers criticized her progress. Drake wished that Angelique had known how to read and write better, as "there are many moments she might employ" those skills in her classes.[125]

Ironically, the only time Angelique succeeded with her compositions and, more broadly, received any "positive" attention from her peers, was on account of her Dakota heritage. She informed Stephen Riggs that the girls liked her "compositions about the Indians. . . . [They] all want to copy it so they can read it fore their composition some times."[126] Martha Riggs also noted that some of the girls "pay her considerable attention because she is an Indian, and I'm afraid it won't be so good for her."[127]

The girls' interest in Angelique likely was grounded in two competing stereotypes that often appeared in nineteenth-century children's literature. On the one hand, children's school readers and textbooks frequently romanticized American Indians and their lives, portraying them as "noble savages."[128] On the other hand, they also were told that Indians lived outside of the political and cultural mainstream of American life and as such were doomed to vanish due to their lack of "civilization."[129] For example, the most popular readers of the era, known as *McGuffey's Readers*, provided long excerpts of romantic stories featuring Indians. One such story, published in the sixth level of the *McGuffey* series, featured a young girl named Magawisca who lived in an idyllic village at the summit of a hill with a "stream that glided around our hill, and so near it that the still nights we could hear its gentle voice." Unfortunately, over time, Magawisca's people were "extinguished" in the name of "progress."[130] Thus, by the age of twelve, Angelique's peers certainly had been exposed to many of these "romantic, yet doomed" stereotypes of American Indians, which undoubtedly fueled their fascination with Angelique and her "Indian stories."

At the same time the girls viewed Angelique as a "romantic savage," they also would have been exposed to literature which portrayed Indians as violent, "uncivilized heathens." For instance, the fourth level *McGuffey* reader included a story featuring "prowling savages" who "plundered the cabins of settlers in their absence" and kidnapped a young girl while her parents were away.[131] The "savage" stereotype undoubtedly led "one of the girls" to ask Anna Jane Riggs during her time at the College "if my mother was an 'Indian squaw' and if we lived like other folk in civilized lands or like the Indians. Another girl asked me if 'we ever talked English at home.'"[132] One can only imagine that Angelique, an actual Dakota, received far worse questions and assumptions than Anna Jane, a white missionary daughter who grew up among the Dakotas.

Unfortunately, the negative stereotypes associated with Indians led some of the girls to treat Angelique as unintelligent and slow. While sewing was not an academic course, the girls frequently sewed and knitted, especially for charity. The girls criticized Angelique's sewing skills, even though she had learned to sew from her Dakota relatives and had continued sewing at the Riggs home from the age of six. Angelique reported that her classmates were "making up a box to send to a Hospital in Louisville." She must have sewn slowly, however, as Martha ended up taking over Angelique's project for her. "Martha has got my dress done all the girls say it is very pretty it is black and white plads and trimed with red buttons. they think Martha is very smart." Angelique reported that the girls asked Martha "if I do not know how to sew." It appears that the missionaries were not the only ones who asked Martha to speak for Angelique. In the end, Angelique decided not to try at all. She "was going to knit a pair of socks" for the charity box but decided not to, as she "was affraid it would take me so long that they would not want them."[133]

It is not surprising that Angelique gave up on sewing. It appears that she may have done the same in some of her other academic classes. Martha complained that Angelique "doesn't see any use in studying this or that, and so won't apply herself as she should."[134] While couched in negative terms, Martha may have been correct that Angelique did not see the relevance of these classes to her life in Minnesota. Angelique also may have struggled with classes that were conducted in a second language and filled with younger students who treated her as either a "noble savage" or as an "uncivilized" Indian. Perhaps it was easier for her to not try at all, than to fail at classes she did not like or feel comfortable taking in the first place.

Her situation worsened by the end of the spring term. The school held exams at the end of each session, which determined the student's advancement to the next stage.[135] It does not appear that Angelique passed her spring exams. She apologized to Stephen Riggs, writing, "I was very much disappointed about my reports for I had studied very hard and tryed to get them. I hope I will have better ones the next time."[136]

Many of the problems that plagued Angelique in her academic classes also affected her social interactions with her peers. The negative evaluations, however, went both ways. Angelique did not understand or appear to like most of the girls in the school. She characterized them as vacuous and silly, especially regarding boys. Angelique explained that "Marthas cousin Charly sent her his picture and she showed it to some of the girls and they all fell in love with it . . . one of them said Oh: what sweet boys if they were here I would like to kiss them and another said she would like to kiss them."[137] Another time,

Angelique observed, "The little girls here are so crazy when they see a boy good many of them have got themselvs in to trouble."[138] Angelique found it even more perplexing that the girls did not act like Christians. Many of the girls swore, which Angelique "thought only boys and men did."[139] She also did not understand why the girls made "fun of the Bible" and teased her for being "so religious."[140]

The girls' behavior made no sense to Angelique. Evangelical missionary culture certainly would have frowned on the girls' actions that did not conform to the missionaries' strict definitions of correct behavior for women. Moreover, like Martha, Angelique had been taught to treat the Bible with reverence and conversion to Christianity as the highest goal. As a recent convert to the mission church right before she left for Ohio, Angelique did not understand the girls' negative reactions to her Christian beliefs. For her part, Angelique "resolved that I shall always show them that I am and hope I'm a christian."[141]

The girls' conduct also contradicted Dakota cultural norms. Missionary Samuel Pond observed that Dakota girls and women valued decorum and modesty. He observed that "as a general rule [Dakota girls] were chaste in their conversation and modest in their behavior both home and abroad. Many of the young women were diffident and bashful and very much afraid they should say or do something unbecoming."[142] Angelique had been raised in a bi-cultural environment that combined evangelical Protestant and Dakota culture, neither of which appeared to have prepared her to understand her peers at the Ohio Female College.

Angelique viewed the younger girls, with whom she had to spend much of her time, as silly and immature. Their immaturity had a harsh edge, as the girls frequently acted unkindly, judgmentally, and even cruelly. Angelique complained that during meals "I sit at Miss Copelands table it is one of the nosiest table all the little girls sit there. They order me around so much I do not like it they think I must do it sometimes I think I wont do what they tell me to and then they commence and scold me." The little girls' bullying made her much "vexed."[143] Angelique never mentioned if the teachers or matrons stepped in to support her or to discipline the other girls. It appears they did not, as she remained with the younger girls throughout her time at the school.

In particular, Angelique had problems with Kate Wood, one of her roommates. Indeed, Kate was the only girl except Martha Riggs she referenced by name in her letters. Although Kate was much younger than Angelique, she was placed in a higher-level class.[144] Martha, Angelique's other roommate, called Kate a "very pleasant" and "delightful" little girl, although she did "pout" especially when interacting with Angelique. Angelique, however, saw Kate as anything but delightful. She informed Stephen Riggs, "Kate Wood gets mad very quick at some things that I just say in fun and do in play so I have come to the conclusion that I will not be so any more."[145] Perhaps there were cultural differences in humor that were lost in translation. Or, Kate Wood may have "vexed" Angelique for the simple reason that she was a Dakota. She also was part of the younger group that bullied Angelique at meals. Again, it appears that neither the teachers, nor the matrons, nor Martha stepped in, as Angelique attempted to resolve the situation herself. "[O]ne thing I have improved in is that I have learned to controle my temper thear was for a while that I thought I would never get along well with Kate Wood . . . but I just thought thear was no sense in doing that way so I have stoped though it is very hard to sometimes."[146]

While Angelique tried hard to get along with Kate and the other girls, she confessed to Alfred Riggs that she lived in constant fear that "the girls will make fun of me."[147] She walked on eggshells, afraid to say anything that would lead to teasing or worse. She admitted that the girls "frighten me sometimes."[148] Being constantly on guard must have been exhausting and emotionally draining for Angelique. Indeed, she could not understand why "at home" she "never felt the way I do now" while at school "any little thing always would make me angry."[149] All her struggles accumulated to make Angelique unhappy and seemingly depressed at the school much of the time. Martha Riggs noted that Angelique was very homesick and slept much more than she should.[150] Instead of focusing on her negative treatment from the little girls and especially Kate, Martha advised Angelique to deal with her unhappiness by always thinking "of her duty to God" and "endeavor to glorify God in these little things."[151]

As illustrated by Martha's frequent advice, she played an outsized role in Angelique's life at Ohio Female College. On the positive side, Martha was Angelique's roommate, confidante, and link to home.

Angelique was proud of Martha and supported her at school, especially when she was chosen as class president. She informed Stephen Riggs, "I expect you will feel honored to know that one of your daughters is a president there were a good many up to hear her Inaugural address."[152] In another letter, Angelique wrote that she felt "quite honored to room with the president."[153]

Martha and Angelique shared some moments of laughter in their dorm room, especially at the expense of F. Y. Vail. During Anna Jane Riggs's time at the Ohio Female College, she had described Vail as "nervous figgity and jerky."[154] Echoing Anna Jane, Angelique found him to be "such a queer man." One morning, the water leaked through the ceiling of their dorm room. Angelique reported,

> Mr Vail came up to see what was the matter soo as he saw what the matter was he ran down stairs and had the servants come up with buckets and he went around and got all the dirtpans and then he came in our room and took all our towels. I do not know what he did with them. After he got through he came in our room and thought it was his he looked all around and saw that we were in the room he fund out that he had maid a mistake he had taken off his spectacles and was going to sit down he found out that he had maid a misstake he looked so funny we couldn't keep from laughing.[155]

Both girls also enjoyed their time away from the school on breaks. Because they could not afford to travel back to Minnesota, they remained in Ohio over the winter and spring breaks. They mainly visited their old mission teacher, Lucy Spooner Drake, and her husband William. Over winter vacation, Angelique reported that they took a sleigh ride with Mr. Drake, rode the omnibus, and "saw a good many wonderful things when I was in the city we went the slaughter house and saw the performance there." She "had a very pleasant time in vacation."[156] During another break, Angelique reported that "we saw Mrs. Bodly and she asked us to come there some Saturday and stay till Monday."[157] Angelique had "the funyest time" once when she had her picture taken.[158] Martha enjoyed these vacations too. Over winter break, Martha wrote, "We spent our two weeks of freedom from study in East Walnut Hills and in Jamestown—and enjoyed ourselves very much."[159]

On a less positive note, both Martha and Angelique also agreed that the other girls at the school spent way too much money on frivolous items. Martha felt "bitter" and "wrong" about associating with girls who "have never known any privation—nor trouble who scoff at work and poverty, and complain daily about food and other things."[160] Angelique also commented on the girls' spending. "I should hate to be the one to pay up the bills of some of the girls . . . I always thought little children were the ones to eat candy nearly every saturday the girls go in to the city and when they come home their baskets are filled then on Monday mornin a good many of them are sick."[161]

Even though both girls agreed that their classmates spent too much money, Martha and her father believed that Angelique could not resist following their bad behavior. Of course, this was a common stereotype about Indians; they supposedly could not help themselves from adopting the behavior of profligate whites who drank, smoked, spent too much money, or ignored the Sabbath. Like other Indians on the frontier who learned the worst from white society, the Riggses feared Angelique would unthinkingly follow the lead of the college girls and frivolously spend her money. As her guardian, Stephen Riggs vowed to teach her the value of money and frugality. Indeed, Riggs only begrudgingly provided her with clothing and spending money, even though he had sold her land to support her at school. For example, Angelique wrote Stephen Riggs asking for a dress, as she had outgrown all her clothing. "I do not know what I am going to do with myself," she wrote. "I am getting so fleshy that not one of my dresses is larg[e] enough and I think I must be growing . . . my new calico dress is very short and their is not a bit that I can let down unless I facet."[162] To save money, Riggs asked Martha to make her a dress, again having his daughter handle situations for Angelique; at the same time, he implicitly called into question Angelique's sewing skills by not entrusting her to sew her own clothing.

Stephen Riggs also believed that Angelique spent too much money on small items, and he cautioned her to spend less. Angelique apologized to Riggs for buying some apples. "I never thought that I was using up so much money untill I received your letter. I expect that if Martha was not here I would use more especially when the apple woman comes some times I want some so badly that I do not know what to do then Martha does with out then so I can."[163] When Angelique continued to want to purchase apples and other items, Martha acted as her father's surrogate and lectured her on the virtue of frugality. Martha seemed to grow frustrated in this role, complaining to her brother that Angelique was "forever wishing that she had something I can't afford to let her have."[164]

Over the months, Martha's frustration with Angelique increased. "It takes as I expected it would—a vast deal of patience to get along with her, for she most surely does not lack in contrariness, and is by no means easily contented," Martha complained to Alfred. She "didn't have to do this, or could do that. . . . Sometimes I get almost completely discouraged." Martha could not understand why Angelique "pouted" and "sulked" so often when she told "her as kindly as I can of something she ought or ought not to do. I should have supposed she would be ashamed to act so—without ever thinking of her duty to God."[165] Meanwhile, Angelique grew tired of Martha's constant advice and lectures.

Despite the missionaries' rhetoric of uplift and acceptance, they (and their children like Martha) still harbored negative evaluations of even those Dakotas who were closest to them. Instead of acting as her peer at school, Martha still saw Angelique as a child who needed to be told how to behave. Martha informed Alfred that despite her frustrations with Angelique, she had much to "be thankful for. I'm sure the one thing that Angelique is away from the influence of some of her relatives is quite sufficient to make one thankful for a time at least."[166] Echoing her parents' rhetoric about their sacrifices to the Dakotas, Martha proclaimed that her trials with Angelique would be worthwhile if it promoted her "civilization" and continued adherence to Christianity.

For many reasons, Angelique clearly did not have a good year in Ohio. At the end of the second spring session, it is unclear if she was asked to leave the school or not. There appears to have been a letter written by the school to Stephen and Mary Riggs, along with another letter containing Angelique's response. Unfortunately, both letters were lost in transit due to the disruption caused by the U.S.–Dakota War of 1862.[167] Although these letters were lost, Mary Riggs must have had an inkling that Angelique could not return to the Ohio Female College. Before the spring semester even ended, she wrote a letter to Helen Peabody, the principal of the Western Female Seminary, inquiring if Angelique could be admitted to the school the following fall. Again, Riggs promised to use Angelique's scrip to pay for her tuition. She also asked what Angelique would need to study to prepare for admission. Peabody told Mary Riggs to have Angelique "study American geography several hours every day—also to review Arithmetic." If Angelique studied and Riggs turned over her scrip, the Western Female College promised that "that some arrangement can be made so that she can enter the Seminary in September."[168] After learning this information, Mary Riggs again asked Martha—not Angelique—to decide Angelique's placement for the next fall term.[169]

Mary Riggs never explicitly linked Angelique's troubles at the College to her Dakota heritage. Angelique herself did not weigh in on this issue, but the evidence certainly suggests that she was treated differently from the other non-Indian girls. From the time she arrived at the school, her teachers placed her in the lowest class with the youngest students, despite her preparation at Lac qui Parle and Hazelwood. She sat with the youngest students at meals, her peers made fun of her academic and sewing skills, and the younger students bullied her. She was constantly scared and on edge when interacting with the other students. Numerous times, both adults and students asked Martha to speak for Angelique as if she was not in the room. The only time her "Indian-ness" was an asset was when the girls wanted to copy her compositions or ask questions about her "Indian" life. The missionaries had based their entire program on the supposition that race did not matter, and Angelique's time at the seminary was supposed to illustrate that "civilized" Christian Indians could be integrated into the larger American society. Instead, her experience in Ohio refuted the missionaries' promises of acceptance and equal treatment for assimilated, Christian Indians. Even Martha became exasperated with Angelique's lack of "progress."

The school year took a toll on Angelique, who wanted to give up on the missionaries' experiment and go home to her Minnesota family, especially Therese, Daniel, Agnes, and Thomas. At first, she equivocated, likely not wanting to disappoint the Riggs family. Right after the end of the spring semester, she asked, "Am I going to stay or come home[?]" In answer to her own question, she wrote, "if I was to choose I do not think I could for I want to come home and would like to stay."[170] Later, she provided a more definite answer. According to

Lucy Drake, Angelique "never before expressed any desire even when pressed on the matter" to continue her education.[171] While Stephen Riggs probably would have ignored Angelique's wishes to withdraw from school, the College's decision to not allow her to return forced their hand. The Riggs family needed to come up with an alternate plan to continue Angelique's "progress" toward civilization. As her guardian, Stephen Riggs did not need to consult with Angelique, her mother Therese, or other Renville kin about new plans for his ward. He decided it was best for Angelique to remain in Ohio for another year.

::: 4 :::

THE DRAKES, WAR, AND HOME TO MINNESOTA

June 1862–September 1863

In June 1862, at the end of the school term, Angelique Renville probably did not pass her final exams. At the very least, these results meant that she would not have advanced to the next class level; it is more likely that she would not have been allowed to return to the Ohio Female College the following fall even if she had wanted to. This outcome was not unexpected, as she had struggled with her classes, teachers, and peers during her months at the school. In contrast, Martha Riggs had excelled both academically and socially, serving as class president and participating in multiple clubs and societies. This divergence in experiences continued at the end of the year; Martha Riggs graduated from the Ohio Female College and returned home to Minnesota, while Angelique waited to find out the Riggses' plan for her.

Angelique watched from the sidelines as Martha and seventeen other senior girls began planning for graduation in the spring. While Martha was excited to graduate, she was anxious about several issues leading up to commencement. First, she did not have the funds to pay for the mandatory senior photographs, nor could she afford the required "Society diploma." Although she professed to not "care a pinhead" about those items, her long letters to her brother Alfred indicated otherwise. Her continued poverty weighed heavily on her mind.[1] She also worried about President Day's decision to read the girls' final essays aloud at the commencement ceremony. Martha nonetheless pushed this concern aside, reasoning that she "came somewhere near the last end, so I should have the pleasure of not being listened to at all."[2]

While Martha worried about several aspects of graduation, she was excited that her father and brother Alfred planned to attend her commencement exercises. After the mid-June ceremony, Stephen Riggs did not mention anything about Martha or Angelique in his letters home to his wife, although he "was very much charmed with the essay and appearance of Miss Eliza Wicks of Marietta." He regretted that Alfred had left early and missed the "opportunity of [her] acquaintance."[3] Perhaps Riggs thought that Eliza Wicks would have made a suitable missionary wife for Alfred. Although he never managed to orchestrate a meeting between Alfred and the charming Miss Wicks, Riggs watched as his daughter played a key role in the pageantry of the graduation ceremony as class president. After the festivities, Martha left Ohio with her father, visiting various friends and missionary acquaintances as they made their way home. They arrived back in Minnesota at the beginning of July.[4]

Angelique did not return to Minnesota with Stephen and Martha Riggs. Instead, she remained in East Walnut Hills, a neighborhood in Cincinnati, boarding with William and Lucy Spooner Drake and their children. Of course, Angelique knew Lucy Spooner Drake from her time as a teacher at the Lac qui Parle mission in the 1850s; she also had spent several of her school breaks with the Drake family to save on school fees. Stephen and Mary Riggs and Lucy Drake had decided that Angelique would remain in Ohio so that she could work on remedial schoolwork in preparation for further studies. Lucy had attended Ohio Female College in the early 1850s; the Riggses hoped she could tutor Angelique for her future return to school.[5] Again, no existing letters indicate that Angelique, her mother, or other relatives were part of this decision. As her legal guardian, Stephen Riggs continued to make all the choices for the still underaged Angelique.

Angelique lived in the Drake home for over a year. Unfortunately, her time with the Drakes brought more anguish and distress, which was a familiar refrain during her time in Ohio. She never completed her remedial studies, for multiple reasons including frequent illnesses (her own and especially Lucy Drake's), her constant domestic labor for the Drake family, and her growing disinterest in continuing her education. Her anguish increased once the U.S.–Dakota War of 1862 began a few months into her stay with the Drake family. Angelique certainly would have found it difficult to concentrate on remedial arithmetic or reading as she worried from afar about her family in Minnesota. Angelique begged the Riggses multiple times to send funds so that she could return home.

They refused to send her travel money, deciding it was best to keep her in Ohio. Though it shielded Angelique from the violence, this choice also kept her separated from her mother and siblings. While the missionaries had tolerated Therese visiting her children at the Lac qui Parle and Hazelwood Missions, her presence was contingent on her deference to the Riggses in all parental matters. During the war, however, Therese made decisions for her children that went against the missionaries' wishes. They demanded that she step back and relinquish control over her children—especially Agnes. The Riggses also worked to keep Angelique away from her mother, even after she came of age. In September 1863, Angelique finally prevailed and returned to Minnesota and her mother. Her traumatic year in Ohio, however, drove a permanent wedge between herself and the Riggs family.

Much of the tension between Angelique and her guardians started even before the school year ended, when Mary Riggs began making plans for Angelique to remain in Ohio. In May 1862, Mary Riggs wrote to her husband—who was away on missionary business—informing him that "Mrs. Drake *would like* to have [Angelique] remain with her a year." Knowing that her husband always worried about the cost of Angelique's care, Mary Riggs promised that "Angelique *could earn her food and clothing*" while with the Drakes. Mary Riggs thought that it was best for Angelique to remain with Drake, "unless there is an opening at Rockford [Seminary]. I have not formed this opinion hastily, and without consciousness of the objections—but it is a deliberate conclusion not withstanding objections."[6]

Perhaps the missionaries' biggest objection to this plan was that Angelique would no longer attend school. However, Mary Riggs reasoned that "a year with [the Drake family] may be just as well for her, as to be at school."[7] Indeed, Lucy Drake promised that Angelique would continue to move forward with her studies. She planned for Angelique to "review Arithmetic, Ancient geography and perhaps *Watts on the Mind*."[8] While the majority of the work would be completed on her own, Drake hoped to engage a young teacher to "assist

Angelique."[9] Drake also assured the Riggses that Angelique would keep up with her singing and sewing. After a year of remedial instruction, Angelique would either stay in Ohio and attend the Western Female Seminary or move to Illinois and join Julia Laframboise and Anna Jane Riggs at the Rockford Female Seminary. Mary Riggs had already contacted both schools to discuss Angelique's enrollment, using her remaining scrip as payment.

Angelique's time with the Drake family started inauspiciously. In June 1862, she arrived at their home extremely ill, having caught a terrible cold the previous winter and never recovered. At the time, Martha blamed Angelique for her own illness. She informed Alfred that Angelique caught a cold "by sitting on the ground for half an hour or so one evening to watch the boys skate. I wish she would ever learn to be even decently careful of herself but haven't much hope she will until she has ruined her constitution."[10] Alfred must have written to Angelique reprimanding her for carelessness, as she wrote back apologizing and promising to take better "care of my health I do not think I have been so careful as I ought to be it is so different here than it is at home if I get my feet wet I have no stove to dry them by so I go till they get dry, and then the consequences that I have a very bad cold."[11]

Regardless of how she caught the cold, Angelique arrived at the Drake home weak and ill. Like Martha, Drake initially blamed Angelique for her own illness. Although she admitted that Angelique had been sick at school, she "aggravated" her cold by overloading her "stomach with unripe peaches." Because Drake was sick herself at the time, she sent Angelique to her neighbor's home, where her neighbor diagnosed Angelique with "an attack of bilious fever" and "treated her homeopathically and as soon as she was able to be moved we brought her home."[12] Back at the Drake home, Angelique's condition worsened. Drake worried because there "seemed to be some trouble with her lungs. . . . She is extremely languid most of the time and has little appetite. She eats so little when she is well that I have not felt alarmed on that account, but her cough was the most alarming and she tells me she has not felt well since last winter when she had such a bad cold." She called the local doctor who prescribed quinine powder, after which Angelique seemed to improve.[13]

During her extended illness, Angelique did not have the strength to work or study. Drake had planned for her to commence reviewing ancient geography the week she "was taken sick." Drake did not press the issue, and "neither of us have been able [to be] student or teacher since." Although the worst of her illness passed and she seemed to improve, Angelique continued to tire easily and needed frequent breaks. While her studies remained stalled, Drake slowly put her back to work performing various domestic chores. She informed Mary Riggs that Angelique's tasks were "very moderate indeed, for . . . the weather was so warm, that it seemed hard work for her to be very active."[14] Angelique struggled even with these accommodations. Three months after her arrival, Drake still was "quite discouraged" with Angelique's lack of "energy."[15]

Although Angelique recovered, Lucy Drake continued to suffer from debilitating illnesses. In an understatement, Stephen Riggs commented that Lucy Drake experienced "a large share of personal physical suffering."[16] In summer 1862, when Angelique first arrived, Drake reported that her "health gave way" and for several weeks she was "confined to my room."[17] A few months later she again became ill. From December until early March she was "not able to read or write . . . on account of my eyes. . . . [I] was entirely blind for one week. Most of the time the pain was excruciating so that my nervous system is again much shattered."[18] In May 1863 she was sick yet again for another month. During her May illness, Angelique wrote that "Mrs Drake has been sick for four weeks."[19] As a result of her continuous illnesses, Drake's "nervous system" was extremely "frail." She felt "violent pulsations through my entire body brought on by the slightest exertion."[20]

Drake admitted that due to her ill health, "Angelique has been obliged to work more than I would like to have had her."[21] Angelique confirmed that she frequently took over most of the household duties because Drake was "not able to do any work" due to her extended illnesses.[22] In a 20 March 1863 letter to Mary Riggs, Angelique described her many daily responsibilities: "Mr. Drake gets up and makes the fires and then calls me. I have been getting the breakfast all the winter." After breakfast, "Mrs Drake sometimes goes visiting and leaves me to take the bread. so if I try very hard I can bake it nearly as nice as she can but sometimes I get in a hurry and burn the bread." In addition to cooking, Angelique did the washing by herself, which she thought "is to much and wish I did not have to."[23] These everyday chores increased during Drake's frequent illnesses. In May, Angelique wrote that she spent so much time "cleaning house" that she did not have "time to write much."[24] Ironically, the one domestic chore Drake did not assign to her was sewing, a skill that was important for success at the female seminaries. Angelique promised Mary Riggs, however, that "I still know how" to sew.[25]

Lucy Drake must have worried about the content of her correspondence to Mary Riggs, as she demanded that Angelique share her letters before she placed them in the mail. After reading Angelique's 20 March letter detailing her numerous chores, Drake dashed off a response to Mary Riggs defending her actions. While Drake did not outright accuse Angelique of lying, she informed Mary Riggs that she "now sees plainly that I have depended to much on her writing not that she means to misrepresent but does not state items plainly." Drake did confirm, however, that Angelique spent the majority of her time on chores rather than on schooling. Drake said she wished it could "have been otherwise, for I was very anxious for her to spend half the time with her studies and music." Still, Drake defended the arrangement. Although Angelique was "not [doing] as well in her studies as I would like, I think she is not losing much by not being in school."[26]

Moving forward, Drake promised Mary Riggs that Angelique would both perform her household chores and progress in her studies. Angelique, however, wanted to do neither. She tired of the constant chores, especially the washing; she also refused to start her remedial coursework. Lucy noted that Angelique "has never before expressed any desire [to study] even when I pressed the matter." After Angelique had spent close to six months in Drake's home, Drake finally sat Angelique down and lectured her on the importance of recommitting to her education. Drake "talked plainly to [Angelique] and was obliged to urge her beyond what I wished." Drake proclaimed that her lecture "was just what [Angelique] needed . . . and she is now anxious to commence her studies."[27] Following their talk, she finally engaged a young tutor. Although Angelique agreed to study with the help of the teacher, she disagreed with Drake over the content of the lessons. Drake wanted Angelique to "learn to write and also to read better."[28] But Angelique asked to study Latin, which had been her favorite class at the college. Perhaps due to the divergence in expectations over the content of her schooling, the young teacher did not work out. Drake blamed Angelique for being "not communicative enough."[29]

In addition to conflicts with Lucy Drake over her work and schooling, Angelique missed her friends and relatives in Minnesota. She especially worried that baby Cornelia Riggs would not remember her. She closed one letter asking Mary Riggs, "Give a kiss to baby for me and tell her that Anlik wants to see her very badly."[30] Angelique even sent a hat to Cornelia, proudly noting that she "worked and earned the money to buy it I am sorry to say that I could not get any pretty ribbons but blue I wanted to get white but it cost so much & I thought I could not get it."[31] While she knew that baby Cornelia could not write her back, Angelique expressed her anger at the older Riggs for not sending her news. She wondered if "Thomas got the letter written to me yet I am looking for it."[32] She was especially upset at Isabella Riggs, who "does not write to me or she never sends me any word. I begin to think that she is so glad I am her that she does not care any thing about me."[33]

Angelique's anger with Isabella and the rest of the Riggs family for their lack of communication paled in comparison to the trauma she suffered from being separated from her Dakota kin—especially her mother Therese, sister Agnes, and brothers Daniel and Thomas—during a time of war. On 17 August 1862, only a few short months after Angelique arrived at the Drake home, the U.S.–Dakota War broke out in Minnesota. Events there framed her entire stay in East Walnut Hills and certainly contributed to her to lack of energy, inability to focus on her studies, and growing desire to return home. Despite her increasingly frequent pleas to return to Minnesota, Stephen and Mary Riggs and Lucy Drake decided that it was best for Angelique to remain hundreds of miles away and separated from her Dakota family.

Although Angelique did not directly experience the U.S.–Dakota War, she had lived through many of the events and issues that caused the conflict.[34] By the time Angelique was sent to Ohio in 1862, the Dakotas had lost 90 percent of their traditional homeland, following a series of problematic treaties ratified in 1837, 1851, and 1858.[35] After the last treaty, Dakota families were confined to an impermanent reservation 140 miles long by ten miles wide. The new reservation was divided into two portions: approximately 2,300 Dakotas resided on the Lower Sioux Agency near the Minnesota River, while 4,000—including Angelique and her kin—lived on the Upper Sioux Agency near the Yellow Medicine River. Settlers eager for more farmland, however, threatened even the remaining reservation lands.[36] The number of white farms established in just one short decade illustrates the transfer of Indian lands to non-Indian farmers: in 1850, Minnesota had only 157 recorded farms; ten years later, that number had jumped to 18,081.[37]

Land loss and confinement to a small reservation made it difficult for Dakota families to continue their traditional subsistence practices of farming, hunting, and gathering, which led to food shortages. The fur trade also continued to decline, leading Angelique's uncles and other relatives to seek new opportunities around Minnesota, including establishing family farms on the upper reservation. The lack of animals for fur and food made other Dakota families dependent on government rations and other supplies. In the summer of 1862, just before the outbreak of the war, government annuities were delayed, and traders threatened to cut off Dakota purchases.[38] According to ABCFM missionary John Williamson, the government "had no rations for them. There were four stores at the agency . . . but they would not give credit to the Indians."[39]

In addition to dealing with corrupt Indian officials and missing rations, Dakota men, women, and children faced increasingly aggressive "civilization" and Christianization programs. Prior to the 1860s, the ABCFM missionaries' outreach had been limited and affected only a few families like Angelique's. In the years leading up to the war, however, government agents expanded their efforts to "civilize" all Dakotas. Officials authorized the construction of a government-run boarding school and urged Dakota men to cut their hair, put on "pantaloons," and begin farming. This increasingly led to a divide between "civilized" Dakota farmers and those who rejected Euro-American culture, religion, and gender roles. Wambditanka (Big Eagle) described the anger that many Dakotas felt over these intensified "civilization" programs. "The whites were always trying to make the Indians give up their life and live like white men . . . and the Indians did not know how to do that, and did not want to anyway," he explained. "If the Indians had tried to make the whites live like them, the whites would have resisted, and it was the same way with many Indians."[40]

Growing tensions among the Dakotas, Indian officials, Protestant missionaries, and settlers set the stage for war. On 17 August 1862, violence began on the Lower Agency. The U.S.–Dakota War itself was quite short. On 19 August, Minnesota governor Alexander Ramsey appointed General Henry Hastings Sibley—a Minnesota fur trader, settler, politician, and former employer of Angelique's father—to lead a volunteer army against the Dakotas. The following month, President Abraham Lincoln sent Major General John Pope to join Sibley after Pope's defeat at the Second Battle of Bull Run (the American Civil War had begun in April the previous year). Under the leadership of Sibley and Pope, the Army fought battles with the Dakotas at Fort Ridgely, New Ulm, Birch Coulee, and other locations. On 23 September, Pope and Sibley's forces defeated the Dakotas at the Battle of Wood Lake. Dakota scholar John Peacock called the military events of the war "asymmetrical . . . with a foregone conclusion." It was only a matter of time until U.S. forces prevailed due to their larger numbers and military capability.[41] Although the war ended fairly quickly, approximately four hundred to six hundred white settlers and soldiers died. Around sixty Dakotas also perished in the fighting, although their fatalities increased substantially following the war.[42] In the first two weeks of the war, fifteen to twenty frontier communities were almost emptied; by the end of the war, settlers had abandoned their homes and fields in more than twenty-three southwestern Minnesota counties.[43]

While Angelique remained separated from the war, her family experienced it firsthand. Just before the war began, Angelique's immediate family remained in close contact with the Riggses' Hazelwood mission: her sister Agnes lived in the Riggs home, her brother Thomas attended the mission boarding school, and her older brother Daniel lived near the mission. Their mother Therese also continued to reside close to the Riggs family in her government-issued home so that she could visit her children. When she learned of the violence on the Lower Agency, Therese immediately ran to the mission and took Agnes and Thomas away with her.[44] Over the next several weeks, Therese and her children joined the rest of their Renville kin, most of whom refused to join the war effort and even rescued the missionaries and numerous white settlers. For instance, when the war first broke out, Angelique's uncles John B. and Antoine Renville warned the Riggs and Williamson families to flee to safety.[45] After alerting the missionaries, John B. "assisted in the final safety of two hundred fifty five captives."[46] Although Mary Riggs worried that Angelique's brother Daniel was "among the suspected criminals," she later learned that he had rescued Sophia Huggins, a missionary teacher whose husband Amos was killed in the fighting.[47] Gabriel, Antoine, and Michel Renville also rescued white settlers. As such, the Renvilles played a key role in the complex story of the war where, according to historian Carrie Reber Zeman, "Dakota people simultaneously *took* captives, [*rescued* captives], were held *as* captives, and were rebelling *against* cultural captivity imposed by outsiders and by their own kin."[48]

Following the decisive Battle of Wood Lake, over a thousand Dakotas, including Therese and her children, congregated at what became known as Camp Release (located near present-day Montevideo, Minnesota) under the command of General Sibley.[49] Sibley informed those who surrendered that they would be treated fairly and humanely. He promised that he had "not come into this country to injure any innocent person, but to punish those who have committed cruel murders upon innocent men, women, and children." He assured those who "hoist[ed] a flag of peace" that they would receive protection.[50] He did not want "to make war upon those who are innocent, but upon the guilty."[51] Those who surrendered would be "counted good Indians, friends of the whites."[52] At this point, Therese and the Renville relatives would not have feared for their safety, as Sibley and other officials designated them as "good" and "friendly" Indians.

Despite his promises of fair treatment, General Sibley created a five-man commission to try Dakota men.[53] These commissioners were military officers who had each fought against the Dakotas just days earlier, which presented a clear conflict of interest.[54] On 28 September 1862, when the trials began, Sibley gave the commissioners a short set of instructions. They were to "summarily try" the Dakota men and pass judgment on those found guilty of "murder and other outrages."[55] Those found guilty would be executed without delay.[56] While Sibley conceded that immediate executions might "perhaps

. . . be a stretch of my authority," he argued that "necessity must be my justification."[57] Several of Angelique's relatives testified in the trials, both for and against the Dakota defendants who were on trial for "murders, robberies, and outrages committed by the Sioux Indians on the Minnesota frontier."[58] When the trials ended on 3 November, a little over a month after they began, the military tribunal had brought 392 Dakota men before the panel and convicted 323. Of those convicted, 303 were sentenced to death; 20 received prison sentences; and only 69 were acquitted.[59] If Sibley had executed all of those found guilty by the tribunal as he planned, it would have meant the immediate elimination of approximately 10 percent of the total male Dakota population in Minnesota.[60]

As the trials proceeded, Sibley increasingly questioned the "friendly" status of all Dakotas at Camp Release even if they had saved white settlers or provided testimony at the trials, as many Renvilles had done. Sibley promised "to purge" the camp "of suspected characters."[61] Instead of only targeting "suspected characters," however, Sibley and Pope decided to relocate all Dakota men, women, and children from Camp Release. Military guards marched the 303 condemned Dakota prisoners to Mankato, about 85 miles southwest of Minneapolis-St. Paul. At the same time, troops removed a separate contingent of more than 1,600 women, children, elders, and "friendly" Dakota men to Fort Snelling, located south of present-day St. Paul.[62] On 26 December 1862, military officials simultaneously hanged thirty-eight Dakota men at Mankato in the largest mass execution in United States history.

While no members of Angelique's immediate family were hanged, many of her kin participated in the forced march to Fort Snelling. The Fort Snelling prison census of October 1862 listed Angelique's mother, brothers (Daniel, Thomas, Joseph), and sister (Agnes). Other Renville kin at Fort Snelling included Antoine, Michel, Gabriel, Sophia, Rosalie, and Isaac Renville.[63] In all, twenty-nine Renvilles were imprisoned at Fort Snelling.[64]

All the prisoners—even those who had rescued white settlers like some Renvilles had—lived under terrible conditions during their months at Fort Snelling. Government officials chose a poor, damp location for the prison camp. Stephen Riggs noted that the prison stood on a "low, flat place in parts of which the water stands."[65] Officials also allocated only three acres for approximately 1,600 prisoners, which led to severe overcrowding.[66] A fence twelve to fourteen feet high surrounded the enclosure, with one guarded gate as its only exit.[67] The prisoners also ate an insufficient and unhealthy diet. According to Thomas Williamson, the prisoners' diet "constipates their bowels and almost universally they are suffering from hard coughs."[68] Because of the crowded, unhealthy conditions and poor diet, diseases spread quickly including "lung fever" (pneumonia) and measles.[69] These diseases led to a high death rate, especially among the children. David Frenier recorded, "[f]rom two to four of the Indian children are dieing [*sic*] every day."[70] Stephen Riggs described the mortality rate at Fort Snelling as "fearful. . . . The shock, the anxiety of confinement, and the pitiful diet were naturally followed by sickness."[71] John Williamson reported, "Within 6 months, more than 200 have died [at Fort Snelling], many of them in consequence of their confinement."[72]

Over seven hundred miles away, Angelique learned about the terrible events in Minnesota from both the missionaries and her relatives back home. Throughout her time at Ohio Female College and during her residence with the Drake family, Angelique corresponded with her Renville relatives, especially her siblings, cousins, and mother. While her siblings and cousins had learned to read and write in both Dakota and English at the mission schools and thus could have corresponded in either language, Therese probably was not literate and thus depended on her relatives or the missionaries to read and write letters for her.[73] Angelique's and the missionaries' correspondences refer to these letters between Angelique and her kin. For example, in November 1862, Lucy Drake noted that Angelique sent letters to both Martha Riggs and her brother Daniel.[74] Angelique also wrote frequent letters to her cousin Sophia Renville, who had lived with her at the Lac qui Parle mission beginning in 1851.[75] In return, her Dakota relatives, including her siblings and a cousin, sent her letters.[76] Her uncle John B. Renville also corresponded with her in Ohio.[77]

These letters from home kept Angelique informed about the health and welfare of her relatives during and after the 1862 war, but they also were a double-edged sword because she could not do anything to help her relatives from afar. Angelique was particularly upset when she read a letter informing her that Therese had married a Dakota man named John Other Day (Anpetutokeca) while imprisoned at Fort

Snelling. She did not approve of her mother's marriage and initially refused to believe the news. Angelique wrote a letter back to Mary Riggs, stating that her mother had promised her "before I came away that she should not get married or listen to any thing while I was away unless I wanted her to." Angelique breathed a sigh of relief after receiving another letter informing her that "Mother has not Other day for a husband. I knew almost that she would not have him." She angrily chastised those who spread this rumor about Therese, as "people have no business making up such lies about her she has enough trouble with out them. I do wish folks would mind their own business and not be tending to others."[78]

Unfortunately, Angelique later learned that the rumor was true, and her mother had indeed married John Other Day. At the time, Other Day was—and still remains—a controversial figure. In his early days, according to a Dakota contemporary, he was "a desperate character among his own people and was both feared and hated."[79] Henry Sibley concurred, noting "when a young man [Other Day] was passionate and vengeful, and withal addicted to intemperance." He also had a "wild and wayward temper."[80] Angelique may have formed a negative opinion of Other Day based not only on his reputation but also when he forced Mary Cloud, the little Dakota girl who lived with Angelique at Hazelwood, to return to the mission against her and her mother's wishes. In 1858, during a trip to Washington, D.C., Other Day caused a further scandal when he "brought back with him a white woman [named Roxanne or Rosanne] he took out of a house of ill-fame whom he married after he got back on the reservation."[81]

After Other Day and Roxanne moved to Minnesota, they lived on a farm located near the Yellow Medicine Agency. Even before his trip to Washington, D.C., Other Day had adopted "the habits and dress of the whites" and attended the mission church.[82] His decision to farm further linked him to the Christian and "civilized" faction of Dakotas. When the war broke out, Other Day "returned his wife to her own people" and rescued sixty-two settlers.[83] For his actions in the war, the Minnesota press rehabilitated his once dubious reputation, calling him a "hero," "noble," and a "good" Indian.[84] One article described him as "a Christian, and one of God's noblemen."[85]

Perhaps because it does not fit into Other Day's "hero" narrative, few sources mention the relationship between Therese Renville and John Other Day. Instead, several historians highlight Other Day's long relationship with Roxanne, stating that she remained with him after the war until his death from tuberculosis in 1869.[86] The evidence is more ambiguous, however, and Roxanne may have left him during the war and never returned.[87] Even so, the marriage between Therese and Other Day was likely polygamous, as there is no indication Other Day obtained a divorce from his first wife. As such, the Protestant missionaries would have harshly evaluated his marriage with Therese. The missionaries continued to strongly denounce polygamous marriages during the war, even going so far as to force all church members incarcerated at Fort Snelling and Mankato to renounce polygamy and "put away" all but one spouse before joining the church.[88] Mary Renville, who was held at Camp Release with Therese and visited her at Fort Snelling, received a "very bad" scolding from the missionaries for failing to halt Therese's marriage to Other Day. Mary defended herself, saying that she and her husband "had tried to pray" for Therese.[89] Praying evidently was not enough to break a polygamous union with a Dakota man of "questionable" character.

On 4 July 1863, while still held at Fort Snelling, Therese gave birth to a daughter named Georgina Maria Other Day. On 24 August, a Catholic priest baptized Georgina. The baptismal record indicated that the little girl was severely ill.[90] Besides her short baptismal record, I could not find any other references to Georgina. Thus, it is my supposition that Georgina passed away at Fort Snelling, given the lack of other records, her recorded illness, and the horrible mortality rate for children there.

In their copious letters, the missionaries failed to comment on the birth and probable death of Georgina. Perhaps the omission stemmed from the missionaries' views of both polygamy and Catholicism. The missionaries would have condemned Therese's marriage to Other Day, as he was already married to another woman at the time, and the Protestant missionaries would have sharply criticized Therese's decision to have Georgina baptized by a Catholic priest. Records indicate that Angelique's older brother Joseph also had his son Agnus baptized at Fort Snelling.[91] The missionaries already viewed Therese as an unfit mother for taking her children away from the missionaries at the beginning of the war; her association with a Catholic priest would have only confirmed their opinion of her choices. While the missionaries never directly commented on Georgina, Angelique likely heard about her baby sister from her Dakota relatives. Her uncle John B. Renville wrote a letter "to all my relatives" about the situation at Fort Snelling where "many babies are dying and there is much sickness."[92]

In addition to the marriage of Angelique's mother and the birth and probable death of a baby sister she would never know, Angelique learned from afar about the death of her closest sister Agnes. When the war first broke out, Therese removed Agnes from the Riggses' home. After the war ended, Stephen Riggs found Agnes "living with the Indians" at Camp Release.[93] He visited the camp and begged Agnes to leave Therese and return to his home. He eventually convinced Agnes to leave with Julia Laframboise. In November, Mary Riggs wrote to Lucy Drake, asking her to pass a message to Angelique about her sister. She wanted Angelique to know that she should "rejoice that Agnes is with us. She came here with Julia a little more than two weeks since. Julia went immediately to Rockford, only spending one night with us. . . . I hope Angelique will write to Agnes soon."[94] Assuredly, Mary Riggs wanted Angelique to tell Agnes to stay with the Riggs family. However, Agnes "only remained at [the Riggses'] house a few weeks" before she "ran away" and returned to her mother, who had by then been relocated to Fort Snelling.[95]

The Riggses wanted to "withdraw [Agnes] from the Indian camp and from her mother's influence."[96] The missionaries called Fort Snelling "a very dangerous place for girls especially Agnes['s] age." They did not believe that Therese could properly "guard her" at the prison, nor did they think that she was a proper role model for her daughter due to her polygamous relationship with John Other Day and her ties to Catholic priests.[97] Despite their firm belief that Agnes would be better off living with them, the Riggses worried that if they successfully "rescued" Agnes, she would only run back to her mother. Thus, they "devise[d] a plan to send her to school if practicable," as they had done with her older sister.[98] On multiple visits, the Riggses tried to convince Agnes to leave her mother, but "she declined returning home with us, but I have some hope she may come after awhile." Although they failed to persuade Agnes to leave her mother, they were "very thankful Angelique is in Ohio and shall be glad to have her stay next summer, if Mrs. Drake is willing."[99]

The missionaries unfairly accused Therese of having a negative influence on Agnes. They were correct, however, that Fort Snelling was a terrible place for children, much as it was for adults. In November, Agnes caught the measles during a widespread outbreak at Fort Snelling.[100] She lingered ill until January. After a long delay, she finally saw "Doc Wakefield," the Fort Snelling physician, who said that there was nothing he could do and that she would not recover.[101] At this point, Therese asked David Frenier, who was literate in Dakota and English, to write to Stephen Riggs asking him to bring Agnes some warm clothing and to find another doctor.[102] Unfortunately, by the time Riggs received the letter, Agnes had passed away on 14 January 1863.[103]

The missionaries blamed Therese for Agnes's death. Mary Renville had seen Therese many times "during our captivity" and did not "have much confidence in her." Mary counseled Stephen Riggs that while Agnes's death was tragic, we "feel better about it than we should if you had given her consent to go to the camp." The missionaries believed they had done everything to rescue Agnes; it was not their fault that she, and especially her mother, had chosen not to be saved. The missionaries, however, could still "save" Angelique. Mary Renville asked Stephen Riggs to "never let Angelique go back ever to her Mother, if you can help it."[104] Stephen Riggs agreed, writing Lucy Drake that "it was so much better for her to be with you than to have had her come here and be a captive to the Indians."[105]

While the missionaries fervently believed that Angelique was better off in Ohio, they worried about informing her of Agnes's death. Mary Renville predicted that "Poor Angelique will take it hard."[106] The missionaries were correct on this point; Angelique was devastated. Martha Riggs reported that Angelique "feels Agnes' death very sorely."[107] In March, Angelique wrote Stephen Riggs to ask him for more information about her sister's death. "I would like to know all about sister Agnes sickness how she felt about dieing when she knew that she could not live. Did she have any word to send me?"[108]

Agnes's death underscored the terrible conditions at Fort Snelling and spurred the remaining Renvilles to increase their efforts to get away from the prison camp. Angelique's relatives considered various strategies to obtain their release. One possible avenue to freedom was to sell their remaining "half breed" scrip. When the war began, the Renvilles still collectively held over three thousand acres.[109] Mary and John B. Renville wrote Stephen Riggs openly suggesting that he sell their relatives' scrip in return for their release. They asked Riggs to help "my Brothers and their families . . . move from that Camp. They have scrip and they have some horses . . . we both feel as if we must not let them die . . . Mr. Riggs see what can be done, don't let them stay in that camp till they all die."[110]

Historian William Millikan suggests that Riggs followed through with Mary and John's request and sold their scrip. For example, Gabriel Renville sold all of his 480 acres in November 1863.[111] Likewise, Stephen Riggs, with the help of Henry Sibley, sold the scrip of Antoine and Michel Renville, both perhaps taking a portion of the profit from the sale.[112] Although there are no letters directly confirming that the sale of their scrip led to the Renvilles' release, circumstantial evidence suggests that this was the case, given the dates of their scrip sale and their release from Fort Snelling.[113] However, Millikan argues that even if the Renvilles successfully traded their scrip for their freedom, they received little else. By 1867, most of the Renville kin lived in poverty on the Lake Traverse reservation in Dakota Territory. In the end, as Millikan surmised, any financial benefits from the scrip went almost entirely to white Minnesotans.[114]

In addition to selling their scrip, other Renville men volunteered to serve as scouts for General Sibley in return for their release from Fort Snelling. Even though the war had ended, the U.S. military vowed to carry on the fight against those Dakota men who supposedly were continuing their war from Dakota Territory. From inside Fort Snelling, Gabriel Renville approached General Sibley to recommend that "some mixed-bloods be picked out as scouts." In February 1863, Gabriel, Michel, Daniel, and Isaac Renville left Fort Snelling to join Sibley as scouts.[115] By spring 1863, the number of scouts increased to approximately thirty men, including Joseph, John B., Victor, and Antoine Renville. The scouts' families accompanied them as they moved from Minnesota into Dakota Territory. Thus, several Renvilles offered their work as scouts in exchange for freedom for themselves and their families, a decision other Dakotas at the time and since have condemned.[116]

As these tragic events unfolded in Minnesota, Angelique increasingly demanded that she be allowed to return home to her family. In March 1863, three months after Agnes's death, Angelique told Lucy Drake, "I want very much to see them all."[117] Therese also desperately wanted her oldest daughter to come home. Jane Williamson chastised Therese for "unremittingly" laboring "to keep the first place in [Angelique's] affections."[118] If Therese truly cared about her daughter, she would realize that the missionaries knew what was best for Angelique and stop attempting to bring her home to Minnesota. While Stephen Riggs still had the force of law on his side as Angelique's legal guardian, his guardianship would end when Angelique turned eighteen on 1 April 1863.[119] In what would supposedly be one of his last decisions as her guardian, Riggs overruled Therese and Angelique and decided that it was in his ward's best interests for her to remain in Ohio as long as possible. In part, Riggs correctly argued that Ohio was safer than Minnesota for a young Dakota woman in the aftermath of the war.[120] More importantly, however, he wanted to keep her away from her "uncivilized" mother who would influence her in negative ways, as she had allegedly done with Agnes. According to Jane Williamson, Therese illustrated that "a mother's influence (the source of so much good) should sometimes be thrown on the wrong scale."[121]

Angelique had little choice but to follow Riggs's decision, as he simply refused to send funds for her to travel home to Minnesota. Meanwhile, he planned to sell more of her scrip to reimburse the Drakes for hosting her in their home. Stephen Riggs hoped "to sell another portion of her land last fall, and so support and educate her [at the Drakes' residence] without drawing any thing more for her from the Board." Unfortunately, he acted too late, and the war "made the land valueless at present." Despite the lack of funds, Riggs reasoned that "Angelique is seventeen years old and will render some help to Mrs. Drake."[122] Indeed, Angelique continued to perform the labor of a domestic servant without pay.

Riggs worried, however, that Angelique's domestic labor was not enough to defray the expenses of her care. He frequently wrote letters apologizing to Lucy Drake for his failure to provide financial support for Angelique. "It has not been at all according to my wish that I have not sent Angelique some money to buy her clothes and to defray other expenses," he explained. "When the outbreak took place I was making arrangements to sell a portion of her land, but that taking place stopped all proceedings and indeed had made the land valueless for the present."[123] A month later, he again worried about Angelique's cost to Lucy Drake. "I feel some concern about it. I fear you have been bearing a burden which I ought not to have let you have—and certainly would not, if God's providences had been different."[124] In January 1863, Riggs asked the ABCFM to provide him with fifty dollars for Angelique's care. The board granted his request, and he forwarded the funds to Lucy Drake.[125]

In the absence of travel money and access to her scrip, Angelique tried to find other ways to return home. In March 1863, Hugh and Mary Cunningham, ABCFM Dakota missionaries, visited the Drake family. Angelique planned to travel back to Minnesota with the Cunninghams but was devastated when they left without her. Lucy Drake informed the Riggses that "Mr. and Mrs. Cunningham were here two weeks ago and after they left [Angelique] seemed very unhappy and said to some of the family that she was going back with them as that would be the only opportunity she would have."[126] Drake tried to placate Angelique, telling her that "we had no idea of sending her home, that we wanted her to stay with us . . . I have said to her repeatedly that I was glad that she was with us for Providence had so dealt with me, that it was necessary for me to have some one that I could rely upon."[127] While Angelique worried about her mother and other relatives, Drake apparently valued the free domestic labor she provided over her well-being. Angelique lamented, "If my mother could feel that I thought as much of her by not going home I would not care as much."[128]

In late spring 1863, Mary Riggs tentatively arranged passage for Angelique to Minnesota and requested that her husband send a draft for travel expenses. Mary informed Lucy Drake about these plans, adding, "There will be a possibility if she should come then of her seeing her mother, but we are very doubtful that is best."[129] Perhaps because of Angelique's plans to see Therese, Stephen Riggs overruled his wife and requested that Drake destroy the draft that Mary had sent to pay for Angelique's travels. Once again, Angelique expressed discouragement with the change of plans. She told Lucy Drake, "'I will stay for I know it is for the best though I want very much to see them all."[130]

In July 1863, Mary Riggs again decided Angelique could return home. She wrote Stephen, "Angelique is very desirous to come home the first good opportunity. I think you requested Mrs. Drake to destroy the draft you sent her for Angelique's travel expenses last spring. Will it be convenient for you to send me one to replace it?"[131] Despite his wife's insistence that he send the money, two additional months passed before Stephen Riggs finally sent Angelique twenty-eight dollars for her passage home to Minnesota. He dutifully recorded the amount in his guardianship log (adding to her debt), even though she was then five months over the age of eighteen, and thus her guardianship should have legally ended.[132] Although Riggs continued to control her finances, he decided that she was mature enough to travel by herself. "I think she is woman enough to come to Chicago after some one sees her aboard the cars and has her trunk all checked. . . . She had better take good care of what little money she has."[133] As Angelique prepared to finally depart Ohio, Riggs expressed to Lucy Drake his hope that Angelique "not fail to thank you and Mr. Drake for the home you have furnished her for so long a time."[134]

Why did Stephen Riggs finally give in and allow Angelique to return home after refusing to provide travel funds for over a year? It may be that Angelique said what the missionaries wanted to hear to finally orchestrate her return to Minnesota. During her years with the Riggs and Drake families, Angelique had learned the value of her household labor. Indeed, Lucy Drake herself told Angelique that she had come to rely on her to keep the household running. In fall 1863, Mary Riggs, like Drake, fell ill and needed a "chief housekeeper." Angelique enthused to Lucy Drake that "it would be her greatest care and delight to relieve" Mary Riggs from her domestic chores.[135] Martha Riggs supported this plan, noting, "it seemed but right that Angelique, having enjoyed the privileges of home, should lend a helping hand when needed."[136] Thus, the missionaries would allow Angelique to return to Minnesota so that she could relieve the ailing Mary Riggs of her household duties.

As Angelique finally prepared to return to Minnesota, the Riggses believed that she would continue as their dependent and ward as she had for the last decade. From 1851 to 1863, the Riggs family decided where Angelique lived, what she studied, how she dressed, the language she spoke, the sale of her scrip, and the use of her money. During her early years, Angelique, like most young children, appears not to have spoken out against the Riggs family and dutifully behaved as a "proper" Christian and "civilized" girl as their "adopted" daughter. She attended the mission school, then Ohio Female College, and joined the mission church according to the missionaries' plans for her. At Ohio Female College, Angelique wanted to make the Riggs family proud even as she struggled. Her letters indicate that she saw the Riggs family as an extension of her Dakota family, but cracks in the relationship began to appear during her time with the Drakes. She was frequently ill and disliked the constant domestic labor. She especially did not want to continue her education. For the first time, she began to question the missionaries' plan for her and quietly to refuse to do some of what was asked of her.

The war heightened Angelique's desire to break with the missionaries. She missed her relatives, was devastated by her closest sister's death, and wished to reunite with her mother. Therese remained relatively quiet during the mission years so that she could continue to see her children, but she increasingly asked that her daughter be returned to her and her Dakota family. As a result, a struggle ensued among the Riggs family, Angelique, and Therese Renville. Angelique and her mother wanted her to return to Minnesota; the Riggses refused, and Stephen remained her legal guardian.

In fall 1863, Angelique finally could return to Minnesota, but she did so by promising to transfer her domestic labor from the Drake family to the Riggs family on her return. More broadly, she vowed to continue to side with "civilization," Christianity, and the Riggs family over her own. In the context of Angelique's assurances that she would remain an obedient and grateful daughter, the missionaries had little warning for what she had planned once she arrived in Minnesota.

::: 5 :::

DAKOTA TERRITORY

Marriage and Christianity

1863–1876

In December 1863, Lucy Spooner Drake wrote a letter to Mary Riggs expressing her shock at Angelique's actions after she returned to Minnesota. Angelique not only had broken her promise to work for the Riggses as their "chief housekeeper," but had turned her back on everything the missionaries had worked to teach her over the years. "Poor misguided girl," Drake lamented, "how she may be kept from evil until she has time to reflect." The news was so shocking that Lucy's frail nervous system kept her from responding for several months; she could not even tell her children about what Angelique had done, as they had grown quite attached to her during her year in their home. Instead of the awful truth, Lucy lied to her children. "We speak of her as being on a visit with her mother," she explained, "and her stay may be all winter."[1] Thirteen years later, after Angelique had passed away from tuberculosis, Martha Riggs echoed Lucy Drake's shock and disappointment in Angelique's obituary. While obituaries typically celebrate the life of the deceased, Martha's article dripped with barely contained anger over Angelique's "betrayal" upon her return to Minnesota in September 1863. Martha reported that Angelique "threw away whatever opportunity she might have had for being and doing good." All of her "training was worse than wasted." She ended up living a "wasted life."[2]

What was Angelique's unforgiveable betrayal? When she arrived in Minnesota, she initially stopped at the Riggs home, but left after only a week to join her numerous relatives in Dakota Territory where they worked as scouts for General Henry Hastings Sibley, including her brothers Joseph, Daniel, and Thomas, and their families. After their long separation, Angelique finally reunited with her mother. The missionaries did not want Angelique to live with Therese, as they still saw her as a poor role model and blamed her for Agnes's death. They also worried about Angelique returning to "savagery," as she now resided in tipis and reclaimed the gender roles and cultural practices of her youth.

Although undesirable, Angelique's reunion with her mother and Dakota kin was not the missionaries' main concern. Rather, once she arrived in Dakota Territory, Angelique lived with (and later married) a Dakota man named Charles Crawford (Wakaninape/Appearing Sacred; also called Charly/Charlie/Charley and Crawford/Renville/Brown) who worked as a scout alongside her relatives. The missionaries ideally wanted Angelique to marry a Euro-American man who befit her status as a "civilized" and Christian Dakota woman. The problem, however, was not that Charles was a Dakota man, nor that he was a scout. His unforgivable sin was polygamy; he was married to another Dakota woman named Tasinahewin at the time. When he married Angelique, he did not "put away" Tasinahewin, as the missionaries demanded of all church members. Over ten years earlier, the missionaries had excommunicated Angelique's father Joseph Hrana for polygamy. The Riggses supposedly had taught Joseph's daughter to know better. They hoped that she would realize the gravity of her mistake, renounce her new husband, and return at once to the mission fold.

Angelique never left her husband or returned to the church. At first, she apologized to the missionaries for her actions and expressed regret. But as the months passed, Angelique became increasingly irritated with the missionaries over their response to her marriage and gave up her initial attempts at reconciliation. The missionaries' unbending cultural and religious expectations collided with Angelique's desire to remain with her new husband and her Dakota kin. Moreover, Angelique became increasingly angry over Stephen Riggs's duplicitous handling of her and Agnes's scrip, as well as his continued guardianship even though she legally should have been emancipated. Indeed, in 1869, she even hired a lawyer to sue Riggs—and several others—for illegally taking her and her sister's land.

The missionaries intended to promote Angelique as one of their proudest success stories; instead, she became a reminder of their failure despite all the resources and effort they had devoted to her transformation. They had hoped to create a perfect Christian wife and mother who would pass her religion and Euro-American culture to other Dakota women and to her own children, but after more than ten years of the missionaries deciding her path for her, Angelique made the choice to separate herself from them and live with her Dakota mother, husband, and kin. The missionaries failed many times to convert Dakotas to Christianity, but they took Angelique's rejection personally. As such, she became a forbidden topic. Throughout the 1850s, the missionaries prominently featured Angelique in their correspondence. After her "betrayal," however, they returned to the early years when they referred to her only as a "half breed girl," or, more often, neglected to mention her at all.

The reaction of the ABCFM missionaries to the union of Angelique Renville and Charles Crawford provides insight into the larger nineteenth-century debate over interracial marriage. Though the missionaries hoped Angelique would marry a white man, or at least a "civilized" Dakota man, many nineteenth-century authors, scientists, physicians, and others adamantly opposed all intermarriages between American Indians and Euro-Americans, even if the Indian partner had adopted "civilization." Those opposed to miscegenation (a term coined in 1863), argued—among other things—that the offspring of interracial unions would be biologically and socially inferior.[3] "Mixed blood" children supposedly suffered from infertility more than Euro-Americans and could not become "civilized." Intermarriage also threatened racial purity, the social order, and could even lead to national degeneration.[4] The fears associated with "racial mixing" led fourteen states and territories to ban intermarriage between Euro-American and Indian people in the mid- to late nineteenth century, although Minnesota was not one of them.[5]

Other commentators, however, endorsed intermarriage as a way to advance "civilization" and hasten the absorption of American Indians into the "dominant majority."[6] Thomas Jefferson, for one, viewed intermarriage as the key to solving the "Indian problem" through assimilation and the eventual dilution of American Indian blood and the creation of a new, unified American people.[7] Even among those who supported the intermarriage of Euro-Americans and Indians, however, there was a gender divide. Marriage between white men and Indian women was usually tolerated, while a union between a white woman and a Native man was viewed as scandalous and unnatural.[8]

Protestant missionaries, like the general population, offered diverse, ambivalent, and often contradictory evaluations of intermarriage.[9] On one hand, missionaries, like those to the Dakota Nation, viewed intermarriage as a way to cement the status of those who had already taken steps to become "civilized" Christians.[10] An article in the *Word Carrier*, a Dakota missionary newspaper, explained that the missionaries had "no objection to the marriage of whites and Indians, provided they are properly mated." A "proper" union resulted from the marriage of two "civilized" people (generally a white man and a "civilized" Dakota woman). The missionaries condemned marriages between "uncivilized" Indians and Euro-Americans as "merely for the gratification of the animal passions."[11]

Dakota girls who had been raised among the missionaries, like Angelique Renville, counted among those who could (and should) marry white husbands. Indeed, the missionaries touted marriage to a white man as the culmination of the civilization process for Dakota girls. The missionaries, for example, described Jane Lamont as a "wild Indian girl as degraded as others. She was an Indian in action, in language and in thought" before she came to live with the Pond Family. After residing with the Ponds for several years, she "benefitted and indeed . . . has become a child of God through faith in Jesus Christ."[12] She also attended the mission school, where she learned to speak and read English. When she came of age, she married Moses Starr Titus, the nephew of ABCFM missionaries Samuel and Gideon Pond.[13] Jane's marriage to Moses cemented her status as a "civilized" woman, and she remained "a Christian mother guiding her household in the way of life, [and] an influential member of the Presbyterian church."[14] Two of her sons even became "prominent and wealthy bankers."[15]

Another Dakota girl named Lucy Prescott "obtained a pretty good English education," and married Eli Pettijohn, an assistant missionary at Lac qui Parle.[16] Like Jane Lamont, Prescott remained a "Christian woman" after her marriage.[17] She also "properly" raised her sons, who became "vigorous . . . active, intelligent, and influential men."[18] By 1857, the missionaries boasted that four other "mixed blood girls" who received instruction at the missions married "American citizens all having considerable property." They also belonged to the mission church.[19] Stephen Riggs summarized his view of proper marriages. Missionary-educated "half-breed girls who made wives for white men," he wrote, "did good in the world."[20]

As a second choice, the missionaries hoped their female students would marry a "civilized" Dakota man. Stephen Riggs dutifully recorded notes on many of the children who lived in the missionaries' homes or attended the small Hazelwood boarding school. At the end of his entries, Riggs frequently noted the eventual marital status of the female (but not the male) students. Of course, those who married white men, like Jane Lamont and Lucy Prescott, received Riggs's highest praise. Riggs lauded other students for marrying mixed-ancestry Dakota men, but only if they both remained committed to Christianity and "civilization." Nancy McClure, for example, married a mixed-ancestry trader named David Faribault. After her marriage, the missionaries described her as "very friendly, ladylike in her appearance, and able to speak English."[21] Some students, however, did not marry "proper" men and suffered long-term consequences. Margaret Renville, who had attended the mission church and school, was "induced" to marry a "Roman Catholic half-breed," who was then "unfaithful" to her.[22] She left the church and failed to live up to the missionaries' high expectations. In sum, the missionaries cared less about a potential husband's "blood" than his adherence to "civilization" and Protestant Christianity. With that said, the missionaries tacitly assumed that "white blood" tended to be linked with both "civilization" and an acceptance of Christianity.

If the missionaries approved of a marriage, they next attempted to convince the couple to "solemnize" their union in "civilized form," which meant marrying according to both church practices and state law.[23] In the nineteenth century, Minnesota statutes defined marriage as a "civil contract" between a man who was at least eighteen years old, and a woman who was at least fifteen years old. The marriage ceremony needed to be performed by a justice of the peace, a judge, or an ordained minister, and have two witnesses. Within one month after the marriage ceremony, the clerk of the district court where the marriage took place needed to receive the couple's certificate of marriage. If the newlyweds lived far from a judge, minister, or justice of the peace, the marriage could still be valid, provided the couple submitted a marriage contract to the district court.[24]

Minnesota law also stated that marriages could not be contracted if either person had "a husband or wife living."[25] Of course, this outlawed polygamous relationships, a restriction the missionaries whole-heartedly endorsed. As was evident in their treatment of Angelique's father, the missionaries believed that polygamy went against Christianity; it also undermined the "Divine constitution of the family."[26] Polygamy was "not a state of marriage;" rather, it was "a state of continued adultery" which exploited and degraded women.[27] As such, the missionaries demanded that a husband involved in a polygamous relationship choose only one wife and "put away" all others before he could become a church member, though Dakota women involved in polygamous marriages could remain members of the church and have their children baptized, as the missionaries did not hold them responsible for the sins of their husbands.[28]

Dakota women who entered "civilized" marriages also were expected to follow Euro-American practices which legally and socially restricted women. According to the legal doctrine of coverture, women surrendered most of their legal rights to their husbands after marriage. Married women could not sign legal documents, file lawsuits, be sued separately, or make contracts on their own.[29] In most cases, husbands controlled their wives' property and income. Moreover, Euro-American women had difficulty obtaining a divorce if the marriage failed. Like marriage, courts handled divorce as a legal matter. Those couples wishing to divorce filed a complaint with their local district court. Minnesota law spelled out specific grounds for divorce, including adultery, impotency, imprisonment, willful desertion, and cruel and inhumane treatment. The court determined if a divorce would be granted and whether alimony would be paid.[30]

Dakotas viewed marriage, divorce, and a women's place in society very differently from their Euro-American counterparts. Dakotas did not view marriage as a legal contract regulated by the state, but as an agreement affirming the importance of kinship and their community as a whole.[31] Instead of simply linking together one man and one woman, Dakota marriages solidified ties between families and strengthened webs of kinship.[32] A couple did not need to marry in front of a judge or a minister, nor did they need to file paperwork with a county clerk. Married Dakota women did not lose their legal identities according to coverture. Dakota couples who wished to end their marriage did not need a judge or court to decide their fate.

Although kinship played a very important role in their marriage practices, Dakota women made their own decisions about who they married.[33] Amos Oneroad, a Sisseton-Wahpeton man, described Dakota courting and marriage customs. While Dakota parents watched their daughters very carefully, they allowed them to speak with young men at dances. After the couple had "met several times and found that they cared for each other, the parents of the boy would try to arrange a *wohanpi* or ceremonial marriage."[34] According to Ella Deloria, the noted Dakota anthropologist, the marriage ceremony was not "boisterous." Rather, it "was a private matter between two persons, not a thing to foist upon the public attention."[35] While understated, marriage ceremonies involved the distribution of gifts to the girl's relatives and poorer members of the community at a public feast.[36] According to historian Sarah Carter, the exchange of gifts validated the marriage and established the reciprocal obligations of both families.[37] After their marriage, the couple generally lived near the bride's family.[38] Although they resided near kin, Deloria notes that the newlywed couple began their marriage without the interference of their relatives.[39]

Most Dakota marriages were between one man and one woman, though polygamous marriages did exist. Carter, in her book on indigenous marriage, argues that polygamy needs to be understood from a Native point of view. According to Carter, polygamous marriages did not oppress Native women or lead to inevitable conflict between the co-wives, as the missionaries and other nineteenth century commentators insisted. For Dakotas and other indigenous peoples, polygamous marriages were another option for marriage that created desirable family units.[40] Kinship obligations that stressed respect, goodwill, and kindness extended to both single and plural marriages, which generally produced a harmonious relationship for the wives, their husband, and their children.[41] Indeed, there was little quarreling in these families.[42] In most cases, husbands consulted their first wives before they married a second (or third) wife. Frequently, the second wives were the sisters or relatives of the first wife. Women involved in polygamous relationships benefitted by sharing work, childcare, and companionship.[43] Especially during times of male population decline, as occurred following the 1862 U.S.–Dakota war, plural marriages provided marriage partners for women who might have otherwise remained single. The children of plural marriages regarded themselves as brothers and sisters although they had different mothers.[44] If one mother died, the co-wife raised her children as her own.

Finally, Dakota women involved in both plural and non-plural marriages generally enjoyed more autonomy than their Euro-American counterparts. In her biography of Daybreak Woman, a mixed-ancestry Dakota woman, historian Jane Lamm Carroll described Dakota girls as spirited and independent.[45] Ella Deloria confirmed that for Dakota men and women, "each was ever a separate person and both had the right to be independent."[46] Dakota women like Daybreak Woman "had extensive autonomy over their own bodies, their labor, the food they gathered and produced, and everything they manufactured—which included the family's shelter, household goods, tools, and clothing."[47] Dakota women also retained power in cases of divorce. While most couples remained married, divorce was relatively easy and not a legal issue.[48] If either couple wished to separate, the husband simply returned to his relatives' village.[49] In cases of divorce, Dakota mothers retained control over their children and their homes.

In sum, the missionaries and Dakota people held very different ideas about marriage, divorce, legal traditions, and gender roles. The missionaries wanted Dakota women like Angelique to enter heterosexual, monogamous, paternalistic relationships that lasted for life. They taught that marriage was both a legal contract adjudicated by the state and sanctioned by the church. The missionaries viewed all Dakota marriage practices—especially polygamy—as contrary to Christianity and "civilization" and oppressive towards women. Carter, however, describes Dakota marriage and divorce practices as "complex, diverse, flexible, and adaptable."[50] They were rooted in kinship, allowed for amiable divorce, and gave Dakota women and their children considerable legal and social autonomy.

The union of Angelique Renville and Charles Crawford illustrated the vast divide between missionary and Dakota conceptions of marriage. At first glance, however, Charles seemed to be the type of suitor the missionaries would support, given his previous interaction with both the missionaries and the United States government. His mother, Winona Crawford, was the mixed-ancestry daughter of a Sisseton Dakota mother and a British fur-trader father. Winona originally married Narcisse Frenier and had a daughter named Susan. She then married Victor Renville and had a son named Gabriel. After Renville's death, she married a Wahpeton man named Akipa, who later was given the name Joseph Akipa Renville, even though he had no biological ties to the Renville family. Winona and Akipa had two sons, named Charles (born 1838 at Lake Traverse, Minnesota) and Thomas Crawford (born 1839).[51]

Charles Crawford initially lived near Lac qui Parle and established close ties with the ABCFM missionaries and the Renvilles.[52] He learned to read and write in the Dakota language from the missionaries. Beginning in 1854, Charles, along with several Renville families, resided near the Hazelwood mission in a separate village. In 1856, Stephen Riggs pressured the village residents to officially become their own band, separate from other "uncivilized" Dakotas. To achieve this goal, the residents wrote a constitution and formed the Hazelwood Republic. In the constitution, members of the Republic promised (among other things) to put their faith in one God, to wear "pantaloons," to establish individual farms, to support education, to follow Euro-American cultural norms, to protect private property, and to obey the laws of the United States government. The constitution also established a system of government with a president, a council, a secretary, and three judges.[53] Seventeen Dakota men signed the constitution, including Charles Crawford (signing as "Charles Renville" after his father, Joseph Akipa Renville) and Michel, John B., Gabriel, Antoine, and Isaac Renville, and Angelique's brother, Daniel.[54]

Charles later served as a treaty delegate and translator. In 1858, he traveled to Washington, D.C., with a group of Dakota men as part of a small treaty delegation.[55] In Washington, government agents detained the delegation until they signed a treaty relinquishing additional reservation lands. According to the new treaty, the Dakotas lost 550,000 acres from the upper reserve and 4,500 acres from the lower reserve. For this land, the Dakotas received 30 cents an acre—approximately one-twentieth of what the reservation land was then worth. Most of these reduced proceeds went directly to the traders, just as had occurred following the treaties of 1851.[56]

Back in Minnesota, Charles and his family continued to interact with both the ABCFM missionaries and government officials. In 1861, Thomas Williamson "married Charles Crawford's mother and her husband . . . and they call themselves Mr. and Mrs. Crawford I understand. They have a son of theirs at Dr. [Williamson's named] Thomas Crawford."[57] Of course, Charles's parents had been married according to Dakota custom for years, but Williamson's ceremony made their union legal according to Minnesota law and missionary practice. Charles's brother Thomas also began attending the mission school.

While his parents and brother established close ties with Thomas Williamson, Charles served as a government translator on the upper reservation around Hazelwood. Martha Riggs informed her brother Alfred that a government official "has taken Charles Crawford for his interpreter and right hand man, and we see them frequently driving around the county."[58] Charles also continued to interact with the Riggs family. In 1861, Martha noted that Charles Crawford "very kindly brought us up our mail yesterday afternoon. He has been attending church very regularly all winter—either here or at Dr. W's and has not unfrequently walked up here and walked back."[59] Martha Riggs worried, however, that he was not a true Christian. "Whether he feels any especial interest in the best things I cannot say," she informed her brother Alfred. "[S]ome think he does while others are of the opinion that he comes to see some one of the so called 'fair sex'."[60]

Although she did not have specific information at the time, Martha's comment proved to be prescient, as the woman Charles Crawford likely came to visit was none other than Angelique Renville. Indeed, once the missionaries sent her to live in Ohio, Angelique and Charles kept up a clandestine correspondence facilitated by Angelique's cousins in Minnesota. While she probably communicated with Charles during her time at the Ohio Female College, Lucy Drake first accused Angelique of acting "very strangely" about her correspondence in spring 1863. When she confronted Angelique about these "secret" letters, Angelique assured Drake that the letters were from her Renville cousins, but Drake "knew from her actions at the time that she was trying to deceive me consequently I watched her closely as possible."[61]

After monitoring her letters, Drake found out that Angelique was not corresponding with her cousins, but with Charles Crawford. At this point, Drake did everything she could to stop the budding relationship. In her correspondence, Drake never explained why she discouraged the courtship. Assuredly, Lucy Drake and Stephen and Mary Riggs wanted Angelique to marry a Euro-American man. She also may have known that Charles was already married to another Dakota woman. Whatever the reasons, Drake took various actions to halt Angelique's association with Charles. First, she asked Hugh and Mary Cunningham (ABCFM missionaries to the Dakotas) to speak to Angelique during their visit to Ohio in summer 1863. The Cunninghams' intervention appeared to work; Drake reported that Angelique "often talked of [Charles] to me, with the most bitter hatred after Mr. and Mrs. Cunningham were here during the summer." Next, Drake asked Angelique's uncle John B. Renville to write her a letter "concerning [Charles Crawford]." After John B.'s admonishments, Angelique seemed to be even "more embittered at him than ever and seemed at times to lose all control of herself."[62] Angelique's vehement protests certainly could have been designed to placate Drake and stop her from monitoring her correspondence. Indeed, Angelique's other statements contradicted her adamant claims that she wanted nothing to do with Charles; at the same time Angelique assured the Cunninghams, her uncle, and Lucy Drake that she "hated" Charles, she also told people that she was engaged and might even "be married before Martha."[63]

The irony of Angelique using the missionaries' education to correspond with someone they deemed unsuitable appears to have been lost on Lucy Drake and the Riggses. The missionaries had taught Angelique and Charles (and other Dakota children) literacy to promote "civilization" and especially Christianity. The pair, however, used missionary-taught literacy to conduct their forbidden correspondence. Furthermore, even though they both spoke English, Angelique and Charles likely wrote their letters in Dakota; indeed, all of Charles's existing letters are written in Dakota, although he sprinkled in English words which he frequently underlined.[64] Lucy

Drake, therefore, would not have been able to read most of the letters' content when she intercepted them. Angelique's cousins at the Hazelwood mission helped to facilitate their correspondence and keep their communication secret for several years.

The letters paused during the U.S.–Dakota War while Charles faced warfare, arrest, two trials, and imprisonment. In the months before the war, Charles lived with his parents and brother at the Yellow Medicine Agency, where he worked as a clerk. Once the war began, Charles and his father Akipa rescued Major Joseph Brown's children and his wife Susan Frenier Brown, who happened to be Charles's half-sister. He witnessed multiple battles during the war along with Angelique's brothers Joseph and Daniel. Like the Renville brothers and other "friendly" Dakotas, he also helped to rescue several settlers. When the war ended, Charles relocated to Camp Release with his parents, brother, and Angelique's mother, siblings, and numerous other Renville relatives.[65]

Despite his ties to "friendly" Dakotas and the Brown family, Charles was arrested for "participation in the murders, robberies and outrages committed by Sioux Indians on the Minnesota Frontier." On 5 October, the five-member military commission appointed by General Sibley tried him for his alleged crimes.[66] Lorenzo Lawrence, a Dakota man and member of the ABCFM mission church, testified against Charles, swearing that he "was in on the Battles since the outbreak and fired upon the Whites." More specifically, Lawrence alleged that he "killed one Dutchman [German immigrant]." Charles defended himself, stating that he "never told an Indian I killed White people, I saved what property I could." Two women affiliated with the Brown family testified in his defense. Despite Lawrence's damning testimony, the commissioners found Charles not guilty.[67]

Only ten days later, soldiers arrested Charles yet again and charged him with the same general war crimes. During his second trial, he defended himself by stating that he was with Daniel, Antoine, Michel, and Gabriel Renville, who could vouch for his innocence. Michel (Michael in the trial transcript) and Gabriel Renville backed up his version of events, testifying that Charles was with them throughout the war and that "Charley [did not] fire a gun." The tribunal once again found in his favor, ruling that the charges were "not proven." Although the military commissioners had acquitted

As a child living with her relatives, Angelique would have played with handmade dolls such as this one to learn Dakota gender roles. This doll was made around 1860, composed of a stuffed leather body with a cotton dress, white beads stitched around the face and boots, and a silver belt. *Minnesota Historical Society*

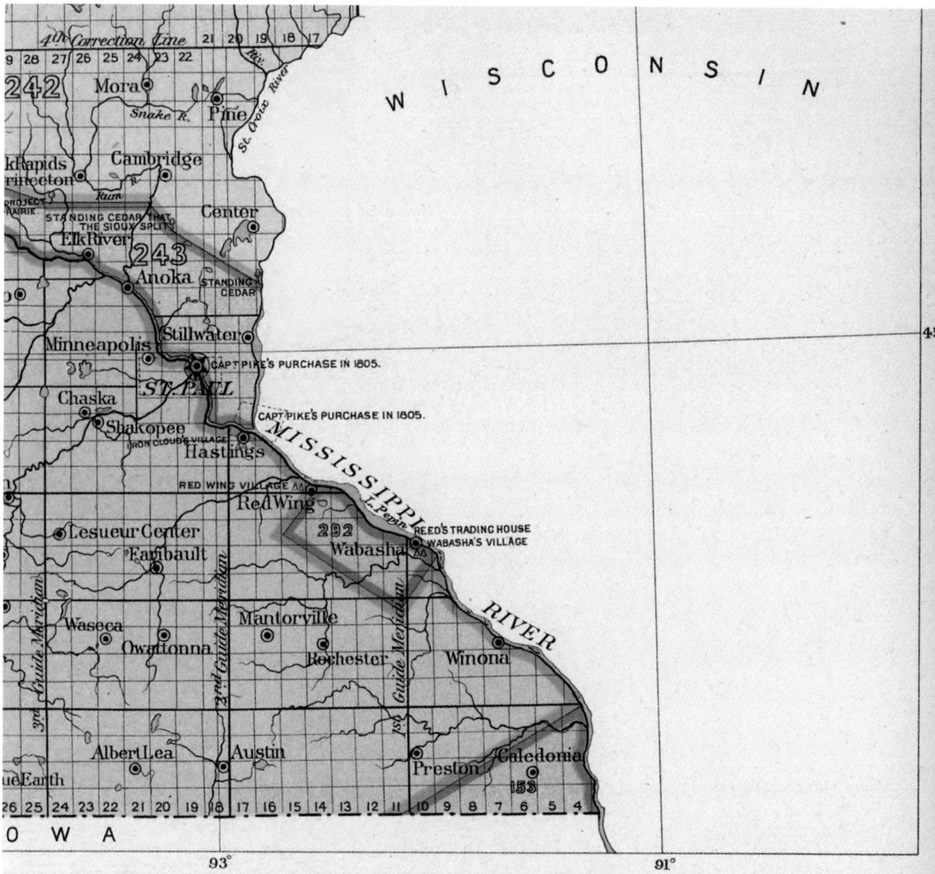

Created by the Treaty of 1830, the "Half Breed Tract" originally comprised 320,000 acres in Minnesota near Wabasha, as seen in a detail from Minnesota Map No. 33 by Charles C. Royce. Government agents distributed scrip to the Dakotas in exchange for the land, based on arbitrary calculations of "blood quantum."

Library of Congress

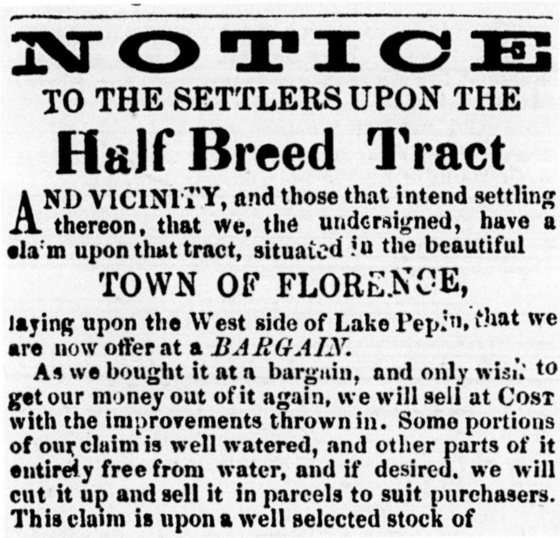

NOTICE

TO THE SETTLERS UPON THE

Half Breed Tract

AND VICINITY, and those that intend settling thereon, that we, the undersigned, have a claim upon that tract, situated in the beautiful

TOWN OF FLORENCE,

laying upon the West side of Lake Pepin, that we are now offer at a *BARGAIN.*

As we bought it at a bargain, and only wish to get our money out of it again, we will sell at COST with the improvements thrown in. Some portions of our claim is well watered, and other parts of it entirely free from water, and if desired, we will cut it up and sell it in parcels to suit purchasers. This claim is upon a well selected stock of

On 9 February 1856, the *Red-Wing Sentinel* ran this notice of the sale of scrip in the "Half Breed Tract." *Library of Congress*

This photograph of Thomas Williamson's Yellow Medicine Mission, located only a few miles from the Hazelwood Mission, is indicative of the type of house Angelique lived in with the Riggs family from 1854 to 1861, as well as the clothing she would have worn. *Presbyterian Historical Society*

As her legal guardian, ABCFM missionary Stephen Riggs controlled Angelique's education, living arrangements, and real estate, which he sold to pay for her education. Riggs, seen here, maintained his guardianship over Angelique (and her sister Agnes) long after she should have been legally emancipated. *South Dakota State Archives*

INTRODUCTION.

THE DAKOTA ALPHABET.

a	(ah),	sound of *a* in *far*.
b	(be),	same as English.
c	(che),	sound of *ch* in *chin*.
c̣,		an exploded c, not in English.
d	(de),	same as English.
e	(e),	sound of *e* in *they*.
g	(ghe),	sound of *g* in *give*.
ġ,		a guttural, not in English.
h	(he),	same as English.
ḣ,		sound of *ch* in German *ach*.
i	(e),	sound of *i* in *machine*.
k	(ke),	same as English.
ḳ		an exploded k, not in English.
l	(le),	same as English.
m	(me),	same as English.
n	(ne),	same as English.
ŋ	(in),	a nasal sound, nearly similar to *n* in *ink*. In Dakota it is only used at the end of a syllable.
o	(oh),	sound of *o* in *go*.
p	(pe),	same as English.
p̣,		an exploded p, not in English.
s	(see),	same as English.
ṡ	(she),	sound of *sh* in *she*.
t	(te),	same as English.
ṭ,		an exploded t, not in English.
u	(oo),	sound of *oo* in *ooze*.
w	(we),	same as English.
y	(ye),	same as English.
z	(ze),	same as English.
ż,		sound of *z* in *azure*.

A few letters are sometimes followed by a short hiatus. Such are marked thus, *s'*.

Gideon and Samuel Pond created an alphabet to transcribe the oral Dakota language into writing. By 1839, Samuel Pond had collected three thousand words for an English–Dakota dictionary.
John P. Williamson, An English-Dakota Dictionary: Wasicun Ka Dakota Ieska Wowapi (New York, American Tract Society, 1902), iii.

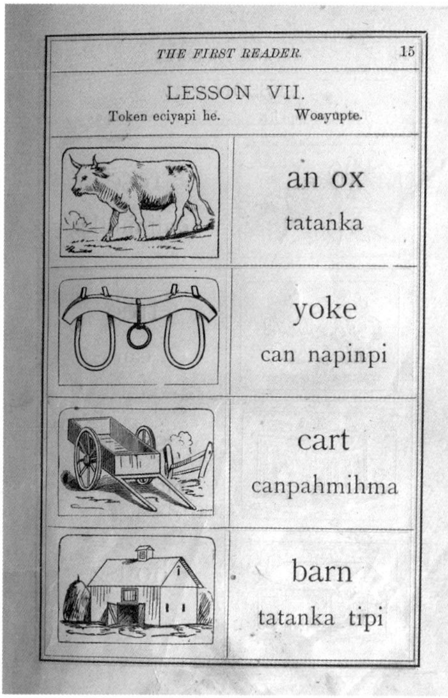

THE FIRST READER. 15

LESSON VII.

Token eciyapi he. Woayupte.

an ox
tatanka

yoke
can napinpi

cart
canpahmihma

barn
tatanka tipi

Dakota children like Angelique and Agnes learned literacy in English and Dakota using readers written and published by ABCFM missionaries, such as this 1873 example by Stephen Riggs. *Stephen Riggs, Model First Reader: Wayawa Tokaheya (Chicago: Geo. Sherwood and Co., 1873), p. 15.*

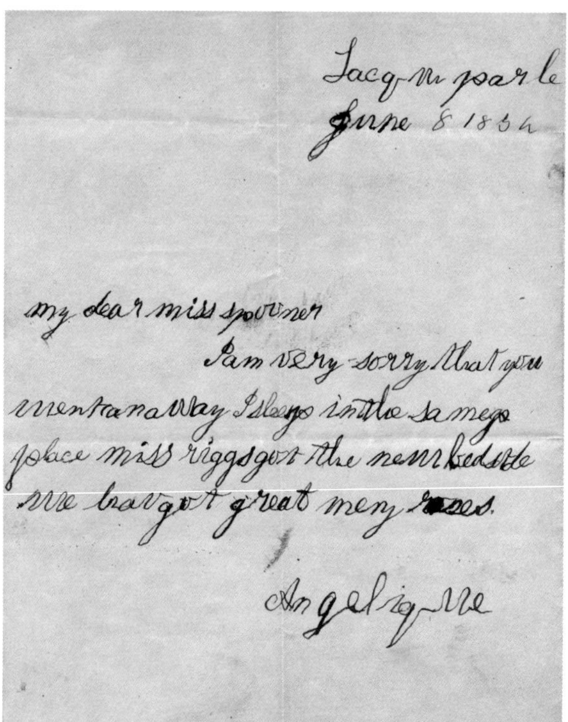

Lacqui parle
June 8 1854

my dear miss spooner
I am very sorry that you
went a way I sleep in the same
place miss riggs got the new bedstede
we bav got great meny roses.

Angelique

This short letter to Lucy Spooner Drake is the first known letter by Angelique. She was nine years old and had been with the Riggs family for three years when this was written. *Center for Western Studies, Augustana University, Sioux Falls, South Dakota*

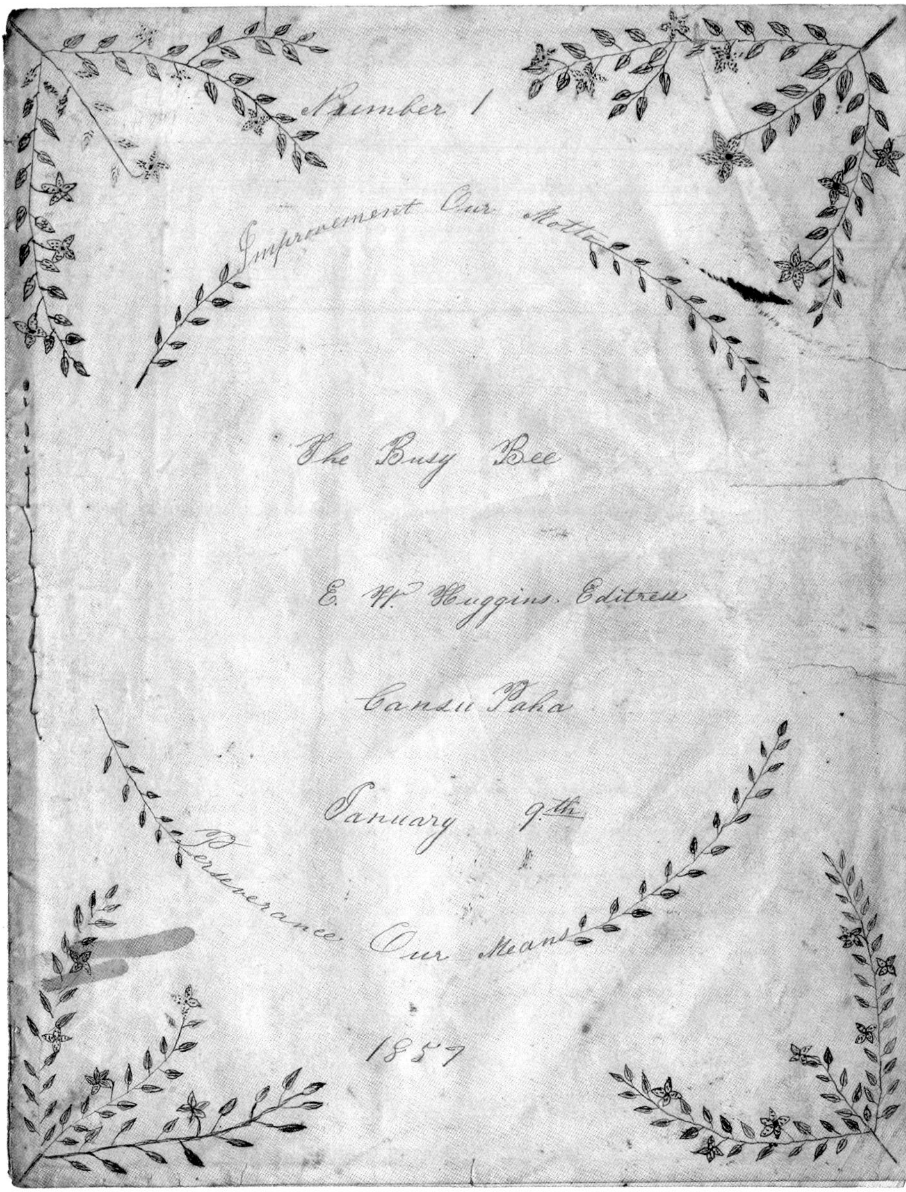

Angelique and the other missionary students at Hazelwood produced *The Busy Bee*, a weekly book of essays, poetry, and compositions, edited by Eliza W. Huggins.
Minnesota Historical Society

The ruins of Peabody Hall at the Western Female Seminary in Oxford, Ohio, after a January 1860 fire destroyed it. The Riggs family were forced to send their daughters, including Angelique, to the Ohio Female College instead. *Walter Havighurst Special Collections, Miami University Libraries, Oxford, Ohio.*

As befitting a school for the affluent, the Ohio Female College boasted that it had been built on "one of the most beautiful and healthful positions in all the Western States." Here it is seen in an artistic rendering by Middleton, Strobridge, & Co., ca. 1858–1865. *Yale University Art Gallery*

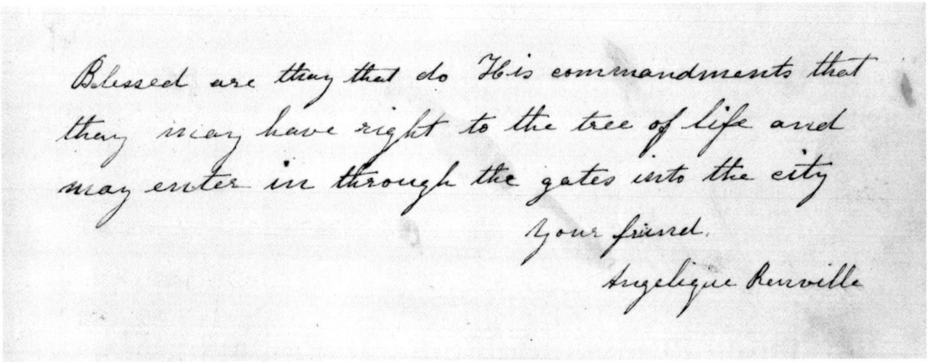

Blessed are they that do His commandments that
they may have right to the tree of life and
may enter in through the gates into the city
Your friend,
Angelique Renville

Just before she departed to study at the Ohio Female College in May 1861, Angelique signed Mary Ann Huggins's autograph book, demonstrating her literacy and knowledge of the Bible.
Minnesota Historical Society

ELLA I. BRIGGS,	Harrison.
MARION L. CALDWELL,	Newport, Ky.
MARY E. COBB,	Cincinnati.
KATE E. CROOKSHANK,	Cheviot.
JANE ELIZABETH DICK,	Melville.
MARTHA DICK,	Melville.
MARTHA JANE DICKSON,	Cincinnati.
MARY ELIZABETH DUCKWALL,	Pleasant Hill.
MARY F. FESSENDEN,	Pleasant Run.
SARAH M. FRANCIS,	College Hill.
VIRGINIA HART,	Union Corner.
BELLE HURD,	Kankakee City, Ill.
CATHARINE INGALSBE,	San Francisco, Cal.
HARRIET INGALSBE,	San Francisco, Cal.
EMMA KENDALL,	Mansfield.
JENNIE KOONS,	Logansport, Ind.
ROSA E. LOTZE,	Cincinnati.
JOSEPHINE MALLERY,	Hamilton.
ISABEL NOBLE,	Tiffin.
MARY ANN PEEL,	Cincinnati.
SARAH S. PEPPER,	Memphis, Tenn.
ANGELIQUE RENVILLE,	Pajutazee, Min.
MARGARETTA L. SCHMIDT,	Wilkinsonville, N.Y.
EMILY WISE,	Cincinnati.

FIRST PREPARATORY.

HANNAH ATKINS,	Cincinnati.

Despite her education at the mission schools, when Angelique arrived at the Ohio Female College she was placed into the lower two-year course with much younger girls, as seen in this school catalogue.
The Ohio Female College . . . with the Plan, Reasons, and Encouragement for its Permanent Endowment. . . (New York: Edward O. Jenkins, 1862), p. 15.

When the U.S.–Dakota War broke out in August 1862, several of Angelique's relatives rescued white settlers from massacre. Thousands of people were made refugees by the fighting; a group of them eat dinner on the prairie in this photograph by Adrian John Ebell. *Library of Congress*

In all, twenty-nine of Angelique's relatives were imprisoned at Fort Snelling, Minnesota, in the aftermath of the U.S.–Dakota War. Terrible living conditions and rampant disease there claimed many lives, including Angelique's sister Agnes, prompting her to return to Minnesota. *Minnesota Historical Society*

While imprisoned at Fort Snelling, Therese Renville married John Other Day (Anpetutokeca), seen here. Angelique did not approve of the marriage, probably due to Other Day's dubious reputation. *Minnesota Historical Society*

In 1858 a group of Dakota men attended treaty negotiations in Washington, D.C. Charles Crawford (Wakaninape), whom Angelique would later marry, stands on the far right.
Minnesota Historical Society

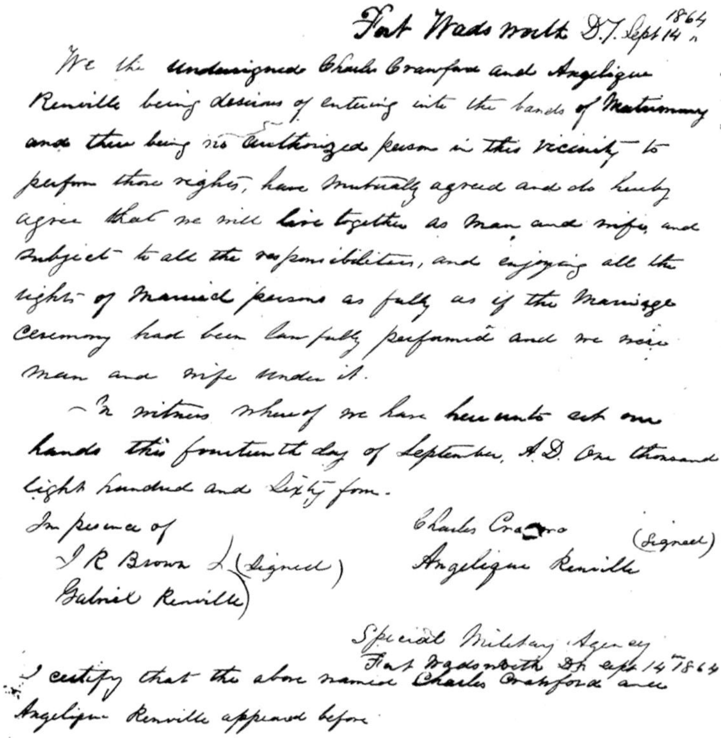

Fort Wadsworth D.T. Sept 14 1864

We the Undersigned Charles Crawford and Angelique Renville being desirous of entering into the bands of Matrimony and there being no authorized person in this vicinity to perform those rights, have mutually agreed and do hereby agree that we will live together as man and wife, and subject to all the responsibilities, and enjoying all the rights of married persons as fully as if the Marriage Ceremony had been lawfully performed and we now man and wife under it.

In witness whereof we have hereunto set our hands this fourteenth day of September, A.D. One thousand eight hundred and sixty four.

In presence of
J R Brown } (Signed)
Gabriel Renville

Charles Crawford (Signed)
Angelique Renville

Special Military Agency
Fort Wadsworth D.T. Sept 14 1864

I certify that the above named Charles Crawford and Angelique Renville appeared before

Angelique legally married Charles Crawford on 14 September 1864, as their marriage certificate attests, despite already being married according to Dakota customs for nearly a year. She may have wished to silence the missionaries' objections to the union, or perhaps to undermine Stephen Riggs's continued guardianship over her.
Minnesota Historical Society

John B. Renville (back row, far left), Daniel Renville (back row, second from left), and Charles Crawford (back row, third from left) posed for this photograph in 1886 along with other members of the Good Will Mission. *Presbyterian Historical Society*

Julia Laframboise, like Angelique, lived with various mission families for years and attended female seminaries in Ohio and Illinois. She later taught at the ABCFM's Santee Reservation school until her 1871 death at the age of twenty-eight. *Hennepin History Museum*

The children of Stephen and Mary Riggs followed in their parents' missionary footsteps. For example, Thomas Riggs, seen here, founded a mission at Oahe near modern-day Pierre, South Dakota.
South Dakota State Archives

him twice, Charles was imprisoned with the rest of the convicted Dakota men in Mankato from January until April 1863. In April, soldiers transferred him to Fort Snelling, where he reunited with his family and Renville allies.[68]

While imprisoned at Fort Snelling, Gabriel Renville had proposed to General Sibley that several Dakota men work as scouts. On 28 May 1863, Sibley added to his list of scouts, including Antoine and John B. Renville, Angelique's brothers Joseph, Daniel, and Thomas, and her new stepfather John Other Day, although he was listed as "absent" on the roles. Sibley's list also included Joseph Akipa Renville and his sons Charles and Thomas Crawford.[69] All of the scouts, and many of their wives and children, traveled into Dakota Territory to continue the government's fight against "hostile" Dakotas.

As her relatives and Charles Crawford signed on as scouts and left for Dakota Territory, Angelique finally convinced the Riggses to send her travel money, and she began to make her way from Ohio to Minnesota. After travelling most of the way on her own, she arrived in Minnesota in September or October 1863. She initially stayed at the Riggses' home in St. Anthony, where she had promised to work as their "chief housekeeper." On 3 November, however, only a few short weeks after her arrival, Mary Riggs informed General Sibley that Angelique had run away from their home while her husband was away in Iowa on missionary business. "[H]is ward, Angelique Renville, niece of Mr. J.B. Renville," Mary wrote, "left us and joined her mother at the camp of the Sioux Scouts." At first, Mary and Stephen blamed Therese; they assumed "that it was through her mother's influence that she left us." Although they were angry that Angelique had chosen her mother, Stephen Riggs decided "it was useless to take any measures for her return."[70]

The Riggses subsequently discovered that Angelique did not leave just to reunite with Therese and her brothers. "We have since learned to our great grief," Mary Riggs lamented, "that she was probably influenced to leave us by a licentious half breed." That "licentious half breed" was Charles Crawford, who was already married to another Dakota woman. Desperate for her to return, Mary wrote to General Sibley in Dakota Territory, pleading with him to "use the means and influence of your position in the cause of justice and mercy" to rescue Angelique. Mary even came up with a plan. Angelique's uncle

John B. Renville "is desirous to attempt her rescue, if any plan can be devised to enable him to do so safely." She asked Sibley to provide government resources so that John B. could save his niece. She suggested "making him the bearer of dispatches to the Sioux scouts, or even giving him an escort and a requisition for rations and forage at the Forts on his route [to rescue Angelique]."[71]

The missionaries believed that Charles had manipulated Angelique into marrying him. No other reason could possibly explain her decision to willingly become part of a polygamous union. Martha Riggs wrote that Angelique was "influenced to leave the home [of] love and life."[72] She had been induced to do so by Charles, who "whispered words to her, which perhaps she carried in her mind and heart."[73] Lucy Drake called Angelique a "Poor misguided girl," who did not know what was good for her.[74] Because Angelique had been manipulated, it was up to the missionaries to bring her back to her proper home where she would have the "opportunity . . . for being and doing good."[75] Once away from Charles, Angelique could reflect on her unfortunate choices and realize the "privileges" and "opportunities" she received as "one of the [missionary] household."[76] In the missionaries' initial appraisal, Charles had led Angelique astray; she had no agency to make her own choices or decisions. After her rescue, she would undoubtedly repent and return to dutifully following the missionaries' plan.

At first, Angelique did not disabuse the missionaries from their idea that she was a victim who felt ashamed of her actions. On 8 February 1864, she sent an apologetic letter to Stephen Riggs from Dakota Territory. She began by stating that she would have written earlier but was "very ashamed of what I have don. and I wish very much that I had not don it. If I had taken a second thought I would not have don so." She hoped that "you and Mrs. Riggs will foregive me I do not desearve to be foregiven. but I ask to be forgiven." Perhaps to placate the Riggses, she promised that she would continue to follow their teachings. She informed them that she "read [the Bible] all the time and do pray that God will help me to do what is right." She vowed to teach some of the women at the scout camp to read, even though she had no books, paper, ink, or pens.[77]

Despite her effusive apologies, Angelique gave no indication that she planned to return to the Riggses' home or had any desire to be "rescued." Indeed, she asked Riggs to "send me my trunk or my dresses if you can not send the trunk." She also wanted Riggs to forward her "album . . . and my two books." She even promised "to pay all that it costs" to mail her trunk and other items. She requested that Riggs honor her request as soon as possible, as "I need my clothes very much." She concluded her letter by reminding Riggs that she was still part of his family, even if she no longer lived in their home. She requested that "baby Cordelia" write her. She also wished that the Riggs boys were near her, as "we live by a very large lake. and it is such a good skateing I wish sometimes that they were here. it is larger then the one at Lacquaparle." Although she missed the Riggs family, she firmly stated that while she "would like to come back but I cannot do it. . . . I have no more to say. so Good bye."[78]

Angelique's next letter, written about a month after the first, was starkly different in tone. She demanded that the Riggses stop harassing her and telling her to leave Charles and her family. She told Stephen Riggs that she did "not like it one bit When you write me letters you scold me all the time. instead of telling me news." Angelique also rebuked Martha for lecturing her and calling her a liar. "Martha told me to give back all the presents that Charly C. gave me," she wrote, but "He has never given me a single thing since I have been here. any body that told her so told that was not the truth."[79]

Stephen Riggs had ignored her previous request to send her trunk, perhaps thinking that this would make her see the error of her ways. She reproached Riggs for his refusal to forward her trunk to Dakota Territory. "I did not like it because you did not send my trunk," she angrily wrote. "I am never comeing back there again. so you will oblige me very much by sending my trunk." In addition to refusing to send her trunk, Riggs must have told her she could teach at one of the mission schools if she came back. Angelique again shut down this idea, telling Riggs to have "Aunt Mary . . . give the school to her Niece. that I am not going to come back. . . . I shall look for my trunk."[80]

Another month passed and Riggs still refused to send her trunk. Angelique wrote another letter, again demanding that he forward her trunk, music, books, and album. She also informed Riggs that she had enough "sense" to make her own choices; she knew what she wanted and that did not involve returning to the mission.[81] Finally, in May 1864, three months after her initial request, Riggs mailed her trunk with some supplies to Fort Abercrombie in Dakota Territory. Even though she had promised to pay the shipping charges, Riggs dutifully recorded the mailing expenses of $9.50 in his long-standing "guardian's log." This new charge for her trunk added to her running debt, which totaled $224.04 by 1864.[82]

While Angelique angrily defended her choice to remain in Dakota Territory, she did not have an easy transition. After living with the missionaries for ten years in Minnesota, and then in Ohio for two years, Angelique had been indoctrinated to view "uncivilized" Dakotas as inferior and "savage." She initially carried some of these internalized prejudices with her to Dakota Territory, admitting to Stephen Riggs that "I even was scared my self when I came to the tents."[83] Angelique needed to readjust to living with her Dakota kin in tipis, participating in bison hunts, and returning to the gender roles and subsistence patterns of her youth. Many of the cultural, religious, and gender norms that she had learned from the Riggs family no longer applied in the scout camps in Dakota Territory.

Angelique experienced conflict with some members of the scout community, probably due to her long absence and years living with the missionaries. She did not know the internal workings of the community, nor the personalities and history of its members. For example, she was drawn into a conflict between Simon Anawagmani, a scout and Christian Dakota, and Gabriel Renville over a school in the scout camp. She complained that Simon Anawangmani "tells more lies then he is worth Becaus Gabril wanted me to teach school he was jealous he wanted his daughter to do it. and he did all he could to have all aginst me. So I have stoped and told them that I would not teach any more." Anawangmani viewed Angelique as an outsider who tried to take over a position that belonged to his daughter. Angelique had merely done what Gabriel had asked her to do. Despite her anger at Riggs, Angelique asked him to step in and give Simon "a lecturing. and have him stop telling lies or telling things that are not so."[84] After being gone for over ten years, Angelique still had one foot in each camp; she resolutely refused to go back to the Riggses, and yet she struggled to find her place within the scout community in Dakota Territory.

Despite these difficulties, her immediate and extended Renville relatives and new husband helped to ease her transition to her new life in Dakota Territory. For the first eleven months after she left Minnesota, Angelique lived with Charles Crawford and his other wife Tasinahewin according to Dakota marriage practices. In other words, a sanctioned official did not legally marry Angelique and Charles, nor did they file any paperwork with the court. They certainly did not take "Christian vows of marriage."[85] Of course, the missionaries did not see Dakota marriage practices as legal. As such, they hoped that that Angelique would finally come to her senses and leave Charles. Indeed, Martha Riggs continued to beg her to return to Minnesota. She hoped that once Angelique realized that Charles's "promises [were] false, she could have bravely left him, and truly and bravely lived afterward."[86] If Angelique made the correct decision and left Charles, she would "be an example to the women around her."[87] Ironically, Martha pinned her hopes on the same Dakota marriage practices that she condemned. Because Angelique had married according to Dakota custom, she could simply leave her husband and return to her previous life, an option unavailable to many Euro-American women at the time who needed to obtain a legal divorce through the court system.

Angelique dashed the missionaries' hopes by legally marrying Charles on 14 September 1864 at Fort Wadsworth in Dakota Territory. Their marriage contract stated:

> We the undersigned Charles Crawford and Angelique Renville being desirous of entering into the bonds of Matrimony and there being no authorized person in this vicinity to perform these rights, have mutually agreed and do hereby agree that we will live together as man and wife, and subject to all the responsibilities, and enjoying all the rights of married persons.

The document contained four signatures: Joseph R. Brown (the government representative) and Gabriel Rinville (Renville) as witnesses, and Angelique and Charles.[88] It is unclear why they decided to marry according to Euro-American practices after eleven months of following Dakota customs. Perhaps Angelique wanted a contract to finally halt the missionaries' lectures about the illegitimacy of her marriage. She may have internalized the need to legally marry, after having spent over ten years with the missionaries. It is also possible that

Angelique knew that a legal marriage would lead to her emancipation from Riggs, as guardianships ended once female wards married. This interpretation certainly would fit into Angelique's impending protracted fight with Riggs over her guardianship.

After Stephen and Mary Riggs learned about the couple's marriage at Fort Wadsworth, they expended much ink with other members of the mission community debating whether the document counted as a legal marriage. At first, the consensus appeared to be that it was not a legally binding marriage. In a letter to Lucy Drake, Mary Riggs called the ceremony "informal" and wondered if it was "truly a marriage."[89] She also wrote to Thomas Williamson, asking him "If you can consistently ascertain whether Maj. Brown had any legal power to perform the marriage rite."[90] Stephen Riggs finally sent a letter to the secretary's office in Dakota Territory, asking if the marriage was legal according to Dakota territorial law. The clerk wrote back that he "knew of no law in Dakota [Territory] requiring a license to marry. . . . There is no law requiring the bans to be published. There is no return required to the Clerk of the court or any other officer."[91] According to the clerk, Angelique did not need the Fort Wadsworth document to be legally married in Dakota Territory.

Stephen and Mary Riggs finally, and reluctantly, admitted that Angelique's marriage would probably "stand in law."[92] This admission, however, did not stop the Riggses from continuing to condemn her marriage to Charles. Indeed, Stephen lectured Angelique about her marriage each time he visited her camps in Dakota Territory. In 1865, Riggs noted that he talked to Angelique about her marriage. "I gave her advice as her case seemed to require," he informed his wife. "I feel sorry for her. And yet I can't but hope that she will do some good in the world."[93] Mary Riggs supported her husband's efforts to overturn her marriage, as she was "very desirous that all proper means be used to help Angelique to walk in the narrow way which headeth unto life."[94]

Angelique pointedly ignored Riggs's lectures and settled into life with Charles, Tasinahewin, and the other Dakota women of her community. From 1864 to 1866, she lived and worked as part of a largely female community, as Charles frequently traveled on hunts and as a government scout. During her husband's protracted absences, Angelique performed traditional Dakota gender roles and subsistence patterns with Tasinahewin and other women in her camp. During a visit to Angelique's camp, Riggs noted that "the great stable of this camp is *meat*."[95] On 4 July 1866, "the buffalo hunters from this camp came home with an abundance of meat and skins. They have been gone about 16 days. One man has just gone around singing the praise of a woman who gave him a bundle of meat and tallow."[96] After the men returned, "the women are up and dressing their buffalo skins in the cool of the morning."[97] On another trip to the scout camp, Thomas Williamson confirmed that "most of the men and many of the women [were] absent on a Buffalo hunt."[98] The men also hunted ducks and geese, while the women picked gooseberries, strawberries, and blackberries.[99] In addition to practicing traditional subsistence patterns, Riggs was horrified to report that some of camp members continued their "heathen" ceremonies, including the sacred Sun Dance.[100] In other words, Angelique lived much as she had as a young girl, participating in traditional subsistence patterns, working with other female members of her camp, and participating in (or, at least witnessing) Dakota religious ceremonies.

It is somewhat unclear if Angelique lived with Tasinahewin or not during the first years of her marriage. In October 1864, John Williamson traveled to the scout camp on the James River about fifty miles west of Fort Wadsworth. The camp consisted of about thirty lodges. Williamson informed Stephen Riggs that he found "Charly Crawford and Angelique Renville keeping house . . . and his other wife gone."[101] Two years later, an 1867 census for the newly created Lake Traverse Reservation supported Williamson's observation, listing Tasinahewin as a single woman living with one child.[102] Another two years later, the January 1869 Lake Traverse census listed Charles Crawford as living in one household with Angelique, Tasinahewin, and two children.[103]

Perhaps the discrepancy stems from the fact that Williamson did not understand (and forcibly condoned) polygamous relationships. As previously discussed, outside observers often ignored Dakota family relations that did not conform to Euro-American ideals. Perhaps Tasinahewin was never "gone" (in the sense of divorced) but resided in a separate household according to Dakota custom. Mary Riggs explained that a woman involved in a polygamous marriage frequently had her own fields and "her own skin or bark lodge—takes care of her own children—provides her own fuel, and c."[104] Williamson also may have privileged Angelique's marriage to Charles by simply erasing his other wife. In both scenarios, it is likely that Angelique, Tasinahewin, and Crawford remained married despite missionary comments and ambiguous census reports to the contrary.

Unfortunately, Angelique did not leave any letters stating how she felt about Charles, Tasinahewin, or her marriage in general, but her actions give some clue. From the beginning, she strongly defended her relationship with Charles and refused to return to Minnesota. She remained with her husband and Tasinahewin until she passed away in May 1876. In the intervening years, she never gave any indication that she wanted to dissolve her marriage, even though according to Dakota divorce practices, she could have easily left Charles if she had wanted to do so. Charles even explicitly stated that he would make changes if she was not happy in the relationship; in 1866, Stephen Riggs reported that Charles Crawford wrote to him "that he will put away [his other wife] if [Angelique] desires it."[105] Angelique appears not to have taken Charles up on his offer. Indeed, she remained with Charles when he married at least two other women. In 1868, Angelique's uncle, John B. Renville, wrote that Charles "reported on a list of names himself and his wife Angelique and two . . . women, now these are his wives too."[106] Of course, the fact that Angelique remained in the marriage does not provide any insight into her intimate family relations or how she felt about her Charles in general, though it does indicate her commitment to the marriage and her family as they constructed it, especially when faced with relentless condemnation and pressure from the missionaries to dissolve the union.

Perhaps her relationship with Charles grew stronger when Angelique gave birth to their daughter Augusta, probably sometime in 1865. Tasinahewin also had at least one child at this time. Augusta and Tasinahewin's children would have been raised together by their mothers.[107] According to Dakota anthropologist Ella Deloria, "Children from polygamous marriages did not separate themselves in a different camp from their half-siblings. They were all brothers and sisters without distinction."[108] The women would have taught their daughters to pick fruit and berries, process the buffalo hides and meat, and sew, much like their own female relatives had done. If Tasinahewin's child was a son, he would have learned from his male relatives. It is likely that the two women shared labor and childcare responsibilities between them, along with other women in their camps.

Unfortunately, as was common with polygamous marriages, existing documents make it difficult to determine the names, ages, and even number of Charles's children with Angelique and those with his other wives. In 1865, Stephen Riggs wrote that Angelique had a little girl named Augusta, but no Augusta Crawford (or Augusta Renville) appears in any census records that match the years around her birth. In 1871, Riggs mentioned in a letter that Angelique had three children but did not provide their names or ages.[109] An 1872 document listing the Renville lands in Dakota Territory recorded that Angelique had "one child and female heir," so the two other children Riggs referenced may have biologically been Tasinahewin's.[110]

Later census records list Charles Crawford as the father to several children born prior to Angelique's death, including Elizabeth (1865 or 1867); Samuel John (1868); Ida Mae (1869); and Peter (1873). Several questions arise about these children. Given their birth dates, were these the children of Angelique, Tasinahewin, or another of Charles's wives? One record listed Elizabeth's birthdate as 1865; could Augusta have been renamed Elizabeth by the census recorder or the missionaries when they baptized her on 31 March 1878, less than two years after Angelique's death? Or, did Augusta pass away, as was all too common for children who suffered from illness, trauma, and lack of food in Dakota Territory in this era? Perhaps these are the wrong questions, however. According to Dakota customs, Angelique and Tasinahewin would not have divided the family's children into biological and non-biological heirs as did Euro-American census or land records.[111] In sum, hours spent examining census records shed little light on the subject; the existing records are silent (or inconsistent) as to the age, number, and what happened to Angelique's children, including Augusta. Assuredly, some of her children (or even Augusta herself, perhaps now called Elizabeth) survived and were raised by Tasinahewin.

In addition to her family with Charles, Tasinahewin, and their children, Angelique maintained strong ties with her extensive network of Renville kin. From the time she left Minnesota, Angelique always resided close to her numerous relatives. From 1863 to 1866, Angelique lived with her Renville kin in various scout camps located throughout Dakota Territory. In 1866, she resided near Lake Traverse with "Antoine and Michel Renville and their families"[112] She also lived near her brother Daniel, his wife, and their children.[113] Charles's father Akipa and brother Thomas also resided near her at various locations throughout Dakota Territory. Most important, Angelique's mother Therese stayed close to her daughter and her family, and her sons Daniel and Thomas. In fact, it was noteworthy when her mother did not reside near Angelique and her family. In 1871, Stephen Riggs wrote that Angelique's "mother does not live here but some sixty miles down the Coteau."[114]

These close kin ties continued when the Renvilles and other Sisseton and Wahpeton Dakotas moved onto a new reservation. In January 1867, Charles Crawford, Gabriel Renville, Akipa, John Other Day, and several other Dakota men traveled to Washington, D.C., to negotiate a treaty to create a new permanent reservation in Dakota Territory. The resulting treaty established the Lake Traverse Reservation, located between Fort Wadsworth and Lake Traverse. The reservation resembles an isosceles triangle, pointing south and straddling the eastern borders of North Dakota and South Dakota. This reservation was set aside specifically for the many Sisseton and Wahpeton men who had served as scouts following the 1862 U.S.–Dakota War, including many Renville kin.[115] Indeed, following the treaty, the southern area of the reservation became known as the "Renville settlement."[116] An 1867 census of the new reservation listed dozens of Angelique's relatives residing near her, including Gabriel, Antoine, Michel, and John B. Renville, and her brothers Joseph, Daniel, and Thomas.[117] Thus, from the time she left Minnesota in 1863 until her death in 1876, Angelique never lived far from her relatives. Angelique chose her kin, and especially her mother, husband, and co-wife, despite the missionaries' decades-long crusade to separate her from them.

Though Angelique clearly chose her kin over the ABCFM missionaries, over the next decade her life continued to intersect with the missionaries and Christianity. Prior to the creation of the Lake Traverse Reservation, Stephen Riggs, John Williamson, and other ABCFM representatives traveled around Dakota Territory preaching at the scattered Dakota camps. In 1865, Stephen Riggs made a trip to the "scout camp," where "we held meetings of various kinds every day, and preach[ed] in the area of the camp every evening."[118] In April 1866, Riggs held meetings during a trip to Dakota Territory "wherever an opportunity occurred."[119] Later that summer, he went on a two-week tour of the Coteau des Prairies, during which he "held thirteen public [meetings]. Three persons have united with the church. We have baptized two adults and five infants, ordained one Elder and solemnized the marriage of two couples. Yesterday we partook of the holy communion. The women put up . . . two large tents. They all turned out in the morning to a Sabbath school."[120] Once the Treaty of 1867 established the Lake Traverse Reservation, Riggs and a rotating cast of missionaries continued to visit the camps at least once a year.[121]

Angelique often encountered Riggs during his preaching circuits. In June 1866, he stopped at her camp. During his short visit, he made a point of giving her a photograph of his daughter Isabella.[122] Riggs did not explain his motivation for giving her the image; perhaps he wanted to remind Angelique of her ties to the Riggs family, as she had once been very close to Isabella, who by this time held a prestigious posting as an ABCFM missionary to China. Stephen Riggs may have been not so subtly attempting to show Angelique the proper path for mission-educated women.

Angelique did not record her response to Isabella's picture. She did, however, attempt to walk a middle path with regards to Christianity, at least at first. She had grown up attending church, reading and studying the Bible, and had joined the Hazelwood church in her teens. Even though she was extremely conflicted about her relationship with the Riggs family, she continued to attend some church meetings and even led a singing group. During one visit to Angelique's camp, Stephen Riggs asked Ellen Brown if Angelique ever attended church services. Ellen responded that yes, she attended meetings, and she was "the leader of the music." Angelique had always loved to sing and had studied music at the Ohio Female College. Despite her participation in meetings, Ellen told Riggs that "she did not think she was a Christian but she wished she was."[123]

Riggs's refusal to baptize Angelique's daughter Augusta assuredly pushed her further away from Christianity. In 1866, Stephen

Riggs described an encounter with Angelique during one of his mission tours to the scout camps. "We came first to Mrs. Brown's home, which is in the valley between the Minnesota and Lake Traverse," he wrote. "Angelique was there. She picked up her child and came right to me and I think was glad to see me." After visiting a few minutes, Angelique "asked me to baptize her little girl, which she calls Augusta, but I was obliged to decline for the present. Tasinahewin wanted hers baptized also."[124] According to rules established by his own mission, Riggs should have baptized Angelique and Tasinahewin's children. Since the 1830s, the missionaries had baptized the children of female church members who were involved in polygamous marriages, as they supposedly were not responsible for their husbands' actions. As such, it appears that Riggs's personal feelings about Angelique overrode his usually strict adherence to mission policy.

After his refusal to baptize her daughter, Angelique began actively avoiding Riggs. On 23 August 1867, Riggs reported that he "tried to see Angelique but did not get a chance. She did not come in to meeting. After it was over I asked Charley where she was. He said she was there and went out as I told him I wanted to see her. The Brown family [searched] for her and called her but she did not make her appearance—nor did I see Charley afterwards. I cannot account for their conduct."[125] While Riggs appeared baffled by Angelique's refusal to see him, her actions certainly make sense in the context of his longstanding critique of her marriage and his refusal to baptize her daughter.

Although Angelique showed little interest in continuing a relationship with Riggs, she lived near the ABCFM mission until her death in 1876. By 1869, Charles had staked "his claim by the Edge of the Coteau."[126] In June 1870, Stephen Riggs established the Good Will mission within walking distance of Charles's claim.[127] In 1871, Riggs reported that "Angelique Renville Crawford lives in sight of us. . . . What is sad about it, Crawford has another wife also."[128] By 1875, Crawford had established a home and farm located close to the mission buildings. An article in *Iapi Oyate*, a Dakota language newspaper, stated that "In passing from the agency to the Manual Labor Boarding School, we see a two story frame off to the left—that with the large wheat field, belongs to Charley Crawford."[129] By 1876, just before Angelique's death, Charles formally claimed an allotment of 159.20 acres of Sisseton-Wahpeton lands on the Lake Traverse Reservation.[130]

Although Charles Crawford's allotment, wheat farm, and settled home indicated his acceptance of many aspects of "civilization," both the missionaries and government officials targeted him due to his polygamous marriage. Beginning in 1872, Moses Adams, a former ABCFM Dakota missionary, took over as Indian agent for the Lake Traverse Reservation. While he supported all "civilization" programs, Adams singled out polygamy as the "greatest of all barriers to [the Dakotas'] mental moral and social development."[131] Adams hyperbolically accused polygamy of rendering "multitudes of women worse off than widows and scores of children too, whose condition is more wretched and miserable than orphans whose fathers and mothers sleep in the grave."[132]

Adams did not just speak out against polygamous relationships; he attempted to legally control all aspects of marriage on the reservation. In January 1873, Adams issued his "Rules for Reservation," which dictated that all marriages needed to be between "one man and one woman." He also ordered marriages to "be solemnized by either the U.S. Indian Agent [Adams], an ordained minister of the Gospel, or a Justice of the Peace." Finally, he mandated all couples who wished to divorce to "come to the U.S. Agent," who most likely would "command them to remain together as husband and wife."[133] Adams enforced his "Rules" by refusing to provide "aid or support under any treaty stipulations or otherwise" to those couples involved in polygamous marriages. More generally, he favored church members in the distribution of agency goods.[134] According to historian Gary Clayton Anderson, Adams attempted to create a "religious oligarchy" on the reservation which dramatically increased factionalism during his tenure as agent.[135]

In theory, Edward Smith, the commissioner of Indian Affairs at the time, supported ending polygamy. Nonetheless, he ruled that Adams's "order prohibiting polygamy among the Indians under your charge [was] a wide departure from the course pursued by the Government in its dealing with the Indians under its control. [T]he department does not deem it advisable to take such action at present time."[136] Smith also criticized Adams's decision to favor Church members in his distribution of rations, which directly violated the

1867 Treaty that had established the reservation. As such, in spring 1873, he ordered that Adams be "investigated for favoring Christian Indians in agency distributions, contrary to the Treaty of 1867."[137] When he learned of the investigation, Adams defended his actions, angrily informing Smith that the charges did not have "a particle of truth." He contradicted himself in the next paragraph, stating that "some of the church members are more industrious, faithful and prosperous than some of those who are corrupt in practice," and thus deserved additional support.[138]

Ultimately, the threatened investigation never happened, and Adams held onto his position for another year. Meanwhile, the conflict intensified. In winter 1873, a group of Dakota men seized items Adams had issued to church members. He responded by calling troops onto the reservation.[139] Stephen Riggs blamed "the adherents of polygamy and old heathenism" for the crisis, writing that they "have been making determined efforts to get rid of the present Agent, Rev. M.N. Adams, because of his Christian character."[140] Finally, in 1874, the Commissioner of Indian Affairs removed Adams from his post for provoking continuous conflicts during his time as Agent.[141] The ABCFM's press provided a different interpretation of Adams's dismissal, simply noting that he "retired," and that his legacy lived on "in the hearts of the Christian people."[142]

While Angelique did not leave any writings specifically addressing Adams or his contentious policies, her family would have been targeted by Adams's anti-polygamy edict and his favoritism for professing Christians. Her husband's actions during the troubles on the reservations certainly did not endear her family to Adams. As the situation deteriorated, Charles allegedly "assailed and abused the pastor" at the Good Will church.[143] Angelique's estrangement from the ABCFM church, as well as Charles's behavior, would have likely excluded her family from receiving legally mandated treaty goods.

Several of Angelique's relatives also suffered during Adams's tenure. Adams denounced Angelique's uncle Gabriel Renville (also Charles's half-brother), the "Chief" of the reservation, for having "two or three wives" and for making "feasts and practicing at them some of the old customs, which degrade and impoverish people."[144] Adams tried to strip Gabriel of his position, recommending that "no Bigamist nor Polygamist be eligible to this office or Councilman, or

Executive Board."[145] Adams also continued to bar Gabriel, and those who supported him, from receiving their rations.[146] As ABCFM pastors, Angelique's uncle John B. and her brother Daniel should have supported Adams, but even they expressed dismay at Adams's actions. Riggs tried to convince both men that they "were wrong" after they "had worked themselves up to feel so toward Mr. Adams." Riggs lectured that they should "give themselves more fully to the work of doing good themselves, and not engage so much in criticizing others."[147]

Even after Moses Adams left as agent, Angelique and her family continued to face a strong ABCFM presence on the Lake Traverse Reservation. In 1870, Martha Riggs Morris and her husband Wyllys Morris moved to the newly established Good Will mission. Both Martha and her husband worked in the government boarding school as teachers; they also retained their affiliation with the ABCFM.[148] Stephen Riggs divided his time between the Good Will mission and Beloit, Wisconsin, where his family had moved after the 1862 war. With the help of Stephen Riggs and several of his other children, the ABCFM established numerous churches and schools across the Lake Traverse Reservation.

During the 1870s, Stephen Riggs and Martha Riggs Morris collectively wrote hundreds of letters from the Good Will mission. In this copious correspondence, Stephen Riggs meticulously documented the many people he met each day. If he ran into church members and had tea, he recorded their names in his letters. Whenever he preached, he noted where and to whom. He frequently mentioned Angelique's brother Daniel, who had been chosen as pastor of the Good Will church in 1871. Likewise, Martha documented her time at the Good Will mission, where she helped to run the boarding school.[149]

Conspicuously absent in all their detailed correspondence are any further references to Angelique, Augusta, or Tasinahewin.[150] The almost complete omission of Angelique in Stephen and Martha's copious correspondence is initially surprising, given their decades-long relationship with Angelique and her proximity to the Good Will mission. But their silence regarding Angelique in fact speaks volumes about how the Riggs family had come to view her. Because she refused to follow their guidance, they no longer viewed her as worthy of comment. This interpretation is based on the absence of information rather than on quotations from the missionaries themselves. There is undeniably a "before" and "after" in terms of missionary references to Angelique: multiple letters chronicle her acceptance of Christianity and her time with the Riggses and in Ohio. The references became less and less frequent after her marriage to Charles, her movement to Dakota Territory, Stephen Riggs's refusal to baptize Augusta, and Angelique's lawsuit against Riggs, as detailed in the following chapter. It was as if the Riggs family slowly erased Angelique from their world.

Stephen Riggs did not explain whether his lack of contact with Angelique was by his choice, her choice, or a mutual decision to avoid each other. Riggs's enmity towards Angelique had begun in 1864 when she "ran away" from Minnesota, entered a polygamous marriage, and (half-way) renounced Christianity. Meanwhile, Riggs's actions, including his desire to undermine Angelique's marriage, his continued lectures, and his failure to baptize her daughter, which she well knew contradicted the missionaries' own policy, likely drove her away from the church and from the family.

For all these reasons, and many others, Angelique distanced herself from the Riggs family as much as they distanced themselves from her. As such, by the mid-1860s her social and religious emancipation from the Riggses was largely complete. She lived her daily life surrounded by her immediate family and kin and appears to have had only passing contact with the missionaries. At the same time, however, she still was legally bound to Stephen Riggs through his continued guardianship over her and his control of her scrip. Throughout the mid-1860s until her death, Angelique fought for her legal and social emancipation from the Riggs family. She also fought for justice for her late sister Agnes.

::: 6 :::

DAKOTA TERRITORY

Land and Guardianship

1863–1876

In September 1869, Angelique Renville Crawford wrote to Eugene St. Julien Cox, a lawyer practicing in New Ulm, Minnesota. In the letter, she asked Cox to investigate the illegal sale of her remaining scrip. She wrote that she had been "imposed upon" and "shamefully deceived" in the sale of her last acres, as her signature "had been procured under very false pretenses." She specifically claimed that she had unknowingly signed a power of attorney. She angrily called the entire transaction "a Swindle." She asked Cox to "look after this for me. I wish to be paid for my land or I want my land back."[1] While this specific letter referenced her lands that had been sold after she had left Minnesota, the legal issues involved went much deeper and dated back to the early 1860s. While not explicitly stated in her letter, other information reveals that she likely asked Cox to also contest Stephen Riggs's handling of her sister Agnes's estate after her death in 1863. More generally, she challenged the missionary's continuing decade-long guardianship over her and his control of her scrip. Although ultimately unsuccessful, Angelique attempted to reassert legal control over her life and land, just as she had already socially distanced herself from the missionaries.

The fact that Angelique hired a lawyer is extraordinary for several reasons. First, her actions went against Euro-American gender roles of the era. From the missionary point of view, Angelique did not act like a proper woman. Back in 1839, two years after she first arrived in Minnesota, Mary Riggs explained to her sister in Massachusetts how a "true" woman behaved, stating that a woman should "[c]ultivate a meek and quiet spirit, a dove like disposition and it will impart a charm to the plainest features."[2] For over ten years, the Riggs family had worked to teach Angelique Euro-American gender roles. Angelique's letter to Cox shows that she did not internalize all their values even after extensive indoctrination. Her letter was anything but meek and quiet. She used strong language to demand restitution. The fact that she advocated for herself illustrated her adherence to traditional Dakota gender roles that stressed autonomy for women. According to legal historian Bethany Ruth Berger, American Indian women were never legally passive, nor did they submit to men.[3] Angelique certainly illustrated this observation, as she advocated for herself without deferring to her husband.

Second, Angelique challenged legal norms of the era. In the nineteenth century, Euro-American women were not supposed to take the lead in legal matters. According to the concept of coverture, a married woman's legal identity was covered by her husband; she could not sell or control property, for example. Angelique, however, operated under the assumption that she controlled her own property, as was customary for Dakota women. She also acted as her own legal advocate. It appears that she found and hired Cox. She wrote to the lawyer and asked him to investigate her case. She gave Cox specific details to get him started, including that her scrip was filed under her maiden name of "Angelique Renville" instead of Angelique Crawford. Most telling, her husband's name did not appear once in her initial letter. She also followed up with Cox to push him to act more quickly on her case. Nonetheless, once her case began, Cox followed legal norms of the era which dictated that he defer to her husband.

Finally, Angelique used the missionaries' education to challenge the sale of her last acres, and more broadly, Riggs's guardianship and the sale of her sister's land back in the early 1860s. Beginning at the age of six, the missionaries had taught her to read and write in English. She was one of only two Dakota students the missionaries sent to a female seminary to further their education. In Ohio, she took more advanced classes, and (for better or worse) learned the social and cultural norms of upper- and middle-class American society. Even though she ultimately rejected the missionaries when she moved to Dakota Territory in 1863, she had learned how American society functioned and how to operate within that world. More specifically, she understood the American legal system. Dakota legal tradition was based on customs and passed down orally.[4] Angelique learned to navigate a very different legal system that was written and in English, focused on case law and courts, and relied on lawyers to help navigate the legal process. Even after she had largely rejected the Riggses (and they had rejected her), she used mission-acquired skills to advocate for her land and rights.

Angelique's fight for her land, and against her guardianship, can be seen as the culmination of her inveterate struggle for physical, emotional, and legal emancipation from the Riggs family. As a child, she did not have the knowledge or means to challenge Stephen Riggs's guardianship or the sale of her scrip. She does not appear to have questioned their decision to send her to Ohio. Slowly, as she came of age, she began to distance herself from the missionaries and to challenge their authority. In Ohio, she corresponded with Charles Crawford, against their wishes. In 1862, she pleaded with the Riggses to allow her to return to her kin in Minnesota. After arriving home, she walked away from the Riggs family to marry an "unsuitable" man. Her break with the missionaries and Christianity was half-hearted at first but widened over the years as the missionaries lectured her, barred her from important church rituals, and supported reservation programs that discriminated against her family. Angelique also became increasingly infuriated over Riggs's continued guardianship and control of her land and finances. Her desire for emancipation and redress for her stolen scrip climaxed with her legal challenge.

Up until her death in 1876, Angelique fought not only for her own rights, but on behalf of her late sister Agnes. In this way, Angelique followed in the steps of her mother Therese, who attempted to retain control over her daughters' scrip in the late 1850s. Unfortunately, despite her numerous skills and knowledge of American cultural and legal norms, Angelique was no more successful than her mother in receiving compensation for their lands. Despite her age, estrangement, and marriage status, Stephen Riggs also refused to relinquish her guardianship as was legally mandated. Therese and Angelique both experienced a legal system that was stacked against Dakota women who challenged powerful men like the ABCFM missionaries and land profiteers.

On 14 January 1863, Agnes passed away from measles during her incarceration at the Fort Snelling prison camp. Although she died surrounded by her mother and her Renville kin, Stephen Riggs was her guardian at the time, as he had been since 1857 (in practice) or 1861 (when he finally completed the legal process). On 23 February, one month after her death, Riggs wrote to Charles Wagner, the probate judge for Brown County, asking how to finalize his guardianship for Agnes. Wagner wrote back that "in order to wind up your Guardianship you will have to render a final account of your doings in the premises, to the Probate Court of Brown County, and then you may apply to the Judge of Probate of Nicollet County to appoint an administrator for the Estate of your deceased ward."[5]

Riggs quickly completed both these orders: he informed the court that Agnes owed him $83.18 for his guardian expenses, and he handpicked Jonas Pettijohn, a close colleague and friend who had served as an ABCFM missionary at Lac qui Parle from 1845 to 1852, to serve as the administrator for Agnes's estate. The court appointed Pettijohn as administrator on 27 May 1863, and he completed his work about two years later.[6] In the intervening years, Pettijohn, always guided by Riggs, worked to close her estate. This process involved selling her land, paying all the expenses related to the sale, settling her guardianship with Riggs, and finally dividing up any remaining proceeds among her legal heirs.

As his first and most important order of business, Pettijohn needed to sell Agnes's land. Like her sister Angelique and brothers Daniel and Thomas, Agnes had received 480 acres of "half breed" scrip in the late 1850s. Unlike her sister, Riggs had not yet sold any of Agnes's scrip—although he tried to do so in 1861—so she still retained all 480 acres when she passed away. Guardianship laws required Riggs to adhere to a set procedure for selling real estate; likewise, the court mandated that as her estate administrator Pettijohn must follow specific steps to sell her land. First, he needed to apply for a license to sell her scrip. In his petition for the license, Pettijohn explained why he, and not Agnes's heirs, was qualified to oversee the sale. Pettijohn's petition informed the court, "That three of the four heirs at law of Said Estate are wholly without means of support, in education, and totally disqualified to discharge the general duties of civilized life. . . . It is the wish of the Guardian [Stephen Riggs] . . . that this land should be sold by administrator [Jonas Pettijohn]."[7]

Pettijohn's petition for a license to sell Agnes's land is instructive for several reasons. First, the document clearly defines Riggs as the guardian of record, and not her mother Therese, which gave him control over her estate. Second, the text links Riggs to Pettijohn, illustrating the prominent role that her guardian played in closing her estate. Third, and more perplexing, was the reasoning given for disqualifying her heirs from handling her estate. According to the court, Agnes had four legal heirs: her mother Therese and her siblings Daniel, Angelique, and Thomas.[8] Out of these four beneficiaries, two were clearly disqualified according to Euro-American standards set forth in the document. Therese had never attended school, could neither read nor write, and lived as a traditional Dakota woman. As such, the court would have classified her as unable to "discharge the general duties of civilized life." At thirteen years old, Thomas was underage at the time.

Who, then, was the third "uncivilized" heir? Both Angelique and Daniel had attended a mission school, were literate, and had been members of the ABCFM church. By the time Agnes's case worked its way through court, Daniel had become an ABCFM minister and worked closely with both Stephen Riggs and Thomas Williamson. Angelique, meanwhile, had married Charles Crawford, was part of a polygamous marriage, had mostly left the church, and actively avoided Riggs. As such, was Angelique the third "uncivilized" heir? As a woman, she probably would have been disqualified from serving as executor to Agnes's estate, but this is not what the petition stated. The likely explanation is that her actions caused the missionaries—especially Stephen Riggs, who was specifically referenced in the document—to erase her education and reclassify her as someone unable to act within "civilized" society.

The court granted Pettijohn a license to sell her land, thus confirming the "incompetency" of Agnes's Dakota heirs.[9] The license was only the first step. Next, the court required that Pettijohn obtain an appraisal of her land. He selected "Mr. J.P. Smith and Mr. J.C. Ellison . . . as appraisers of the land and valued it all at $2.50 per acre $1200 in all."[10] He also needed to decide whether to sell all her acres at once or split the sale into smaller sections. He initially "asked for an order to sell the whole." Through some mistake, "the lawyer that wrote out the petition asked for only a part to be sold."[11] Because of this error, Pettijohn ultimately ended up conducting two separate sales and accruing several duplicate fees. After the fact, he admitted that "We made a mistake in not selling all the land at once. I would have saved somewhere between $20 or 30 by it."[12]

Pettijohn made another mistake when he failed to advertise the land for four successive weeks prior to the sale, as mandated by the court.[13] He belatedly advertised Agnes's land in the *St. Peters Tribune* and "posted three copies [of the advertisement] in three different and conspicuous places in Nicollet County."[14] After finally checking off all the requirements, he proudly informed Riggs that "The sale is to be the last day of this month."[15] On 19 November 1864, Pettijohn sold the main portion of Agnes's lands (400 acres) "at Public Auction, for cash, to the highest bidder."[16] Her land ultimately sold for $400, or $1.00 an acre, far below its appraised value of $2.50 per acre.[17] The low sale price in fact violated state law, which required "land to be sold for two thirds of its valuation." Pettijohn admitted that he "was not aware of the law," and learned that "The judge can annul, or confirm the sale just as he thinks best."[18] The judge ultimately confirmed the low sale price.

Pettijohn likewise sold the remaining 80 acres for $1.00 an acre. It appears that Pettijohn initially received a much higher offer for Agnes's last acres and subsequently agreed to a steep decrease in the sale price after the fact. He explained to Riggs what happened. "You are doubtless thinking it is time to hear from me in the way of getting money. I am thinking so too, but have none to send yet," he wrote. "The man [who] bought the land appeared to think he had given too much for it, and hemmed and hawed and higgled a number of days before I could find out whether he would take it."[19] The initial land records indicate that the buyer agreed to pay $382 for the remaining 80 acres ($4.78/acre), but the final legal paperwork recorded a sale price of only $80.[20]

On the final account statement submitted to the judge, Pettijohn recorded that he sold Agnes's 480 acres for exactly $480. This was not the final value of her estate, as Pettijohn deducted multiple fees—as was legally allowed—from this amount, including twenty-five dollars for the probate judge and $5.50 for an attorney. He subtracted smaller amounts for stamps, deeds, and probate fees. Because he conducted two separate land sales, some fees appeared several times. Pettijohn charged $22.70 for his work as administrator, although he claimed that "I have not charged near as much as the law allows me; but what I lack in charging, others have made up."[21] By far the largest payment of $83.18 went to Stephen Riggs to close his guardianship account for Agnes. After all these deductions, each of Agnes's four heirs would only receive a one-time payment of $68.25.[22] Pettijohn admitted that her heirs may have been "surprised at there being no more coming to them." He promised that "I have done the best I knew how to do in settling up the business."[23]

While Pettijohn claimed that he had done his best, he admitted that he knew "so little about what can be done or needs doing I hardly know what . . . to do."[24] Indeed, he made multiple mistakes closing her estate, which resulted in rebukes from judges and county clerks. For example, in March 1864 Pettijohn and Riggs came up with a plan to finally "settle the business" of Agnes's estate. The judge rejected it, stating that "he cannot admit of an estate being settled up in such a way."[25] Two months later, they came up with another proposal to dispose "of the land yet remaining." The judge informed Pettijohn that "it cannot be disposed of legally in the way we were talking of."[26] Each of his many errors caused delays which forced Pettijohn to petition the court for at least two extensions.[27] In the end, everything cost more than he planned, and Agnes's land sold for far less than the appraised value. Given all the problems he faced settling her estate, it is no wonder that Pettijohn complained that he just "wanted to have the business all off my hands."[28]

Just when Pettijohn thought that he could finally wash his hands of Agnes's estate, he ran into multiple problems distributing the funds to her heirs. Of the four heirs, Daniel was the only one to quickly receive his payment of $68.25. Pettijohn (through Riggs) simply paid Daniel the amount in cash when he visited Minnesota.[29] Difficulties arose with Therese's and Thomas's shares, since both lived in Dakota Territory instead of Minnesota, and Therese was an "uncivilized" Dakota woman and Thomas was underage. Pettijohn solved the problem by asking the judge if Stephen Riggs could represent both Therese and Thomas. "The Judge says if you will act as agent for Mrs. Renville and send up your hand as guardian for Thomas he will appoint you," Pettijohn explained, "and the business can all be finished."[30] Riggs filed paperwork with the court to serve as Thomas's guardian, just as he had done for his sisters years earlier. In his short guardianship petition, Riggs described Thomas as a fourteen-year-old "half breed of the Sioux or Dakota nation." He resided in the Scouts Camp in Dakota Territory and needed Riggs's guidance as "he is entitled to certain Moneys" from his sister's estate.[31] On 3 May 1864 the court appointed Riggs to act as Thomas's guardian; he also served as Therese's agent.[32] This meant that "a final settlement [could] be made."[33] As guardian, Riggs also assumed control of Thomas's scrip. On 10 March 1873, Samuel Brown, working with several land profiteers, received power of attorney to sell Thomas's land for 60 cents an acre. It also appears that 320 acres belonging to Angelique's brother William, who passed away as an infant in the 1850s, was sold at the same time.[34]

No evidence indicates that Riggs failed to pay Therese and Thomas their shares, but Angelique never received a dime from her sister's estate. By 1864, Riggs's yearly "guardian account" for Angelique recorded a debt of $224.04 ($3,966.34 today). Because of her debt, the judge authorized Riggs "to receive Angelique's share of the sale money."[35] He dutifully recorded $68.25 in his guardian ledger, as well as $20 she received for her articles that had been destroyed during the war, and $30 for the sale of her watch (which she authorized him to sell on her behalf).[36] This left her with an outstanding debt of $118.12.

Angelique's brother Daniel apparently felt that his mother and sister had not been treated fairly in the distribution of Agnes's estate. In a letter to Stephen Riggs, he inquired about the small payments to his mother and Angelique. He asked Riggs to transfer his portion of Agnes's estate to his mother and Angelique. There is no indication that Riggs followed through with Daniel's wishes, as there was no decrease in Angelique's debt to Riggs recorded in his "guardian's account." Of course, it is possible that Daniel transferred his share of the estate to his mother and sister on his own without Riggs's help.[37]

Like Daniel, Angelique did not agree with Stephen Riggs's handling of her sister's estate. Over ten years later, in the early 1870s, Angelique may have initiated a lawsuit against Stephen for his role in selling Agnes's land. There is tantalizingly little information about this litigation; only a few short references alluding to this lawsuit appear in Stephen Riggs's and Thomas Williamson's correspondence. It is clear from these brief references, however, that Riggs was involved in a lawsuit and hired a lawyer to defend himself. In April 1873, Riggs wrote Thomas Williamson about a lawsuit regarding Agnes's estate brought against him by none other than Eugene St. Julien Cox. "In regard to Agnes Renville's land you may remember that [it] was sold by Jonas Pettijohn as administrator. I had nothing to do with that further than to recommend Mr. Pettijohn for administrator," he explained to Williamson. "Cox does not know so much about things as he thinks he does. You will see that in this suit nothing else depends upon it. *I* sold no other land."[38]

Two important inferences can be drawn from these short sentences. First, Riggs named Cox as the attorney of record leading the lawsuit against him. While he did not specifically mention Angelique, it is not a stretch to assume that she was the one who asked Cox to investigate Riggs's role in the handling of Agnes's estate, since she had already hired Cox to handle her own land claims. It would be extremely coincidental if Cox had independently decided to also handle Agnes's case, as her estate had been closed six years earlier. It is more likely that Angelique was looking out for her sister, and the rest of her family, even after Agnes's death.

Second, the letters between Stephen Riggs and Jonas Pettijohn over the course of two years illustrate that his defense clearly was untrue—Riggs was intimately involved in every aspect of probate for Agnes's estate. He hand-picked Jonas Pettijohn as administrator. Their extensive correspondence illustrates that Pettijohn consulted with Riggs every step of the way over the next two years. Riggs came up with the plans, which he then put Pettijohn in charge of implementing. In October 1863, Pettijohn admitted he did not know how to proceed with Agnes's estate, and informed Riggs that "I suppose the best plan is to let you act on your own judgment and responsibility, and I will be satisfied with what you do."[39] In March 1864, Pettijohn presented Riggs's "proposed plan of settling the business" to the judge.[40] Two months later, Pettijohn suggested "disposing" her land "on the cheapest plan I can to conform to the law. It will probably cost from $15 to 25$." He would not, however, make this move without Riggs's assent and asked that he approve his plan.[41] Of course, this correspondence was private; as such, Riggs could plausibly deny that he had played any role in the sale of Agnes's estate.

Even though Riggs proclaimed his innocence, a few months later he hired a lawyer to defend himself against Cox's lawsuit. It appears that Thomas Williamson hired the lawyer for Riggs in winter 1873–1874. In February 1874, he asked Williamson about the "expense [I] incurred last winter in that case of litigation. As I have not the address of the lawyer in whose hands you placed it, I will ask you, if it is not too much trouble, to see him and inquire what steps had better be taken to quiet title, as they call it. Whatever bill there is to pay, if the lawyer will let me know, I will pay it."[42] In addition to the issue of legal fees, Riggs referenced a "Quiet title" in his comments to Williamson. "Quiet title" lawsuits are filed to establish or settle a disputed title to a property. They are particularly used when there is a disagreement about the title and the lawsuit is meant to remove or "quiet" a claim or objection to the title.[43] As such, it appears that Riggs needed to defend his actions regarding the title to Agnes's land. It is not known how the suit concluded, as the existing correspondence from Riggs and Williamson never referenced it again. Court records for Brown and Nicollet Counties do not reference this case, so it is likely that a formal complaint was not filed, and that the case never made it to court. If Angelique did in fact bring the lawsuit against Riggs, it may be that the case was dropped, with no remediation for her sister's lands, after her death in 1876.

Whether Angelique challenged Stephen Riggs's handling of her sister's estate is unclear, but it is clear that tensions between the two increased further over Riggs's continued guardianship and control of her remaining scrip. As early as November 1863, when Angelique left the Riggses' home for Dakota Territory, Minnesota law clearly stated that she should have been released from his guardianship. According to state statutes, a guardianship for a woman ended when she reached eighteen years of age or married.[44] By 1863–1864, Angelique clearly met both criteria. She had turned eighteen on 1 April 1863, and although the missionaries disputed the legality of her marriage, she had a signed and witnessed marriage contract dated 14 September 1864. Moreover, as Stephen Riggs well knew from his correspondence, the laws of Dakota Territory did not require a legal marriage document in the first place. Thus, Angelique had reached both legal benchmarks, and yet Riggs refused to end her guardianship.

Stephen Riggs ultimately wanted her guardianship terminated as well. The sticking issue was her debt, which increased each year as

Riggs paid the annual taxes on her remaining 360 acres of land and continued to charge her 6 percent yearly interest on her outstanding debt. In 1865, he recorded that he paid $15.48 for the taxes on her land. He also charged his usual 6 percent yearly interest totaling $10.59. This left an outstanding debt of $131.99 ($2,250 today). By 1866, her debt increased again when he charged her another $21.60 for land taxes and a yearly interest payment of $9.91, leaving a debt of $161.50 ($2,823 today).

In summer 1866, Riggs began an all-out campaign to end Angelique's guardianship on his terms, even though the law stated that she should no longer have been his ward. He refused to release her until she paid her debt, which by summer 1866 had increased to $178.50 ($2,971 today). Riggs devised a plan: he would have Angelique sign a deed agreeing to let him sell 120 acres of her remaining scrip for $1.50 an acre, for a total of $180. Once she signed the deed, he wrote in his ledger that her debt would be cleared, and the "Amount to be paid by me to Angelique when the deed is signed $10."[45] In sum, if Angelique agreed to his plan, Riggs would have sold half of her acres, leaving her with 240 acres out of her original 480. She ultimately would have received one ten-dollar payment for all these lands; Riggs would have used the rest of the money to pay her decade-long accumulated debt. Of course, Riggs argued that as her guardian the debt was legitimate and legal, as he paid for her care and education. Minnesota guardianship law supported Riggs's claims against her estate, as it allowed him compensation for "honestly and faithfully discharge[ing] his duties" for his ward.[46]

On 26 June 1866, Riggs traveled to Angelique's camp in Dakota territory to settle "with her as guardian." Riggs recorded that at the beginning of their meeting, Angelique showed him "the paper which was written out by J.R. Brown for a marriage covenant and signed by both parties with witnesses."[47] Angelique likely showed Riggs this document to prove that she had legally married Charles Crawford and that her guardianship should end. Riggs did not dispute the document. Rather, he focused on convincing her to sign a deed giving him the right to sell the additional 120 acres. He left their meeting confident that Angelique supported his plan. They agreed to meet the following day at Fort Wadsworth to sign the needed paperwork.

However, this meeting did not go as planned. Riggs informed his wife that "Charly Crawford and Angelique came up here last evening but went back today without going to the Fort to finish our business. They made a great many objections to various things."[48] The couple mainly objected to Riggs's plan to sell her scrip. Riggs blamed Charles for the breakdown in negotiations, noting that "Her husband objected to her making a settlement."[49] Of course, Riggs would have viewed the interaction through the lens of his own society's gender roles, which placed men in charge of legal negotiations, money, and land. Angelique may have let her husband speak for her knowing that Riggs expected it, or Riggs may have ignored Angelique's role in the process and interpreted her husband as being in charge. Ultimately, it did not matter who led the objection, as both walked away from the meeting leaving the papers unsigned. Riggs left Fort Wadsworth unhappily noting that his "heart is sick with the developments of human wickedness around here." He prayed that "God . . . can induce her to do right."[50]

After the ill-fated meeting, Stephen and Mary Riggs devised additional plans to pressure Angelique to repay her debt and end the guardianship over the next several years. In August 1866, Mary Riggs wrote her husband expressing sympathy that "Angelique has not enabled you to close fully and pleasantly your guardianship." She suggested enlisting a third party to help settle that case. "Would not J.R. Brown advise her to settle up as you wished," she asked, "if you would ask him his opinion and influence?"[51] Riggs appears to have followed through with her suggestion. In 1866, he sent Joseph R. Brown an itemized copy of his "guardian ledger." He then asked Brown to help him pressure Angelique to pay her debts and finally end her guardianship. Like Riggs, Brown could not convince Angelique to settle. As late as September 1867, Mary Riggs lamented that "If we only had what Angelique owes us, I think we could use it to educate some one." She again suggested that Riggs attempt to "get a tax title to her land." By this point, however, Angelique refused to even meet with Riggs. Mary Riggs blamed Angelique, and not her husband, for this standoff. "Poor girl," she wrote. "I am sorry she didn't wish to see you."[52]

After 1867, Stephen and Mary Riggs faded into the background regarding Angelique's land. Instead, the story of her scrip shifted from Riggs to three "land sharks"—as they were derisively called at the time—who left a trail of shady and illegal land transactions across Minnesota and into Dakota Territory.[53] On 26 June 1868, a man named Francis Xavier Brosseau purchased the remaining 360 acres of Angelique's land, supposedly for $500.[54] Angelique charged that Brosseau, along with his two co-conspirators, stole these acres from her. According to the facts that she presented to Eugene St. Julien Cox eighteen months later, Brosseau, William H. Grant, and Joseph Campbell came to see her—and other Dakotas who still owned scrip—at her camp in Dakota Territory. The three men informed Angelique that they could "get double pay for [her] land," through a scheme where they would sell her land twice, once to an individual and once to the government. To receive this windfall, she only needed "to sign some papers . . . in order to secure irrevocable title to my land." Once she signed the papers, the "land sharks" promised that the profit made from selling her land twice would be divided between herself and Brosseau.[55]

According to land records, Angelique sold all her remaining 360 acres to Francis Brosseau for $500. William Grant is listed on the land sale document as her "Attorney in fact," which meant that she allegedly signed a power of attorney authorizing him to conduct her land sale.[56] Angelique claimed, however, that she never authorized Grant to represent her. "If it was a Power of attorney that I signed," she explained, "it was unknown to me, and was a Swindle."[57] She also never received the $500 listed in the land documents as the sale price for her acres. Eighteen months later, Angelique wrote the letter referenced in the introduction of this chapter asking "Mr. Cox [to] please look after this for me. I wish to be paid for my land or I want my land back. Please do all you can for me. Yours Truly, Angelique Crawford."[58]

In her 1869 letter, Angelique reached out to Cox, told him the facts of her case, and asked him to help her receive redress for her stolen land. She also involved Joseph R. Brown (and later, his son Samuel) in her case. Both Browns had served as scouts and had links to the Renville and Crawford families. They also had strong ties with the government, the military, and the Indian scrip market. While she advocated for herself and wrote to Cox directly, she also realized that she needed the support of well-connected men to advance her case.

In late March 1870, Cox drew up paperwork to represent Angelique in her quest to overturn the illegal land sale.[59] However, she never received the paperwork and her lawsuit stalled.

In December 1870, Angelique again wrote to Cox, chiding him for dragging his feet on her case. "It has been sometime since I have heard from you or anything about that land," she wrote. "Will you be kind enough to write and let me know the circumstance." She requested that Cox write to Joseph Brown and set up payment for her case.[60] Brown, however, failed to pay the retainer. Cox wrote to Samuel Brown, explaining that "Mrs. Angelique Crawford through Mr. J.R. Brown desired me last spring to commence an action to set aside a Power of Attorney and a [sale] made when and by Grant and Brosseau. I then drew up all the necessary papers and informed her I should be compelled to have an advance of $25.00 and Mr. Brown informed me he would arrange matters in St. Paul in June. I did not see him and matters have been at a stand ever since."[61]

Finally, in February 1871, Cox received his retainer which allowed him to "proceed at once with the case."[62] At this point, however, Cox attempted to sideline Angelique from her own lawsuit. Even though Angelique had initiated the inquiry into her land, Cox chose to deal mainly with Samuel Brown and especially with her husband Charles Crawford. When Angelique contacted Cox, she had followed Dakota gender roles which did not restrict her legally or socially and placed her in charge of her own land. For his part, Cox adhered to Euro-American gender roles which favored men and excluded women from the public and legal spheres, especially regarding property. Cox informed Angelique that a contract was "ready for Mr. Crawford's Signature."[63] Cox, and the court, also captioned all subsequent legal documents with the names "Charles Crawford, and his wife, Angelique Crawford."[64]

Indeed, the crux of Cox's argument to overturn the land sale rested on the dictates of coverture, which held that a husband controlled all property that his wife brought to their marriage.[65] By the mid- to late-1860s, however, many state legislatures, including Minnesota's, had begun to overturn coverture. In March 1869, the Minnesota legislature amended the state statutes, finally granting women the ability to manage and control their own property after marriage.[66] Angelique's case just missed this revision. Brosseau, Grant, and Campbell approached her in 1868, which placed her under the earlier statute which stated that a married woman's land "shall not be disposed of by her without the consent of her husband."[67]

Accordingly, Cox's legal strategy focused on Angelique's marriage status at the time of the alleged sale of her lands. In one of his first letters about Angelique's case, he asked a series of questions about her marriage status in June 1868: "Was she married at the time of executing the Power of Attorney? Did her husband consent to her signing? What is his name?"[68] These questions illustrated Cox's reading of the state law at the time. If Angelique was legally married, she could not sign away her land without her husband's consent. If her marriage was "illegal," she could act as a "femme sole" and the sale would stand. If Angelique won her case using this reasoning, it would not have been because Brosseau and Grant had done anything wrong, manipulative, or criminal, but because women were not supposed to have the capacity to control property or to participate in the legal sphere. Ironically, at the same time paternalism and coverture took away her rights, it might also have saved her land.

After gathering information about the case, on 29 April 1871 Cox filed a complaint with the 9th District Court of Nicollet County against William H. Grant and Francis X. Brosseau. Cox left Joseph Campbell off his lawsuit, noting that Grant and Brosseau simply hired him to help carry out their nefarious "conspiracy." Throughout the seven-page, handwritten complaint, Cox used strong language charging Grant and Brosseau with knowingly conspiring to "defraud" and "cheat" his client by having her sign a "false and fraudulent Power of Attorney." Overall, the two men planned and carried out "a wicked and false cheat and swindle." In addition to illegally stealing her land, Cox claimed that her acres were worth $2,000 (instead of the recorded $500), although she had received no payment in any amount. He demanded that the court force Brousseau and Grant to "reconvey said premises to this Plaintiff" and cancel the deed she had fraudulently signed "the same as if never executed." He also asked that "the defendants pay Plaintiff her costs with one hundred dollars Attorney's fees."[69]

Cox's narrative contradicted the story Angelique had told in 1868. In her initial letter to Cox, Angelique had described a scheme to sell her land twice. In his complaint, Cox never mentioned this conspiracy; rather, he explained that the defendants had told Angelique that the title to her land was defective, and that she needed to sign a power of attorney so that they could preserve the title. While the result was the same—she lost her land with no compensation—Angelique's explanation focused on a larger conspiracy to not only defraud her, but the government as well by selling her land twice. Cox's complaint also continued to focus on her marriage status at the time. He opened his complaint by noting that Angelique and Charles were "at the time of signing the . . . bogus Power of Attorney, Husband and Wife." He also pointed out that Grant and Brousseau had her sign under her maiden name of Renville, when her name was Crawford at the time, which provided further proof that the sale should be nullified.[70]

Thus, Cox again sidelined Angelique in her own case by dismissing her account of what happened and focusing on her marriage. In addition, Cox misrepresented Angelique throughout the complaint in extremely stereotypical ways. He described her as "ignorant," "uninformed," and "naïve and trusting." He wrote that she was "ignorant of the wiles of designing men, being of Dakota blood and but understanding the English language imperfectly."[71] Of course, Cox knew that this was patently false. For two years, she had written him letters in perfect English. Her letters also showed her knowledge of Minnesota land statutes and legal concepts like power of attorney, title, witnesses, and testimony. She met Cox in person during her deposition, where she again testified in fluent English and indicated her knowledge of the law. Contrary to what he knew about Angelique, Cox knowingly chose to portray her as ignorant, naïve, and uneducated. Her lawyer erased her missionary education and time in Ohio at a female seminary, instead depicting her as "uncivilized" and uneducated.

A similar lawsuit brought by another mixed-ancestry Dakota woman named Adele Buckholz used this same demeaning language.[72] In July 1870, Buckholz, along with her husband Emil, also sued William Grant and Francis Brosseau for illegally taking her land. Like Cox, Buckholz's attorney D. G. Shillock accused Grant and Rosseau of stealing his client's property, worth $5,000. While he did not specifically mention other cases like Angelique's, Shillock claimed that his client's case was part of a larger conspiracy "organized and carried out by [Grant and Brosseau] against those Half Breeds . . . which if fully known would appall the community." Their "rascality carried out on a grand scale," allowed the two men to rise "in a few years from abject poverty to riches which they are counting by the hundred thousands." Their crimes cried "to heaven for punishment." While Shillock condemned their actions in no uncertain terms, like Cox, he called his client Buckholz an "ignorant half breed" throughout his complaint. Indeed, he used the word "ignorant" eight times to describe Buckholz. Perhaps both Shillock and Cox believed that the only way to obtain redress for their clients was to play to the trope of "ignorant savages." Or, more likely, these nineteenth century stereotypes were so ingrained that the lawyers could not see the strength and knowledge of both Dakota women in front of them.

Despite the challenges these Dakota women faced from their lawyers, both cases continued to work their way through the courts. Angelique's trial was set for 10 May 1871.[73] The trial must have been delayed, as Cox interviewed Grant, Brosseau, and Campbell in July 1871.[74] After these interviews, Cox informed Angelique (through Samuel Brown) that her case was in trouble. He believed that the three men presented a strong defense of their actions and probably would win if the lawsuit proceeded. Most troubling was the issue of the power of attorney that Angelique had supposedly signed. Cox explained that "I am afraid we are going to have very considerable difficulty because Br[osseau] will [claim that] She signed the power of attorney with full knowledge of its contents and c." Cox also argued that her "illegal" marriage doomed her case. He wrote that her "marriage is certainly very informal if not totally defective and if it was not for cohabitation would be totally void." Given these problems with her case, Cox asked if "Mrs. C. [would] settle with the defendants?"[75]

Angelique categorically refused to settle and pushed forward with her case. Even though he thought that she would lose, Cox scheduled witness depositions for 21 November 1871. He asked that "Mrs. Crawford and her witnesses must be here by the 20th. Those who know of the transaction when Brosseau was there also the Notary who married the parties if possible."[76] These witnesses would address the main problems Cox had outlined: whether Angelique had knowingly signed a power of attorney and if she had been legally married to Charles Crawford at the time of the sale.

As Cox readied his witnesses, Brosseau offered a compromise:

he would "redeed 80 acres of her land." Of course, this would still leave Brosseau with 260 acres. Cox urged Samuel Brown to convince Angelique to accept this offer, as it would "save all further trouble and expense. [If] Mrs. C. will accept the offer let me know at once."[77] Angelique rejected Brosseau's proposal, and her case languished for another six months. During this time, Brosseau continued to press Samuel Brown to convince Angelique to take the 80 acres and end her suit. In June 1872, he informed Samuel Brown that "The deed to Angelie Crawford is all right now and the money is forthcoming—hoping to hear from you soon with all the particulars."[78]

By 14 July 1872, Brosseau had lost patience and demanded that Cox convince his client to settle. He opened his letter demanding to know why "Charles Crawford [was] dissatisfied, didn't you give them enough to please both of them?" He demanded that Cox conclude the case so that "they should [not] cause you any more troubles." He also told Cox to "bring if you can those 2 patents and get Mrs. Crawford to sign the Power of Attorney if possible for I must have it without fail—for it is needed the worst way." To finally conclude the matter, Brosseau suggested Cox "better make friends with Charley Crawford and tell him how the matters stand—and I know that you can make him feel all O.K." Once again, Brosseau saw Charles as the key to settling the case and not Angelique. He also implied that Charles could be manipulated by a profession of friendship and vague promises that the settlement was "O.K." Brosseau closed his letter reiterating the importance of getting Charles to settle the suit: "Wishing that you will get that matter arranged with Charles Crawford—you are able to make him come to time [terms?] and c."[79]

If Cox did not come through, Brosseau developed a backup plan to get Angelique's land patents, involving none other than Stephen Riggs. Brosseau knew that Riggs still held her land patents, which he had obtained in the 1850s when he became her guardian. Brosseau asked Samuel Brown to convince Riggs to send him "the patents for they are necessary to show the claim of title from the government to her and then from her to me." In return, Brosseau promised that he would convince Angelique to notarize "those papers that Riggs wanted her to sign."[80] In other words, Riggs would get what he wanted from Angelique (the end of her guardianship and the payment of her debt) if he helped Brosseau get what he wanted (the patents to her land). Riggs never referenced Francis Brosseau in any of his correspondence. Certainly, a respectable Protestant missionary like Riggs would not have openly associated with a "land shark" like Brosseau. However, even if Riggs refused to publicly acknowledge any kind of relationship, both men shared the goal of using Angelique's land for their own purposes: Riggs to pay off her guardian's debt, and Brosseau to profit off the illegal sale of her land.

At the same time Brosseau approached Stephen Riggs, he continued to pressure Samuel Brown to "try and settle with S. Julien E. Cox . . . and tell him to dismiss the case."[81] Cox may have agreed to settle the case, for a fee. In a letter to Brown, Cox stated that if he received one hundred dollars, "I will dismiss action and pay court costs and officers fees."[82] This letter does not mention Angelique by name, but Cox does reference a case involving 360 acres, the amount of Angelique's claim.[83] While the existing letters are oblique and ambiguous as to whether Cox sold out his client, the result is known: the judge dismissed her case on 26 July 1872 without any compensation for attorney's fees.[84] Brosseau, Grant, and possibly Cox prevailed and profited at Angelique's expense. While Brosseau had promised to re-deed 80 acres of her land if the case was dismissed, no land records show that he carried out this promise. As such, it appears that Angelique lost all her land, without any compensation. Despite her knowledge of American society and legal norms, various men at every level of her court case—Brosseau, Grant, Sam Brown, and perhaps even her own lawyer—conspired to keep her from receiving any redress for her stolen property.

One final chapter in the story of Angelique's scrip returns the narrative to Stephen Riggs. While Cox, Brosseau, and Grant litigated her over her scrip, Riggs finally found a way to clear most of Angelique's outstanding debt. In July 1867, Mary Riggs informed her husband that she had received news about F. Y. Vail, who had purchased 120 of Angelique's acres in the early 1860s. She learned that "Mr. Vail has been sick in this city for a month or six weeks for a time it seemed doubtful whether he would recover." Interestingly, he still held his "120 acres of prairie land in Minnesota."[85] Two years later, Vail passed away. After his death, Stephen Riggs wrote the Auditor's Office of Nicollet County asking about the status of Vail's purchase and if the land was available for transfer. The auditor responded that "The Vail property has not been redeemed. . . . if it is not redeemed by June you can get deed from State as absolute property. The tax on the property for this year is $9.08 and delinquent. Taxes and charges are $14.46 making in all $23.54."[86] The auditor informed Riggs that if he paid the back taxes by "June 1, 1869 . . . I will send you the deed."[87]

This is exactly what Riggs did. Land records indicate that he paid $23.71 (a few cents higher than the original auditor's estimate) for Vail's 120 acres on 30 June 1869.[88] The land documents explained this transfer: Vail's lands had "been forfeited to the state of Minnesota for non payment of taxes . . . and remained unsold and unredeemed at the expiration of the period of redemption." Stephen Riggs's offer to purchase these lands for $23.71 "was accepted, that being the highest offer for said lands."[89] It is debatable whether there was competitive bidding on these lands, as Riggs's sale price equaled less than 20 cents an acre. The documents, however, indicate that this low price was acceptable to the county land office and Riggs received the 120 acres. Three years later, on 4 May 1872, Riggs turned around and resold these same 120 acres for $100 to his son-in-law Wyllys Morris (Martha's husband).[90] Riggs does not appear to have forwarded this money to Angelique. Instead, he undoubtedly credited her outstanding "guardian's account," as he had been attempting to do since the early 1860s.

In effect, Riggs achieved what Brosseau had promised Angelique: he profited by selling her land twice, first in 1862 to F. Y. Vail, and again in 1872 to Morris. Of course, this was entirely legal according to the land policy of the time. Nonetheless, Angelique never saw a penny of the profits from this double sale of her acres. Riggs set himself apart from "land sharks," such as Brosseau, but he used the legal system to achieve his own goal of clearing Angelique's debt to him for her years of education and Christianization. Ironically, Angelique had unambiguously rejected Riggs's efforts to recoup her debts, as well as the Christianity of her youth. Through a circuitous process, he had also found a way to finally end her guardianship in his favor. The legal system of the time supported and legitimized his actions at every turn.

As Eugene St. Julien Cox, Francis Brosseau, Stephen Riggs, and others fought over her remaining scrip and her guardianship, Angelique became increasingly ill with tuberculosis, a progressive and terrible disease which also had taken her father's life back in the mid-1850s. Beginning in the 1870s, at the same time Angelique's health began to decline, Indian officials declared an epidemic of tuberculosis among American Indians. While tuberculosis broadly infected many Americans in the nineteenth century, doctors also racialized the disease, arguing that American Indians were uniquely susceptible to the illness. Many even "posited a direct relationship between greater degree of Indian blood and greater risk of infection."[91] Stephen Riggs reflected this thinking, commenting that Indians' "scrofulous bodies" had a "liking" for pulmonary consumption.[92] Others argued that a lack of "civilization" led to the high rate of tuberculosis among American Indians.[93]

While American Indians did not have any genetic or cultural predisposition to the disease, tuberculosis is often spread among those facing poor housing, nutrition, medical care, and poverty—risk factors which affected most American Indians living on reservations in the nineteenth century. The Lake Traverse Reservation, Angelique's home for the final years of her life, certainly suffered from poor economic conditions. Throughout the 1870s, many Dakotas living at Lake Traverse faced starvation as grasshoppers destroyed all their crops, government rations often failed to appear due to graft, and hunters risked "being treated as hostile" if they left the reservations in search of buffalo.[94] Conditions became so severe that several families used their tipis to make moccasins and clothing, which left them without shelter.[95] Agent Moses Adams's policies that distributed available rations only to monogamous, Christian Dakotas certainly worsened the situation for many families.

Literate Dakotas penned letters to the missionaries and government officials to inform them of the terrible conditions on the new reservation and demand remediation.[96] Catherine Totidutawin, one of the first Dakota women to learn to read and write from the ABCFM missionaries, wrote that she and her family were reduced to eating bark from trees.[97] John B. Renville informed Stephen Riggs that "the Indians are trying to be patient and submissive but say they don't think there is any virtue bearing starvation for themselves and their families." He heard "children crying for food and could not get it." Renville offered to travel to Washington, D.C., with the ABCFM missionaries to plead the Dakotas' case.[98]

Faced with these poor conditions and lack of food, many residents on the Lake Traverse Reservation became ill with multiple diseases, including tuberculosis. Unlike other contagious diseases, tuberculosis can lie dormant in a person's body for some time. Once active, tuberculosis kills slowly, "consuming" one's body over time (hence the nineteenth century name, consumption).[99] Angelique's disease likely followed this course, with the illness gradually weakening her over several years. During her last year of life, "her health began failing." By the end, "her sufferings were extreme."[100] She passed away at Iyakaptapi (Ascension) on the Lake Traverse Reservation on 30 May 1876, at the age of thirty-one, surrounded by her family and several missionaries, including Martha Riggs Morris, who worked at the nearby Good Will government boarding school.

A few weeks after her death, Martha Riggs Morris published Angelique's lengthy obituary in *Iapi Oyate*, the missionaries' Dakota/English language newspaper, describing the final moments of her life. This was one of the first extensive references missionary writings made to Angelique since the mid-1860s. According to Martha, Angelique discussed Christianity, sin, and redemption as her health deteriorated. In the last weeks of her life, a missionary woman named Mrs. Curtis visited Angelique and read the Bible and prayed with her. Angelique reportedly derived "great comfort from the Word as read to her, that her only trust was in the Lords, and she was not afraid to die." As her death neared, she became calm. According to Martha, on the Sabbath right before her death, Angelique "had a dream. 'I have seen my father and the Lord Jesus,' she said, 'and now I am glad to go.'" Not content with this statement, however, Martha pressed her one final time to acknowledge that her marriage to Charles was sinful. Angelique stated: 'I feel that my sins are forgiven.' 'What sins?' . . . 'Do you mean living with a man who had another wife?' 'Yes,' she said . . . 'the Lord Jesus has forgiven *all* my sins.'"

While Martha wanted to discuss Christianity and her polygamous marriage, Angelique focused on gathering her relatives in her home. She specifically asked for her brothers Joseph, Daniel, and Thomas. Thus, she died as she had chosen to live the last decade of her life: surrounded by her kin, including her brothers, her uncle, John B. Renville, two of her aunts, and her husband, Charles. While Martha did not mention Tasinahewin, given their close relationship over the years, it is likely that she cared for and visited Angelique during her final weeks. Martha Riggs Morris probably would not have mentioned her presence in Angelique's obituary given her longstanding condemnation of their family relations. At the time of her passing, Charles was away on an errand. According to Martha, on her death bed, Angelique said "'Tell Charley'—and that was the last." Her final words indicated her long and lasting ties to her husband, despite the missionaries' decades-long crusade against her marriage.

Twenty years earlier, Stephen Riggs had recorded Joseph Hrana Renville's death at the Hazelwood mission. Martha Riggs Morris and Stephen Riggs both portrayed the deaths as morality tales that illustrated the cosmic clash between "savagery" and "civilization," between "heathenism" and "Christianity." For Stephen Riggs, Joseph's death ultimately was a story of redemption and the triumph of Christianity over heathenism. He had fallen from the church but had purportedly accepted Jesus Christ right before his death. Martha Riggs Morris, however, did not have the same faith that Angelique had truly changed as she neared the end of her life, in large part due to her refusal to denounce her marriage. Martha "would have been glad to have recorded more decided utterances in regard to her own life all of these years, yet if the Lord forgave, we may well keep silence." Martha went further, again calling Angelique's life "wasted." She ended her obituary on a more positive note, however. Perhaps all was not lost. While Angelique had made the wrong choices throughout her life, her story might influence some other "poor, weak creatures"—especially Charles—to "do right."[101]

Martha's account of Angelique's death summarized many of the themes that guided the missionaries' long and conflicted relationship with their adopted daughter: above all, their focus on her conversion to Christianity; their unrelenting condemnation of her polygamous marriage; and their treatment of Angelique as a recalcitrant child who needed, but rejected, their guidance. In addition to her traumatic relationship with the ABCFM missionaries, Angelique, like all Dakotas, lived through a tumultuous era that included war, removal, and reservation life. She also personally faced legal guardianship, efforts by multiple actors to strip away her land, and changing definitions of race that increasingly focused on "blood" and American Indians' differences from Euro-Americans.

Despite these constraints, Angelique continued to make her own choices, as she had done since she left the Riggs family for Dakota Territory to marry Charles Crawford and return to her kin. Angelique was a strong, unrepentant Dakota woman who lived according to her own values and made her own choices, after decades of missionary efforts to control her culture, religion, and land. Ironically, at the same time she rejected the missionaries, she also used missionary-taught skills to challenge her guardianship and the loss of her lands in ways not open to most American Indians at the time, especially American Indian women. Yet her knowledge of literacy and the legal system did not secure the return of her land, nor did it save her from tuberculosis or the collective struggles that her Dakota kin continued to face living on the Lake Traverse Reservation after her death.

Despite the trauma she faced in her life, Angelique Renville Crawford's written letters and numerous other documents demonstrate her resilience, strength, and ingenuity against multiple actors who attempted to control her life and land. She resisted the prejudicial structures of the era that worked to undermine her autonomy and restrict her choices. She demanded to be treated fairly and with respect. Despite extreme pressure to live a "civilized" and Christian life in Minnesota under the watchful eyes of the missionaries, she chose to move to Dakota Territory to live with her mother, brothers, husband, and other Dakota kin. Her remaining letters and actions indicate that her Dakota kin remained at the center of the life. Certainly, her stories lived on among her relatives and other Dakotas, not as Martha Riggs Morris's cautionary tale, but as a mother, wife, sister, cousin, and friend.

EPILOGUE
Ties that Bind

After Angelique Renville Crawford's death from tuberculosis at the young age of thirty-one, the complicated and intertwined relationships she had established with her kin, Dakota and non-Dakota acquaintances, and the ABCFM missionaries continued without her. Although the documents are silent on some relations—especially her mother Therese and her child(ren)—several relatives, and of course the ABCFM missionaries, continued to figure prominently in the lives of those who survived Angelique. The following brief summaries are by no means a complete accounting of what happened to the important people in her life following her death. Instead, these individuals are among those who had the longest sustained interaction with Angelique throughout her life. These updates illustrate the continued importance of relations among her Dakota kin, as well as their conflicted, multigenerational relationships with the ABCFM missionaries. Like Angelique, their stories illustrate tragedy, hope, compromise, and survival, and the ties that bound together—and separated—her family.[1]

Wakaninape (Charles Crawford)

Charles Crawford's relationship with Christianity and the ABCFM missionaries is perhaps the most surprising and perplexing development after Angelique's death in 1876. While Charles had interacted closely with the ABCFM missionaries, government scouts, and Indian agents throughout his life, he had been barred from church membership due to his polygamous marriages. His relationship with the missionaries abruptly changed after Angelique's death. Martha Riggs

Morris ended Angelique's obituary noting that while Angelique had made unfortunate choices throughout her life, her story might influence some other "poor, weak creatures to do right."[2]

Perhaps Angelique's death pushed Charles to reconsider Christianity, as Martha had hoped. Indeed, in 1877 he joined the Good Will Presbyterian Church. On 4 June 1879, the Dakota Presbytery licensed him to preach and he became the pastor of the Good Will church on 23 June 1881.[3] In 1890, the mission press called Charles the "cathedral church of the missionary bishopric."[4] What led him to convert to Christianity, especially after years of conflict with the missionaries over his polygamous marriages, is not explained in available records. Perhaps Charles reached a rapprochement with Stephen Riggs after the two "had a long talk . . . about the past and present."[5]

In addition to his close relationship with the ABCFM missionaries, Charles kept his ties with Angelique's relatives. Articles in the *Iapi Oyate* frequently linked Charles with Angelique's brother Daniel, her uncle John B., and several other Renville kin, at various church functions and meetings.[6] For example, in the 1880s, Charles Crawford, John B. Renville, and Daniel Renville each presided over a church on the Lake Traverse Reservation, and the men frequently traveled to the ABCFM's annual meeting together.[7] In 1884, Charles, Daniel, John B., Isaac, and Michel Renville attended the Theological Institute in Santee, Nebraska.[8] Charles even helped Daniel Renville after learning of his financial troubles; Charles gave Daniel five dollars and promised to give him another five dollars each quarter.[9]

Around 1891, Charles married Emma Ortley, who was close to twenty years his junior. According to existing census records, he had at least three children with Emma. His marriage to Emma must have been monogamous, as the missionaries would have barred him from the church and certainly not allowed him to work as a pastor if he had additional wives. Emma and Charles baptized each of their children, raised them within the local Presbyterian Church, and sent them to missionary boarding schools, including the Santee Normal Training School in Nebraska, run by Reverend Alfred Riggs, Stephen's son.[10] Charles lectured Dakota children who returned from boarding schools to continue living "civilized" lives. He admonished those "who have finished their schooling and have come home [to] first of all look after themselves and conduct themselves in the proper manner."[11] Emma served as the president of the Women's Missionary Society of the Presbyterian Church.[12] Charles Crawford passed away on 12 February 1920 at the age of eighty-two. He is buried in the Good Will Cemetery in Roberts County, South Dakota. While the missionaries proclaimed that nothing could erase Angelique's betrayal, Charles's acceptance of Christianity and "civilization" after this wife's death would have been viewed as a blessing; from the missionaries' perspective, their years of sacrifice for and hard work on Angelique had not been entirely in vain.

Tasinahewin

On 27 November 1878, two years after Angelique's death and prior to Charles Crawford's marriage to Emma Ortley, the missionaries recorded that Charles and Tasinahewin formally married according to state law and church practice. In their records, the missionaries gave Tasinahewin the English name "Anna Jane Brown Shawl." This "formal" church-sanctioned marriage likely took place alongside Charles's conversion to Christianity, as the missionaries would not have allowed him to become a church member unless he followed Euro-American marriage practices. This is the first record of an English name for Tasinahewin, which would have signified her supposed transformation into a "civilized" and Christian wife.[13] Perhaps her English name "Anna Jane" followed the missionary practice of naming Dakota women after missionary women; Anna Jane was the daughter of Stephen Riggs.

As a mother, Tasinahewin continued to experience both joy and tragedy. According to Dakota cultural practices, it is likely that Tasinahewin took care of any of Angelique's children who survived her. In 1877, just a few months after Angelique's death, Tasinahewin's three-year-old son Peter passed away.[14] In 1878, Tasinhewin gave birth to a girl, whom she named Angelique, likely to honor the relationship and interwoven families and stories of these two women who lived together or near each other for over a decade. In May 1881, Tasinahewin made sure to baptize little Angelique, just as the elder Angelique had tried (and failed) to baptize her own daughter Augusta.[15] Charles and

Tasinahewin remained married until at least 1887, having at least one more daughter, named Lydia. Available records do not indicate what happened to Tasinahewin—and several of her children—after 1887.

Joseph, Daniel, and Thomas Renville

Following Angelique's death, her brothers remained close, residing with their families at Iyakaptai (Ascension), near the Good Will mission. Like Angelique's husband, the mission press lauded Daniel for his work with the ABCFM. Licensed to preach in 1867, he served as a pastor at the Good Will mission on the Lake Traverse and Spirit Lake Reservations. In 1879, Daniel sent his daughter Cora to live with Stephen Riggs in Beloit, Wisconsin, much as his parents had sent his sisters Angelique and Agnes to live with the Riggs family years earlier. Cora only attended the local public school for three months before becoming ill and suffering a "rapid decline." She pleaded to go back to her father and "die with her friends." Unfortunately, on 8 February 1879, she passed away before she could return to Dakota Territory and "was buried among the white people." The mission press, however, made sure to note that throughout her sickness "she daily read her Dakota Testament," and her final words were reportedly, "I trust in Jesus—I love Jesus."[16] Unlike her aunt Angelique, the missionaries publicized that Cora had died a "good death," making sure to confirm her commitment to Christianity before she passed.

Like Cora, her uncles, father, and many cousins remained linked to the ABCFM and Christianity throughout the rest of their lives. They also remained close geographically, residing in South Dakota on the Lake Traverse Reservation. Joseph died in 1881; Thomas in 1887; John B. in 1904; and Daniel in 1909. All were buried in South Dakota.

Stephen and Mary Riggs

On 22 March 1869, Mary Riggs passed away from pneumonia after several years of illness.[17] Three years later, in 1872, Stephen Riggs married Annie B. Ackley, a former teacher at the Hazelwood Mission.[18] At the time of their marriage, Riggs was sixty; his new wife was thirty-seven. At least one of his children did not support the union. His daughter Anna Jane sent her father "an earnest protest" against the marriage. Just before her death, Mary had asked Anna Jane to take care of her sister Cornelia. Anna Jane wanted to honor her mother's request and did not want a stepmother taking over her sister's care. Stephen Riggs sent Anna Jane two long letters to "mollify her views and feelings," explaining that Annie would be a good stepmother.[19] Riggs also hoped that his new wife would continue Mary's missionary work. He informed Annie, "Of course I shall expect you to be more queenly and more noble and more loving and more self sacrificing for the Dear Christ's sake and his poor ones, because you are my affianced. Is that too much? I think the truly good and pure and beautiful in human character is developed by the grace of God through the family relation."[20]

In 1874, Stephen (age sixty-two) and Annie had a daughter named Edna Baker Riggs. After Edna's birth, Stephen Riggs continued to travel extensively to the Good Will mission on the Lake Traverse Reservation and to areas further west, where he helped to establish new Lakota mission stations. He also made multiple trips east to promote his missionary work and Dakota language publications. While Stephen traveled, Annie remained in Beloit. She contributed to missionary work by taking in several Dakota boarders, including Cora Renville, to her Beloit home.

Until his death in 1883, Stephen Riggs remained committed to missionary work. After his death, his and Mary's children continued their proselytizing into the next generation. Isabella Riggs Williams and her husband Mark worked as missionaries in China; an article in the *Iapi Oyate* dubbed their mission "the Chinese Branch of the Dakota Mission."[21] Martha Riggs Morris was perhaps the closest to her father, continuing his mission work on the Lake Traverse Reservation. Indeed, her sister Anna Jane called Martha a "co-worker with [her] father."[22] Martha and her husband Wyllys ran the boarding school at the Good Will mission (1870–1891), assuredly teaching many of Angelique's nieces and nephews. Martha also took multiple Dakota girls into her own home, just as her mother had done.[23] Alfred Riggs ran the Santee Normal Boarding School with his brother Henry, averaging over one hundred Dakota students a year.[24] Thomas Riggs operated a Lakota mission near the present-day Oahe Dam.

Cornelia, who had been close with Angelique before she was sent to Ohio, spent two years working with her sister Martha at the boarding school at Good Will.[25]

Several of the Riggs children—especially Alfred and Thomas—also became prominent figures in the late nineteenth-century "Friends of the Indian" movement, which stressed the "salvation" of all Indians through "civilization" and Christianity.[26] To achieve these goals, the "Friends," especially during their annual "Lake Mohonk Conference of the Friends of the Indian," strongly championed and promoted the boarding school movement. They also supported allotting reservation lands in severalty, which eventually became the Dawes Act. Indeed, in 1877 Alfred Riggs proposed that Congress survey and allot Indian lands in Nebraska and Dakota Territory.[27] Thus, the second generation of Riggs missionaries took the smaller adoption and "civilization" programs of their parents and championed them on a regional and national level.[28]

Lucy Spooner Drake

Angelique lived for over a year with Lucy Spooner Drake and her family in Ohio. During that year, Drake suffered frequent debilitating illnesses that affected her nervous system and led her to rely on Angelique's domestic service. Five years after Angelique left Ohio, Drake's continued ill health may have led her to try to take her own life. In 1868, Moses Adams informed Stephen Riggs that "Cousin Lucy Drake is in a deplorable State of mind and body—that she jumped from the second story through a window and crippled herself for life and is quite deranged. It is distressing to think of her case. We can only commend her to Our Heavenly Father with the assurance that it is all for the best mysterious and affliction as it is."[29] After her accident, she survived another five years, passing away on 17 March 1873.

Angelique Renville, Julia Laframboise, and ABCFM Missionaries

The lives of Angelique Renville and Julia Laframboise intersected in many ways over the years. ABCFM missionaries adopted both girls at a young age; they remained with mission families for about a decade each. Like Angelique, the Riggs family professed to have "a warm affection for Julia . . . [she] called our house one of her homes."[30] After receiving a mission education, Julia, and then Angelique, were sent to female seminaries in Ohio. Both left their respective schools in Ohio after one year. At this point, their lives diverged. While Angelique "ran off" to marry a "polygamist" in Dakota Territory, Julia remained "a noble Christian woman . . . completing her education at Miss Sill's Seminary, in Rockford, Il."[31] Stephen Riggs paid for Julia to attend the Rockford Seminary with her scrip.[32]

After graduating from the Rockford Seminary, Julia devoted her life to teaching Dakota children at the ABCFM mission school in Santee, Nebraska, alongside Alfred Riggs. According to Thomas Williamson, "she went cheerfully, counting it a privilege to be employed in teaching the poor despised Indians."[33] A few years after her arrival at Santee, the lives of Angelique and Julia unfortunately converged once again. On 20 September 1871, at the age of only twenty-eight, Julia also passed away from pulmonary consumption. As the missionaries had done with Angelique and numerous other American Indians, they in part blamed Julia for her own illness, noting, "She was not careful of herself."[34] Unlike Angelique, the missionaries believed there was nobility in Julia's illness, as she supposedly had made herself ill through her devotion to missionary work and Christianity. "After teaching school until one o'clock," Stephen Riggs explained, "she was ever ready to go with the agent's daughters to interpret for them in the case of some sick person, or to relieve the wants of the poor."[35] A missionary woman who witnessed Julia's death praised her devotion to missionary work; she was "thoroughly educated, thoroughly the lady; always loyal to her people . . . always generous in her deeds and words; always to be depended upon. Oh, could we but have kept her to work many years for the ennobling and Christianizing of the Dakota!"[36]

In 1880, Isabella Riggs Williams, from her "Chinese Branch of the Dakota Mission," proposed writing a "Triograph" extolling the virtues of three women associated with the Dakota mission: Eliza Huggins, Nannie Williamson, and Julia Laframboise.[37] These three women represented the perfect expression of what the missionaries hoped to achieve: self-sacrifice in the name of Christianity, the latter two through their early and noble deaths. Conspicuously absent from Isabella's proposed "Triograph" was Angelique Renville. Angelique's early years of training, extensive education, and admission to the church seemingly would have made her a perfect addition to Isabella's work along with Julia Laframboise.

Instead, Angelique's ending differed drastically from that of Julia Laframboise and other mission-educated Dakota women. While the missionaries attempted to divide Angelique and Julia into "good" and "bad" Dakota women, their choices reflected their own concerns and relationships with the Riggs family. Julia Laframboise saw the Riggses as part of her extended family, but also remained in contact with her Dakota kin. She never married, instead devoting herself to her friends and missionary work. Angelique, in contrast, distanced herself from the Riggs family for multiple reasons, including her guardianship and Stephen Riggs's handling of her and Agnes's extended wardship and scrip.

For these reasons and many others, Angelique never fully reconciled with the missionaries or the Christian faith of her youth. Angelique's actions led the missionaries to erase her from their correspondence and Isabella's proposed "Triograph." Instead, Angelique became the cautionary tale of Martha Riggs's obituary that focused on her "betrayal" and "wasted life." Of course, Angelique's life was much more than Martha's obituary indicated, just as Julie Laframboise was more than a "noble martyr" to the missionaries' cause. Both were strong Dakota women who made their own choices. While they ultimately chose different paths, each woman fought for what she believed was right, in a time when women in general, and especially American Indian women, were not supposed to have a voice. While the missionaries sought to control the narratives of Angelique and Julia, the women left letters, written in English, that help to reclaim their identities during a tumultuous period of history that involved war, exile from Minnesota, and the arrival of government officials, settlers, and ABCFM missionaries who all in different ways attempted to remake Dakota land, culture, language, and religion.

The intertwined stories of Angelique and Julia circle back to one of the original points of this book: no single story encapsulates the experiences of all Dakota women, either in the nineteenth century or the present day. By all accounts, Angelique's and Julia's backgrounds should have led to them to make similar life choices. They were both mixed-ancestry Dakota women who grew up around Lac qui Parle, had fathers who worked in the fur trade and Dakota mothers, were adopted by Protestant missionaries with whom each lived for about a decade, and even attended female seminaries in Ohio. They both lived through land loss, the decline of the fur trade, war, and exile. Despite these commonalities, however, they made very different choices regarding religion, marriage, and especially their relationship with the ABCFM in general, and with the Riggs family in particular. As such, Angelique's story is her own, and it does not speak to the experiences of all Dakota women, nor even to all mixed-ancestry, missionary-educated women. Her biography does, however, help to explore the constraints and opportunities one Dakota woman faced during a tumultuous time of economic, geographic, and cultural dislocation.

:::

APPENDIX

Selected Letters/Documents Written by and about Angelique Renville

Lac qui parle
June 8 1853
My dear miss spooner:
I am very sorry that you went a way. I sleep in the same place. miss riggs got the new beds. we have got great meny roses.
Angelique

From: Angelique Renville to Lucy Spooner, 8 June 1853, Stephen Riggs Papers, CWS, Box 3 folder 6

:::

[May 16, 1861], Mary Huggins Autograph Book
Blessed are they that do His commandments that they may have right to the tree of life and may enter in through the gates into the city
Your friend,
Angelique Renville

From: Mary Ann Huggins souvenir autograph book, 1858–1860s, digital version part 3, p. 7, Alexander G. Huggins and Family Papers.

:::

O. F. College. College Hill
Jan: 20. 1862

Dear Mr: Riggs

It has been as much as two months since I received your letter I do not know what the reason is for my not answering it. It keeps raining and raining all the time it does not seem much like winter when thear is not much snow or not any. it snowed little just before school commenced so that the folks called it good sleighing. It was so slipery that Martha and I were afraid to come in the Omnibus so Mr. Lewis Drake brought us back in a sleigh so we had a sleigh ride. Miss Allison says that this school is fuller then it ever was since she has been here. Last tirm there was only ninty that boarded in the College but now there is about a hundred two or three. I had a very pleasant time in vacation. saw a good many wonderful things when I was in the city we went to the slaughter house and saw the performance there. I expect if Old weeping beauty and Kitawinna had been there they could have got plenty of the entrails. My music teacher is changed for the third time and when I am changed I have to practice just what I have been. she does not seem to be as good music teacher as Miss Ketchell her voice is not as strong for when I am singing with her I can hear my voice but when I sung with Miss Ketchell she would think I was not singing when I was doing my best. now I have to do more my self so I expect I will learn more in the singing line.

I expect you will feel honored to know that one of your daughters is a president there were a good many up to hear her Inaugural address. Miss Wallare Miss Allison Miss Lathrop Miss Hendrick wer up and Mrs Rose Pres: Day would have come but he was invited out some whear else.

Miss Vene Smith had been the president before she told Martha she hoped she would fill the chair better than she had done then Martha went up and took the chair. I feel quite honored to room with the president.

We do not hear anything about the war it just seems like thear was no fighting don once in a while Mrs Pyle tells us some thing about it. when they have had a battle.

We room right over father Vail I expect he thinks we are quite noisy sometimes. One morning the tank leaked and came through the seeling and Mr Vail came up to see what was the matter soo as he saw what the matter was he ran down stairs and had the servants come up with buckets and he went around and got all the dirtpans and then he came in our room and took all our towels. I do not know what he did with them. After he got through he came in our room and thought it was his he looked all around and saw that we were in the room he fund out that he had maid a mistake he had taken off his spectacles and was going to sit down he found out that he had maid a misstake he looked so funny we could not keep from laughing. I think he is such a queer man he was preaching on sunday and he stoped in the middle of his surmen and said he was glad the young ladies were paying so much attention. A kiss for baby and a love for all the rest

I am your Affately
Angelique Renville

From: Stephen R. Riggs and Family Papers, digital version, Jan.–July 1862, images 15–17, MNHS.

: : :

O. F. College. College Hill
Feb. 1. 1862

Dear Mrs. Riggs

This is Saturday morning and I have just got my composition done fr which I am very glad.

I do not know what I am going to do with myself I am getting so fleshy that not one of my dresses are larg enough and I think I must be growing to my new calico dress is very short and their is not a bit that I can let down unless I facet. Martha has got my dress don all the girls say it is very pretty it is black and white plads and trimed with red buttons. they think Martha is very smart. they ask her if I do not know how to sew. The ladies on the Hill are making up a box to send to a Hospital in Louisville Mrs Pyle got the girls to contribute some money to buy the things and she got six or seven dollars. Mrs Brooks brought some linen over for us to pick lint she had some linen that Mrs Worthingtons mother spun in the Revolutionary war I was going to knit a pair of socks but I was affraid it would take me so long that they would not want them

Feb 3. Lewis came to see us so I did not get this letter done. he staid nearly all the afternoon.

In vacation we saw Mrs. Bodly and she asked us to come there some Saturday and stay till Monday but we have not done it yet

I saw the silk bed quilt that a lady maid for Pres. Lincoln and a watch case for Mrs. Lincoln the bed quilt is not very large it is little larger then babys. in the center was all embroidered it was made very nice.

Marthas cousin Charly sent her his picture and she showed it to some of the girls and they all fell in love with it one of the girls did [ear it off?]. Tell the boys that the girls think thear picture is a very pretty one of them said Oh: what sweet boys if they were here I would like to kiss them and another said she would like to kiss them. So I expect the boys will feel very much flattered

Friday nights I go up to society to hear them speak and read composition I think it is very fine. Huldah Hill is such a good speaker I like to hear her better than any of the others I sit at Miss Copelands table it is one of the noisest table all the little girls sit there. They order me around so much I do not like it they think I must do it sometimes I think I wont do what they tell me to and then they commence and scold me. I used to think that I was the only one that got vexed at any little thing but since I came here I see others that do and I think how silly it is

Kate Wood gets mad very quick at some things that I just say in fun and do in play so I have come to the conclusion that I will not be so any more. How much larger is baby then she was when we came away? Is Mother well and all the other folks I forgot to tell you that I received a pare of gloves and under sleves for New Years preasant from Mrs Drake. Give my love to all and a kiss for baby

I am your Affately
Angelique Renville

From: Stephen R. Riggs and Family Papers, digital version, Jan.–July 1862, images 29–31, MNHS.

: : :

O. F. College. College Hill
March. 24. 1862

Dear Mr Riggs

We were very glad to hear from home for we had not had a letter fore four or five weeks.

I was very much disappointed about my reports for I had studied very hard and tryed to get them. I hope I will have better ones the next time.

Good many of the girls are going home and those that are not make a fuss because they can not go. I do not see what they would do if they lived so far as we do. The little girls here are so crazy when they see a boy good many of them have got themselvs in to trouble.

28. I have been so busy that I have not had any time to write but today is the last day and I am so glad.

The wonderful exhibition that is going to come off to night and which Martha is the presedent. She is fixing her white dress. April 2. This letter has not got finished yet. Mrs. Drake Hester and lewis Drake came out to the exhibition and staied all night. I went home with them and stayed untill monday Mrs Hasbrook and Phebe Bayliff came to the city with me. Mrs. Drake wanted me to have my picture taken so Mrs. Hasbrook went with me to have it taken. I had the funyest time I did not know the way and got lost a few times untill I came to Comingsvill then I walked the rest of the way.

I am studying lattin I like it very much so far. I never thought that I was using up so much money untill I received your letter. I expect that if Martha was not here I would use more especially when the apple woman comes some times I want some so badly that I do not know what to do then Martha does with out then so I can.

I should hate to be the one to pay up the bills of some of the girls I always thought little children were the ones to eat candy nearly every saturday the girlies go in to the city and when they come home their baskets are filled then on Monday mornin a good many of them are sick.

one thing I have improved in is that I have learned to controle my temper thear was for a while that I thought I would never get along well with Kate Wood because she wanted things one way and I another but I just thought thear was no sense in doing that way so I have stoped though it is very hard to sometimes. There are some girls here that fairly swear I always thought only boys and men did. When I write any compositions about the Indians the girls all want to copy it so they can read it fore their composition some times. Every thing looks so green now. some of the folks have commeced ploughing. I saw one mane plough and a little boy following behind made me think of Robby how he used to do. When I commenced to write the first part always looks different. I do not see what the reason is.

I guess this is the last letter I will write to you. it will be soon untill you come. Am I going to stay or come home if I was to choose I do not think I could for I want to come home and would like to stay. Give my love to all the folks. Angie Renville

From: Stephen R. Riggs and Family Papers, digital version, Jan.–July 1862, images 80–82, MNHS.

: : :

O.F.C. College Hill
April 12, 1862

Dear Alfred,
I have just got in the mood of writing so I am going to answer your letter it ought to have been don long time ago. It will be so nice to have you come with your pa when he comes. You asked in your letter which of my studies I liked the best I like latin the best I think I will like it still more when we get in the reader. Miss Hendrick is my teacher in latin I think she is the best latin teacher here.

About taking care of my health I do not think I have been so careful as I ought to be it is so different here than it is at home if I get my feet wet I have no stove to dry them by so I go till they get dry, and then the consequences that I have a very bad cold. Some of the girls frighten me sometimes at what they talk I do not think their mothers taught them to regard the Sabbath and the Bible. I am sure if I did such things that I would expect to be punished some way. I know that I do not do what is right because I am affraid the girls will make fun of me I know that is not right and I make up my mind that I will not be so sometimes when they see that they cannot do any good by making fun of the Bible and saying I am so religious they stop. I have resolved that I shall always show them that I am and hope I'm a christian. I never felt the way I do now before I know that when I am at home any little thing would always would make me angry now I have tried not to be so and I always feel better afterwards. I can feel as if I was a christian.

Our room is so cold I can hardly write it keeps raining all the time and makes is so disagreeable to have to stay in the house all day. I had my picture taken I had six and I have one left I was going to send it to you but when I heard that maybe you would come so you can see it yourself. Miss Bogin gave me a very pretty piece of music call The Maiden prayer. I have not taken the pieces that you sent me soon as I get this one learned I am going to take them.

Martha and I have been talking about the commencement now the exhibition is over the girls talk of nothing but the commencement. It is only Ten weeks till school is closed the weeks do fly so fast [it] seems to me the weeks and months do go so fast since I came here.

I do not know wheather my writing looks better than it used or not every time I write a letter it looks different.

When Mrs. Pyle taught me how to write she never had me put on any shading or make any flourishes. But since I began to take lessons of Mss. Branson she has us all make them I donot think they are pretty. It seems as if thear was not war. I hear so little. Yesterday Mrs. Pyle read to us about the battle that has just been fought. Martha received a letter from Mrs. Holtzclaw and she said Eli was in the thickes of the battle at Mill Spring but there were only two killed in the Company he belonged.

Have you heard that Andrew Williamson has enlisted in the fifth Minnesota Reg? today is Saturday and I have got to write a composition and I cannot think of anything to write. If you will answer this letter I will try and be more prompt in answering it. I am your affat sister Angie Renville

From: Miscellaneous Letter to Alfred Riggs, box 4, folder 23, Alfred Riggs Papers, CWS.

: : :

Wall nut Hill.
Mar. 20th 1863.

Dear Mrs Riggs.

I am ashamed to say that this is the first letter that I have written to you since I have been here We have had very pleasant weather for two weeks but yesterday and to day are not very pleasant.

Night before last we went in to hear the "Old folks" sing. they did not look as outlandish as I expected they would.

One of the men they call Cousin Ruben he was about the funniest one he had on a long taild coat that came almost down to the floor. Some of the ladies were dressed quite fine one or two of them had on hoops but the rest did not have on any.

I expect you would like to know what I am doing this winter I have done but very little sewing. but I still know how.

Mr. Drake gets up and makes the fires and then calls me. I have been getting the breakfast all the winter.

Mrs Drake sometimes goes visiting and leaves me to bake the bread. so if I try very hard I can bake it nearly as nice as she can but some times I get in a hurry and burn the bread.

Some times I have the washing to do all by myself and I think it is to much and wish I did not have to. When I think a gain I will have to do it sometime in my life and perhaps more to so. I go to work and think it is just as easy or easer now then it will be then

I was very glad to hear that Mother hase not Other day for a husband. I knew almost that she would not have him.

She told me before I came away that she should not get married or listen to any thing while I was away unless I wanted her to.

I think people have no business making up such lies about her she has enough trouble with out them. I do wish folks would mind their own business and not be tending to others.

I would like to know all about sister Agnes sickness how she felt about dieing when she knew that she could not live.

Did she have any word to send me? I have often wished that Mr Riggs had been with her.

I think she would have told him more then any one else it cant be helped now.

Thomas and Henry look so big in that picture that you sent Mrs Drake Robby looks like a little beggar boy his hair is all over his eyes.

Mrs Drake thinks that perhaps Mr and Mrs Cunning ham will be here next week. I will be glad to see them any time.

I have a pretty spring dress Mrs Drake always gets me a dress with out my knowing any thing about it and I am always suted this is a delain one. I have it all made.

Give a kiss to baby for me and tell her that Anlik wants to see her very badly Has Thomas got the letter written to me yet I am looking for it—

Give my love to all folks.

Yours Aff ately.
Angie E. Renville

From: Stephen R. Riggs and Family Papers, digital version, Jan.–Mar. 1863, images 110–112, MNHS.

: : :

[May 1863]

Dear Mrs. Riggs

Mr & Mrs. Cunningham are here and I have a few things to send by them so I thought I would tell you about them.

The hat is for baby I have worked and earned the money to buy it I am sorry to say that I could not get any pretty ribbons but blue I wanted to get white but it cost somuch I thought I could not get it.

The whit dress I have sent for I have no need of eather of these things and I have a new bonnet so I do not need the scarf

Mrs Drake has been sick for four weeks. she is not any better and she is not able to do any work I do not like it because Isabella does not write to me or she never sends me any word. I begin to think that she is so glad I am her that she does not care any thing about me. I feel like I would like to be starting for home this morning but I am willing to stay and am glad to stay. only I think my friends might think of me sometimes.

I have a song it is. Do they think of me at Home. I wonder if they do I think they might.

Tell Thomas that I shall answer his as soon as I can.

Hester and I are cleaning house so I have not time to write much.

Give my love to all the folks and tell baby that Ange sent her this hat and she mus keep it nice.

Your Aff ate.
Angelique E. Renville

P.S. This ribbon is for the strings Martha can fix them on

From: Stephen R. Riggs and Family Papers, digital version, Apr.–Sept. 1863, images 33–34, MNHS.

: : :

Canezawanasapi
Feb 8th 1864.

Dear Mr. Riggs
I received your letter last week. and I was very glad to get it.

I did want to write to you before this time but I felt ashamed to do it.

I feel very ashamed of what I have don. and I wish very much that I had not don it. If I had taken a second thought I would not have don so.

I even was scared my self when I came to the tents.

I do feel ashamed and sorry of what I have don. and I hope you and Mrs. Riggs will foregive me I do not desearve to be foregiven. but I ask to be forgiven.

I am teaching school but I have no books. I have one a b c book and that is all. and theare is a good many that want to learn how to write but I have no paper and ink and pens & holders.

If I only had the books I could have about twenty schollars. even the old women want to learn.

Gabrel told me that I should not teach any body that would not pay.

Oone thing I ask is that you would send me my trunk or my dresses if you can not send the trunk.

I would send you ten dollars but I am affraid you will not get it safe. If you will send it to me I am willing to pay all that it costs me.

I Do not remember how much Marthas trunk cost but I know it cost eather seven or eight dollars I want or would like to have you send my album with what things you send and my two books.

I need my clothes very much I would write to Aunt Mary but I have no paper and I will write to her when I have som.

I did feel very glad to get a letter from baby.

I am very much obliged to Mrs. Riggs for the testment.

I do read it all the time and do pray that God will help me to do what is right.

Tell the boys that we live by a very large lake. and it is such a good skateing I wish some times that they were here. it is larger then the one at Lacquaparle

Give my love to all and tell baby that I will write to her when I have paper and ink. tell her that I would like to come back but I cannot do it.

When you send the things dirrect it in the care of Gabril. and it will get safe to me. I have no more to say. so Good bye.

Yours Aff ate.
Angelique E. Renville

From: Stephen R. Riggs and Family Papers, digital version, Jan.–Mar. 1864, images 42–44, MNHS.

: : :

Canxecaojo
March 24th 1864

Dear Mr. Riggs

I have just received your letter. and I have my dress I did not like it because you did not send my trunk. I am never comeing back there again. so you will oblige me very much by sending my trunk.

And you can keep the money I mean as much as it will cost for sending it. Tell Aunt Mary that she can give the school to her Niece. that I am not going to come back. Martha told me to give back all the presents that Charly C. gave me he has never given me a single thing since I have been here. any body that told her so told what was not the truth.

I do not like it one bit When you write me letters you scold me all the time. instead of telling me news. I get scolded enough here.

I shall look for my trunk

Yours truly
Angelique Renville

From: Stephen R. Riggs and Family Papers, digital version, Jan.–Mar. 1864, images 133–134, MNHS.

⁝ ⁝ ⁝

Cansecaojo
April 186[4].

Dear Mr. Riggs.

I received your letter yesterday. I would like you to send me my trunk. please to send my coans and my music and books. and my albuman.

I woul like Martha to send me a paper of needels. She can take out my bonnet I would like the strings and the triming on the top You may do what you please with the watch.

I suppose you get letters from Simon. and he of corse tells you all about me he tells more lies then he is worth Becaus Gabril wanted me to teach school he was jealous he wanted his daughter to do it.

and he did all he could to have all aginst me. So I have stoped and told them that I would not teach any more. that I did not know enough to teach to go to Mary Simon for I am going to her when she commences. she has not commenced yet.

I heard that he told you all about me and how I acted with the boys here I do not like it atall. for I have not had any thing to do with them.

I suppose because Anna had one for a husband why he thinks that sister Rosalie and I have. we have a little sence yet.

I would like you to give him a lecturing. and have him stop telling lies or telling things that are not so. dirrect my trunk in the care of Gabril and I will get it safe.

Give my love to all.

Yours truly.
Angelique Renville

From: Stephen R. Riggs and Family Papers, digital version, Apr.–Sept. 1864, images 2–3, MNHS.

⁝ ⁝ ⁝

Lake Traverse, Min
Sept 8 1869

E. St. Julien Cox
St Peter Min
Dear Sir

I have just learned through the kindness of Maj. J.R. Brown that the records at St. Peter shows that I gave a power of Attorney to William H. Grant to sell my land and that he same had been sold to one Rosseau that Campbell and Rosseau were the witnesses to my signature.

Now Mr. Cox I have evidently been imposed upon, have been shamefully deceived and that my signature has been procured under very false pretenses.

One Rosseau (said to be of St. Peter) and Mr. Joseph Campbell came to me about eighteen months ago and asked me to Sign some papers which they told me was necessary in order to secure an irrevocable title to my land and that I would some day get double pay for the land that is I could (by their help) Sell one piece of land twice that they desired to help all those who could not help themselves.

It was agreed that if he (Rosseau) for he was at the bottom of all could get the government to pay for land a second time the proceeds should be divided between myself and Rosseau.

Such is the circumstances as far as I know. If it was a Power of attorney that I signed it was unknown to me, and was a Swindle.

Mr. Cox please look after this for me. I wish to be paid for my land or I want my land back.

Please do all you can for me.

Your Truly
Angelique Crawford

Scrip was issued in the name of Angelique Renville.

Angelique Renville to E. St. Julien Cox, 8 Sept. 1869, Joseph R. and Samuel J. Brown Papers, reel 6.

: : :

Lake Traverse, Min.
December 20, 1870
E. St. Julien Cox
Dear Sir,

It has been sometime since I have heard from you. or anything about that land.

Will you be kind enough to write and let me know the circumstances.

I have requested S. J. Brown son of J. R. Brown, to write to you.

But he having buisness on hand he will not have time to write immediately.

Please write to him.

Your Truly
Angelique Crawford

(on bottom—Mr. Brown will be at the "Merchants Hotel" St. Paul)

Angelique Renville to E. St. Julien Cox, 20 Dec. 1870, Joseph R. and Samuel J. Brown Papers, reel 6.

: : :

Account of Angelique Renville with S.R. Riggs, guardian
Samuel J. Brown

July 27 1857
Paid R[obert] McCullough traveling expenses and time in going for Angelique's Scrip $20.24
5 powers of attorney for locating 1.25
For certificate to the same 5
August 4, 1857
Traveling expenses and time in locating 12.30
Paid for Letters of guardianship 1.40
Paid postage in securing Patents $41.18

September 1, 1861
To interest on the above for four years and one month at 6%
$10.04
Cash paid for Angelique's outfit on sending her to school 28.27

January 1862
Paid expenses of selling 120 acres of land at guardian's sale 20.65
April 1862
Paid for recording Patent and Deed 1.75
Paid taxes on 480 acres for 1861 18.84
$120.73

1862
Paid Angelique's passage to Ohio in September of 1861 24.50
June 1862
Incidental expenses up to June 37.50
August 1862
Cash paid Angelique 8.00
Paid tuition and board for one school year at College Hill 100.
$390.73

August 1862
By amount received for 120 acres of land sold at guardian's sale at $1.25 $150.
$140.73

April 1863
Paid taxes for 1863 on 360 acres 11.16
Paid ? 4.25
September 1863
Cash to A. to pay her passage home $28
Interest on $140.73 for two years 16.88
$201.02

March 1864 Paid taxes of 1863 13.52
May 1864
Purchases made for Angelique 4.25
Expressing trunk to Abercrombie 5.25
$224.04
September 1864
By amount received from the estate of Agnes Renville—Angelique's portion from Administrator $68.12
Cash for articles destroyed in the Indian raid 20.
Received on sale of a watch 30.
$105.92
1865 Paid Taxes for 1864 15.48
May 1 1865
To interest on $105.92 for 1 year and eight months up to this date 10.59
$131.99
Paid tax on 360 acres for the year 1865 21.60
May 1866
Interest on 131.99 for one year 9.91
Due me at this date $161.50
June 26, 1866
To cash paid on settlement 8.50
$170.00
By 120 acres of land at $1.50 per acre $180.

Amount to be paid by me to Angelique when the deed is signed $10.

Stephen R. Riggs to Joseph R. Brown, "Account of Angelique Renville with S. R. Riggs, guardian," Joseph R. Brown and Samuel J. Brown Papers, reel 3.

NOTES

INTRODUCTION

1. Angelique often signed her letters "Angelique E. Renville" and "Angie E. Renville." Unfortunately, I was unable to discover what the "E" stood for in my research. For her signature, see Angelique Renville to Mary Riggs, 20 Mar. 1863, Stephen R. Riggs and Family Papers, Minnesota Historical Society, St. Paul (hereafter MNHS).

2. In August 1852, Stephen Riggs wrote, "We have now one half-breed girl in our family." From the context and the timeframe of her residence with the Riggs family, it is certain that the "half-breed girl" was indeed Angelique, but Riggs did not provide her name. This was a pattern throughout his early correspondences. Once Angelique became "civilized" and joined the church, Riggs began to use her name in his correspondences. See Stephen Riggs to Selah Treat, 28 Aug. 1852., mss. 244: no. 283, ABCFM Papers. The original ABCFM papers are held at the Houghton Library, Harvard University; they are also available in microfilm form at various repositories, including Wheaton College. The MNHS possesses typed transcripts of selected papers from Harvard's ABCFM collection related to the Dakota mission. Unless otherwise noted, all citations from the ABCFM papers in this book came from the typed transcripts available at the MNHS.

3. Janet D. Spector, *What This Awl Means: Feminist Archaeology at a Wahpeton Dakota Village* (St. Paul: Minnesota Historical Society Press, 1993), p. 43.

4. Pekka Hämäläinen traced the fluid and expanding nature of Dakota/Lakota society over the course of several centuries in *Lakota America: A New History of Indigenous Power* (New Haven, Conn.: Yale University Press, 2019).

5. Elissa Wahuta, "I Will Write a Bestselling Native American Biography," *Black Warrior Review* 43, no. 1 (Fall/Winter 2016): 152–53.

6. Jameson Sweet, in an unpublished manuscript referenced by Margaret Jacobs in "Getting out of a Rut: Decolonizing Western Women's History," *Pacific Historical Review*: 79, no. 4 (Nov. 2010), notes that Sacagawea remains a subject of popular and scholarly inquiry, with five out of twenty-four biographical studies devoted to her. A quick Google search of "Native American biographies" confirms a strong preference of biographers to write about Native men. For example, two websites listed approximately five times as many Native male as female biographies. See, https://www.infoplease.com/people/famous-native-americans; and http://www.nativepartnership.org/site/PageServer?pagename=pwna_native_biographies, accessed 24 Sept. 2020.

7. Rayna Green, "Native American Women," *Signs* 6, no. 2 (Winter 1980): 249.

8. Elizabeth Cook-Lynn, "Life and Death in the Mainstream of American Indian Biography," *Wicazo Sa Review*, 11, no. 2 (Autumn 1995): 91.

9. Nancy Shoemaker, "Native-American Women in History," *OAH Magazine of History* 9, no. 4 (Summer 1995): 10.

10. Academic presses increasingly publish biographies about American Indians who lived in the twentieth and twenty-first centuries and in regions other than the Great Plains. For biographies that focus on these centuries, see Kent Blansett, *A Journey to Freedom: Richard Oakes, Alcatraz, and the Red Power Movement* (New Haven, Conn.: Yale University Press, 2018); Sean J. Flynn, *Without Reservation: Benjamin Reifel and American Indian Acculturation* (Pierre: South Dakota Historical Society Press, 2018); and David Martínez, *Life of the Indigenous Mind: Vine Deloria Jr. and the Birth of the Red Power Movement* (Lincoln: University of Nebraska Press, 2019). Other authors write about Native peoples who were not warriors or leaders. See Philip Burnham, *Song of Dewey Beard: Last Survivor of Little Bighorn* (Lincoln: University of Nebraska Press, 2018). Authors are also studying American Indians from geographic regions outside of the Plains. See Mary F. Ehrlander, *Walter Harper, Alaska Native Son* (Lincoln: University of Nebraska Press, 2018).

11. For examples of recent biographies about American Indian women published by the University of Oklahoma and University of Nebraska presses, two prominent publishers of American Indian biographies, see Ada Deer and Theda Perdue, *Making a Difference: My Fight for Native Rights and Social Justice* (Norman: University of Oklahoma Press, 2019); Tadeusz Lewandowski, *Red Bird, Red Power: The Life and Legacy of Zitkala-Ša* (Norman: University of Oklahoma Press, 2016); Renya K. Ramirez, *Standing Up to Colonial Power: The Lives of Henry Roe and Elizabeth Bender Cloud* (Lincoln: University of Nebraska Press, 2018); and Linda M. Waggoner, *Starring Red Wing! The Incredible Career of Lilian M. St. Cyr, the First Native American Film Star* (Lincoln: University of Nebraska Press, 2019). Despite these titles, a quick study of the publication lists of these two academic presses indicates that most of their recent biographies continue to focus on American Indian men. As of 2020, both presses together published eight biographies on American Indian men and three on women.

12. Jacobs, "Getting out of a Rut," p. 592.

13. Ibid., p. 586.

14. Antonia Castañeda, "Women of Color and the Rewriting of Western History: The Discourse, Politics, and Decolonization of History," *Pacific Historical Review* 61 (1992): 515.

15. Catherine Denial, "Pelagie Faribault's Island: Property, Kinship, and the Meaning of Marriage in Dakota Country," *Minnesota History* 62, no. 2 (Summer 2010): 50.

16. Clara Sue Kidwell, "Review: *The Encyclopedia of Native American Biog-*

raphy: Six Hundred Life Stories of Important People, from Powhatan to Wilma Mankiller," in *The Journal of American History* 84, no. 3 (Dec. 1997): 1026.

17. Susan Ware, "Writing Women's Lives: One Historian's Perspective," *Journal of Interdisciplinary History* 40, no. 3 (Winter 2010): 423.

18. Theda Perdue, *"Mixed Blood" Indians: Racial Construction in the Early South* (Athens: University of Georgia Press, 2005), p. 71. For additional information on the history of race in antebellum America, see Robert F. Berkhofer Jr., *The White Man's Indian: Images of the American Indian From Columbus to Present* (New York: Alfred A. Knopf, 1978); Joseph L. Graves Jr., *The Emperor's New Clothes: Biological Theories of Race at the Millennium* (New Brunswick, N.J.: Rutgers University Press, 2001); Reginald Horsman, *Race and Manifest Destiny: The Origins of American Racial Anglo-Saxonism* (Cambridge, Mass.: Harvard University Press, 1981); Bernard W. Sheehan, *Seeds of Extinction: Jeffersonian Philanthropy and the American Indian* (Chapel Hill: University of North Carolina Press, 1973); William Stanton, *The Leopard's Spots: Scientific Attitudes Toward Race in America 1815–59* (Chicago: University of Chicago Press, 1960); Ronald T. Takaki, *Iron Cages: Race and Culture in 19th-Century America* (New York: Alfred A. Knopf, 1979); and Alden T. Vaughan, *Roots of American Racism: Essays on the Colonial Experience* (New York: Oxford University Press, 1995).

19. Stephen Riggs, *Mary and I: Forty Years with the Sioux* (Chicago: W. G. Holmes, 1880), p. viii.

20. Vaughan, *Roots of American Racism*, p. 3.

21. According to historian Robert E. Bieder, "The concept of environmentalism—the influence of the natural and social environments on human mental and physical characteristics—infused most thinking in the eighteenth century." Quoted in "The Representations of Indian Bodies in Nineteenth-Century American Anthropology," *American Indian Quarterly* 20, no. 2 (Spring 1996): 166. See also, C. L. Higham, *Noble, Wretched and Redeemable: Protestant Missionaries to the Indians in Canada and the United States, 1820–1900* (Albuquerque: University of New Mexico Press, 2000), p. 33.

22. Higham, *Noble, Wretched and Redeemable*, p. 33.

23. Bieder, "The Representations of Indian Bodies in Nineteenth-Century American Anthropology," p. 169; and Bernd C. Peyer, *The Tutor'd Mind: Indian Missionary-Writers in Antebellum America* (Amherst: University of Massachusetts Press, 1997), p. 123.

24. Peyer, *The Tutor'd Mind*, p. 123; Higham, *Noble, Wretched and Redeemable*, p. 37; and Perdue, *"Mixed Blood" Indians*, p. 81.

25. See James L. Hansen, "A Roll of Sioux Mixed-Bloods, 1855–56," *Minnesota Genealogical Journal* 7 (1984): 613.

26. Michael C. Coleman, "Not Race, but Grace: Presbyterian Missionaries and American Indians, 1837–1893," *Journal of American History* 67:1 (June 1980): 41–60.

27. Amanda Porterfield, *Mary Lyon and the Mount Holyoke Missionaries* (New York: Oxford University Press, 1997), p. 19.

28. Margaret D. Jacobs, "Entangled Histories: The Mormon Church and Indigenous Child Removal from 1850 to 2000," *Journal of Mormon History* 42, no. 2 (Apr. 2016): 27–60; Margaret Jacobs, *A Generation Removed: The Fostering and Adoption of Indigenous Children in the Postwar World* (Lincoln: University of Nebraska Press, 2014); Katrina Jagodinsky, "'In a Family Way': Guarding Indigenous Women's Children in Washington Territory," *American Indian Quarterly* 37, no. 1–2 (Winter/Spring 2013): 160–77; Katrina Jagodinsky, "A Tale of Two Sisters: Family Histories from the Strait Salish Borderlands," *Western Historical Quarterly* 47, no. 1 (Spring 2016): 27–49; and Dawn Peterson, *Indians in the Family: Adoption and the Politics of Antebellum Expansion* (Cambridge, Mass.: Harvard University Press, 2017).

29. Margaret Jacobs, "Breaking and Remaking Families: The Fostering and Adoption of Native American Children in Non-Native Families in the American West, 1880–1940," in *On the Borders of Love and Power: Families and Kinship in the Intercultural American Southwest*, eds. David Wallace Adams and Crista DeLuzio (Berkely, University of California Press, 2012), p. 25.

30. Ibid., p. 604.

31. Edward Valandra, "The As-Told-To Native [Auto]biography: Whose Voice is Speaking?" *Wicazo Sa Review* 20, no. 2 (Autumn 2005): 105.

32. Denial, "Pelagie Faribault's Island," p. 49.

33. Annette Gordon-Reed, "Writing Early American Lives as Biography," *William and Mary Quarterly* 71, no. 4 (Oct. 2014): 509–10.

34. Louis Garcia, "A Message From Garcia: The History and Culture of the Spirit Lake Dakota, Message #29, Lac qui Parle Hymn," 21 Feb. 2008, email to author from Louis Garcia.

35. According to an email message from Louis Garcia, the name "Hrana"—which was recorded on a census and several documents—does not make any sense. He writes: "In the old spelling, 'r' was a gutter H. So 'Hhana' [would have] the second H has a dot over it to show guttural." Email correspondence with Louis Garcia, 14 Apr. 2020. Despite the uncertainty over "Hrana," I have chosen to use it as it appears in the written documents from the time. It also helps to distinguish between the multiple "Josephs" in the Renville family.

36. Unfortunately, I never learned the Dakota names of Angelique, her mother Therese, or her siblings Agnes and Thomas. Her brother Daniel's Dakota name was Zitkadantawa.

37. Martha Riggs Morris, "Angelique Renville Crawford," *Iapi Oaye. The Word Carrier*, 1 Aug. 1876, p. 32.

CHAPTER 1

1. Stephen Riggs wrote that the population at Lac qui Parle was divided into three villages. Samuel Pond gave the names of the three villages as Oteratonwe, Takapsintona, and Wanpetonwan. See Stephen Riggs to Selah Treat, 7 Aug.

1848, mss. 244, no. 239, ABCFM Papers; and Samuel Pond to Selah Treat, 20 Oct. 1848, mss. 244, no. 9, ABCFM Papers.

2. Jon Willand, *Lac qui Parle and the Dakota Mission* (Madison, Minn.: Lac qui Parle Historical Society, 1964), p. 46.

3. Gwen Westerman and Bruce White, *Mni Sota Makoce* (St. Paul: Minnesota Historical Society Press, 2012), p. 120. According to Stephen Riggs, a Dakota man named Eagle Help took "the romance . . . out of the French name," instead noting that "Mda eyaydan did not mean 'Lake that Talks' but 'Lake that Connects.'" Riggs, *Mary and I*, p. 58. Still, Mary Riggs preferred to use the perhaps even more poetic "Lake of the Echoes" in her correspondences. For example, see Mary Riggs to her Mother, 8 Oct. 1837; and Mary Riggs to her Mother, 19 July 1838, Stephen Return Riggs Papers, [microform] 1837–1851, 1876, Presbyterian Historical Society, Philadelphia. (Hereafter Stephen Return Riggs Papers, PHS.)

4. Doane Robinson, "A Comprehensive History of the Dakota or Sioux Indians," *South Dakota Historical Collections*, vol. 2 (1904), p. 176. See also Gary Clayton Anderson, "Joseph Renville and the Ethos of Biculturalism," in James A. Clifton, ed., *Being and Becoming Indian: Biographical Studies of North American Frontiers* (Waveland Press, Inc., 1989), p. 66. Mary Huggins Kerlinger, who grew up among the Dakota as a missionary daughter, reported that about 600 people lived around Lac qui Parle. See Mary Huggins Kerlinger, "Reminiscences of Missionaries Among the Dakotas, circa 1925," parts 3, 77, Alexander G. Huggins and Family Papers, MNHS.

5. Thomas Williamson to David Greene, "Obituary of Joseph Renville Sr.," mss. 244, no. 370, ABCFM Papers. Gertrude Ackermann also described Lac qui Parle as a stopping point for "travelers and wayfarers" in "Joseph Renville of Lac qui Parle," *Minnesota History* 12, no. 3 (Sept. 1931): 240.

6. Various documents spell Therese Renville's first and last names in multiple ways, including Terese, Terresia, Therese, and Theresa; she was also known as Ermetinger, Armentinger, and Armatender, among many other names. Unfortunately, no records I examined indicated her Dakota name.

7. Michael Lansing, "Plains Indian Women and Interracial Marriage in the Upper Missouri Trade, 1804–1868," *Western Historical Quarterly* 31, no. 4 (Winter 2000): 420.

8. Ibid.

9. Entry 529, box 358, Miscellaneous Reserve Papers, 1825–1907, Record Group 75, National Archives.

10. William died 27 Oct. 1857. Unfortunately, the paperwork for William Renville's estate has been lost. See Minnesota Probate Court, Ramsey County, 1849–1925, p. 737, Ancestry.com, https://www.ancestry.com/imageviewer/collections/9070/images/007668461_00737?usePUB=true&_phsrc=IBM243&_phstart=successSource&usePUBJs=true&pId=742338.

11. See "Renville, Angelique," State Census Index: 4367102, Minnesota Historical Society, https://www.mnhs.org/people/statecensus/4367102, lines 30-34, accessed 25 Sept. 2020.

12. See "Minnesota Territory, 1849–1858," MNHS, https://www.mnhs.org/talesoftheterritory/people/count/count4.php, accessed 25 Sept. 2020.

13. Margaret M. Jobe, "Native Americans and the U.S. Census: A Brief Historical Survey," *Journal of Government Information* 30, no. 1 (2004): 66–67.

14. Colette A. Hyman, *Dakota Women's Work: Creativity, Culture, and Exile* (St. Paul: Minnesota Historical Society Press, 2012), p. 31.

15. Samuel W. Pond, *The Dakota or Sioux in Minnesota As They Were in 1835* (St. Paul: Minnesota Historical Society Press, 1986), p. 147. For an in-depth discussion of Dakota kinship practices, see Ella Deloria, *Speaking of Indians* (Lincoln: University of Nebraska Press, 1998), pp. 25–26. Julie Davis, in her study of 1970s Indian activism in Minneapolis/St. Paul, noted that social workers continued to evaluate American Indian families as deficient into the twentieth century. Davis explains, "American Indian concepts of kinship and approaches to child rearing conflicted with White, middle-class ideas about the nuclear family and parental responsibility." Many families continued to leave their children in the care of elders and extended family members, which social workers considered to be unacceptable childcare arrangements. Julie L. Davis, *Survival Schools: The American Indian Movement and Community Education in the Twin Cities* (Minneapolis: University of Minnesota Press, 2013), p. 86.

16. G. D. Sandefur, R.R. Rindfus, and B. Cohen, eds., *Changing Numbers, Changing Needs: American Indian Demography and Public Health* (Washington D.C.: National Academies Press, 1996), https://www.ncbi.nlm.nih.gov/books/NBK233091/#ddd00115.

17. Nick Estes, *Our History is Our Future: Standing Rock versus the Dakota Access Pipeline, and the Long Tradition of Indigenous Resistance* (New York: Verso, 2019), p. 119

18. According to "Sketch of Joseph Renville, a 'bois brule' and early trader of Minnesota," Joseph's mother (Angelique's great-grandmother) left his father and returned to her Dakota community with her son. When Renville was about ten, his father took him from his mother's village and sent him to Canada to study under a priest. See Edward D. Neill, "A Sketch of Joseph Renville, a 'bois brule' and early trader in Minnesota." (St. Paul: Minnesota Historical Society, 1872). Several years later, he returned to Minnesota, according to *Dakota Tawaxitku Kin, or, The Dakota Friend*, 1 Aug. 1852, p. 3–4. For a long obituary on Joseph Renville's life written by ABCFM missionary Thomas Williamson, see Thomas Williamson to David Greene, "Obituary of Joseph Renville Sr.," mss. 244, no. 370, ABCFM Papers.

19. Ackermann, "Joseph Renville of Lac qui Parle," pp. 235–36. While Renville's fur trade post was located in southwestern Minnesota, most of the fur trade posts were constructed further north near the Canadian border. For information on the Minnesota fur trade, see Grace Lee Nute, "Hudson's Bay Company Posts in the Minnesota Country," *Minnesota History* (1941): 270–89.

20. Stephen R. Riggs, *Taȟ-Koo Wah-Kań; or, The Gospel among the Dakota* (Boston: Congregational Sabbath School and Publishing Company, 1869), p. 157.

21. Mary and Joseph Renville's children included Joseph (Angelique's father), Francois Joseph, Angelique Agathe Winona, Antoine, Marguerite, Rosalie, Mary, Michel (or, Michael), and John Baptiste. Many sources list only eight Renville children, skipping Francois Joseph. Eight lived into adulthood; some authors believe that their ninth child died prior to reaching adulthood. See Willand, *Lac qui Parle and the Dakota Mission*, FN 67, 57; and Nicole St-Onge, "Familial Foes? French-Sioux Families and Plains Métis Brigades in the Nineteenth Century," *American Indian Quarterly* 39, no. 3 (Summer 2015): 311.

22. Gary Clayton Anderson, *Gabriel Renville: From the Dakota War to the Creation of the Sisseton-Wahpeton Reservation, 1825–1892* (Pierre: South Dakota Historical Society Press, 2018), p. 2.

23. Jane Lamm Carroll, "'This Higgledy-Piggledy Assembly': The McLeods, an Anglo-Dakota Family in Early Minnesota," *Minnesota History* 60, no. 6 (Summer 2007): 221.

24. St-Onge, "Familial Foes?," p. 303.

25. St-Onge, "Familial Foes?," p. 304.

26. Mary K. Whelan, "Dakota Indian Economics and the Nineteenth-Century Fur Trade," *Ethnohistory* 40, no. 2 (Spring 1993): 246–76.

27. Carroll, "'This Higgledy-Piggledy Assembly,'" p. 221.

28. Catherine Price defined *akicita* as "enforcer of decisions." See Price "Lakotas and Euroamericans: Contrasted Concepts of 'Chieftainship' and Decision-Making Authority," *Ethnohistory* 41, no. 3 (Summer 1994): 449. According to anthropologist William Powers, *akicita* means a soldier or marshal in Lakota; it also means "a messenger of a supernatural being or power." Powers, *Sacred Language: The Nature of Supernatural Discourse in Lakota* (Norman: University of Oklahoma Press, 1986), p. 201. Although both authors referred to the Lakota language, the same general translation is also applicable to Dakota. Stephen Riggs defined *akicita* as a "head warrior" or "warrior or soldier." See Stephen Return Riggs, *A Dakota-English Dictionary* (Washington: Government Printing Office, 1890), p. 26.

29. Anderson, *Gabriel Renville*, p. 4. For the reported name of Renville's soldiers, see Lawrence J. Barkwell, "Renville's Soldiers and the Renville Rangers: The "Tokadantee" or "Prairie Dogs." Metis Heritage and History Research Louis Riel Institute, http://www.metismuseum.ca/media/document.php/07428.Renville%20Soldiers%20and%20Renville%20Rangers.pdf, accessed 23 Apr. 2020.

30. "Sketch of Joseph Renville," 4. See also Stephen Riggs, "Dakota Portraits," *Minnesota History Bulletin* (Nov. 1918): 553.

31. For a description of a Renville's "Soldier's lodge," see, Stephen Riggs to David Greene, 10 Sept. 1839, mss. 141, no. 56, ABCFM Papers.

32. Hämäläinen, *Lakota America*, p. 113.

33. Jonas Pettijohn to Samuel Pond, [date missing, probably 1843], Pond Family Papers, MNHS.

34. Thomas Williamson to Samuel Pond, 16 Nov. 1843, Pond Family Papers.

35. Lansing, "Plains Indian Women and Interracial Marriage in the Upper Missouri Trade, 1804–1868," p. 413.

36. Shirley R. Bysiewicz and Ruth Van de Mark, "The Legal Status of the Dakota Indian Woman," *American Indian Law Review* 3, no. 2 (1975): 256.

37. Bysiewicz and Van de Mark, "The Legal Status of the Dakota Indian Woman," p. 261. For references to Dakota women gathering wild rice, see Lawrence Taliaferro to Samuel Pond, 26 Aug. 1839, Pond Family Papers.

38. Bysiewicz and Van de Mark, "The Legal Status of the Dakota Indian Woman," p. 262.

39. Hyman, *Dakota Women's Work*, p. 44.

40. Susan Sleeper-Smith, "Women, Kin, and Catholicism: New Perspectives in the Fur Trade," in *Native Women's History in Eastern North American Before 1900: A Guide to Researching and Writing*, eds. Rebecca Kugel and Lucy Eldersveld Murphy (Lincoln: University of Nebraska Press, 2007), p. 235.

41. Hyman, *Dakota Women's Work*, p. 40.

42. "Counting Winters. [c]," *Dakota Tawaxitku Kin, or, The Dakota Friend*, January 1, 1851, p. 3.

43. Mary Riggs to Henrietta Longley, 28 Dec. 1839, Alfred Longley and Family Papers, MNHS.

44. Jane Lamm Carroll, "'Who was Jane Lamont?': Anglo-Dakota Daughters in Early Minnesota," *Minnesota History* 59, no. 5 (Spring 2005): 186.

45. Carroll, "'Who was Jane Lamont?,'" p. 189.

46. Carroll, "'Who was Jane Lamont?,'" p. 193.

47. Jane Lamm Carroll, "Naginowenah, Lucy Prescott, and the Wizard of Cereal Foods: Cultural Identity across Three Generations of an Anglo-Dakota Family," *Minnesota History* 63, no. 2 (Summer 2012): 65.

48. Jane Lamm Carroll, *Daybreak Woman: An Anglo-Dakota Life* (St. Paul: Minnesota Historical Society Press, 2020), p. 1.

49. Hyman, *Dakota Women's Work*, p. 4.

50. Denial, "Pelagie Faribault's Island," p. 51.

51. Deloria, *Speaking of Indians*, p. 25.

52. Charles Eastman, *Indian Boyhood* (New York: McClure, Philips, and Co, 1902), pp. 58–59.

53. Eastman, *Indian Boyhood*, p. 3.

54. Charles Eastman, *Old Indian Days* (Lincoln: University of Nebraska Press, 1991), p. 16.

55. Charles A. Eastman, *From the Deep Woods to Civilization* (Lincoln: University of Nebraska Press, 1977), p. 1.

56. Samuel William Pond, Jr., *Two Volunteer Missionaries among the Dakotas or The Story of the labors of Samuel W. and Gideon H. Pond* (Boston: Congregational Sunday School Publishing Society, 1893), pp. 43, 47; and Eastman, *Indian Boyhood*, p. 29.

57. Hyman, *Dakota Women's Work*, p. 4.

58. Stephen Riggs reported that Dakota girls watched their female relatives dressing "down a skin with her bone or iron tool . . . and the little girls must 'play' dressing skins also." Riggs, *Taȟ-Koo Wah-Kaŋ́*, p. 38.

59. Mary Riggs to Henrietta Riggs, 28 Dec. 1839, Stephen Return Riggs Papers, PHS.

60. Anderson, "Joseph Renville and the Ethos of Biculturalism," 70.

61. Thomas Williamson to David Greene, 10 May 1838, mss. 141, no. 5, ABCFM Papers.

62. Hämäläinen, *Lakota America*, p. 112.

63. Rhoda R. Gilman, "Last Days of the Upper Mississippi Fur Trade," *Minnesota History* 42, no. 4 (Winter 1970): 124.

64. Willand, *Lac qui Parle and the Dakota Mission*, p. 116.

65. See Thomas Williamson to David Greene, 19 Dec. 1843, mss. 141, no. 28, ABCFM Papers; Ackermann, "Joseph Renville of Lac qui Parle," pp. 237–38; "Nicollet and Fremont," *South Dakota Historical Collections* 10 (1920): 69–70; and Riggs, *Taȟ-Koo Wah-Kaŋ́*, pp. 158–59. Another letter written by Thomas Williamson provided the same dire economic news: "At the time this mission was commenced [Joseph Hrana Renville] was wealthy or least was supposed to be so. But . . . animals are becoming scarcer every year, and the price of furs [is] almost as steadily diminishing while those who furnish [Hrana] with goods continue to charge him as high a price as ever." Thomas Williamson to David Greene, 19 Dec. 1843, mss. 141, no. 28, ABCFM Papers.

66. Minnesota Probate Court, Ramsey County, *ca. 1849–1925*, p. 283. https://www.ancestry.com/imageviewer/collections/9070/images/007665321_00383?usePUB=true&_phsrc=IBM241&_phstart=successSource&usePUBJs=true&pId=2330997.

67. Thomas Williamson to David Greene, 10 May 1838, mss. 141, no. 5, ABCFM Papers.

68. This is only a partial letter; it does not contain a date. It is signed "Joseph Rinville." Reel 32, last image of the reel, Henry Hastings Sibley Papers, MNHS.

69. Thomas Williamson to David Greene, 14 Aug. 1837, mss. 141, no. 2, ABCFM Papers.

70. "Nicollet and Fremont," p. 69. See also Riggs, *Taȟ-Koo Wah-Kaŋ́*, p. 158.

71. Robinson, "A Comprehensive History of the Dakota or Sioux Indians," p. 186.

72. Riggs, *Taȟ-Koo Wah-Kaŋ́*, 8. See also, Edmund Bray and Martha Coleman Bray, *Joseph N. Nicollet on the Plains and Prairies* (St. Paul: Minnesota Historical Society Press, 1993), pp. 20, 49.

73. Henry Sibley to Martin McLeod, Sept. 1846, box 1, Martin McLeod Papers, MNHS.

74. Henry Sibley to Martin McLeod, 2 Sept. 1848, box 1, Martin McLeod Papers.

75. Martin McLeod to Joseph [Hrana] Renville, 27 Feb. 1849, box 1, Martin McLeod Papers. According to other text in the letter, it was written in English and translated by Stephen Riggs into Dakota for Joseph Hrana.

76. Lac qui Parle Census, 1850. https://www.ancestry.com/interactive/8054/4195937-00018/3324367, accessed 4 Oct. 2020.

77. Stephen Riggs, "My Dear Times," *Minnesota Weekly Times*, 8 Mar. 1856, p. 2.

78. For a copy of the Treaty of 1830, see Charles J. Kappler, *Indian Affairs. Laws and Treaties* (Washington: Government Printing Office, 1904), pp. 305–10.

79. Kappler, *Indian Affairs. Laws and Treaties*, pp. 305–10. See also William Millikan, "The Great Treasure of the Fort Snelling Prison Camp," *Minnesota History* 62, no. 1 (Spring 2010): 8.

80. Millikan, "The Great Treasure of the Fort Snelling Prison Camp," p. 5.

81. For the text of the Treaties of 1851, see Kappler, *Indian Affairs*, pp. 588–93.

82. See Lucile M. Kane, "The Sioux Treaties and the Traders," *Minnesota History* 32, no. 2 (June 1951): 65–80.

83. Executive Documents of the Senate, 1853–54, vol. 9. Senate Document 61, pp. 10–11.

84. Joseph Hrana's brother Michel received $750; his other brother Antoine, $1000; his sister Rosalie, $250. The brothers received individual payments, as well as a sum for their children, while Rosalie and Joseph only received individual payments. It is not recorded how the amounts were determined, as Joseph Hrana also had many children at the time. See Executive Documents of the Senate, 1853–54, vol. 9. Senate Document 61, pp. 10–11

85. See https://www.usdakotawar.org/history/treaties/minnesota-treaties, accessed 4 Oct. 2020. For extensive information on the 1851 Treaties, see William Watts Folwell, *History of Minnesota* 1 (St. Paul: Minnesota Historical Society, 1922), pp. 277–88; and Roy W. Meyer, *History of the Santee Sioux: United States Indian Policy on Trial* (Lincoln: University of Nebraska Press, 1993), pp. 72–87. Dakota historian and activist Waziyatawin calculates that the Dakota were paid only three cents an acre for 24 million acres; however, after further calculations and deductions for the money that went to traders and other non-Dakota, Waziyatawin argues that the payment could have been as low as a penny an acre. Today, the Dakota occupy about less than 1 percent of their original land base. See Waziyatawin, *What Does Justice Look Like? The Struggle for Liberation in Dakota Homeland* (St. Paul: Living Justice Press, 2008), pp. 35, 61.

86. Denial, "Pelagie Faribault's Island," p. 50.

87. In addition to the discussion of the Treaty of 1830 which follows, the later Treaty of 1837 with the Dakota also made "special grants of land to such of the white men living among them as had Indian wives and children by them." Pond, *Two Volunteer Missionaries*, p. 115.

88. For a copy of the "Treaty with the Sauk and Foxes, etc., 1830," see Kap-

pler, *Indian Affairs*, pp. 305–10. See also Millikan, "The Great Treasure of the Fort Snelling Prison Camp," p. 8.

89. "The Half Breed Treaties," *Minneapolis Star*, 3 Aug. 1925. See also Millikan, "The Great Treasure of the Fort Snelling Prison Camp," p. 8.

90. Minnesota Historical Society, Minnesota Treaty Interactive, https://www.usdakotawar.org/static/1862-treaties/mn-treaties.html, accessed 4 Oct. 2020.

91. "An Act to authorize the President of the United States to cause to be surveyed the tract of land in the Territory of Minnesota, belonging to the half-breeds or mixed-bloods of the Dacotah or Sioux nation of Indians, and for other purposes," 17 July 1854, Thirty-third Congress, Session 1, Ca. 82, 83, 1854, p. 304. See https://www.loc.gov/law/help/statutes-at-large/33rd-congress/session-1/c33s1ch83.pdf, accessed 4 Oct. 2020. See also Gustav O. Brohough, "Sioux and Chippewa Half-breed Scrip and Its Application to the Minnesota Pine Lands," (master's thesis, University of Wisconsin, 1906); Millikan, "The Great Treasure of the Fort Snelling Prison Camp," p. 8; and David Ress, *The Half Breed Tracts in Early National America: Changing Concepts of Land and Place* (New York: Palgrave Macmillan, 2019).

92. "The Half-Breed Tract," *Winona Weekly Republican*, 17 Feb. 1857, p. 2.

93. Lizzie Ehrenhalt, "'The Most Satisfactory Proof': Revising an Anglo-Dakota Family History," *Minnesota History* 63, no. 4 (Winter 2012–2013): 153; and Hansen, "A Roll of Sioux Mixed-Bloods, 1855–56," p. 601. See also Jameson Sweet, "Native Suffrage: Race, Citizenship, and Dakota Indians in the Upper Midwest," *Journal of the Early Republic* 39, no. 1 (Spring 2019): 109.

94. Frederick L. Johnson, "'Half-Breed' Tract," MNOPEDIA, https://www.mnopedia.org/place/half-breed-tract, accessed 4 Oct. 2020.

95. Millikan, "The Great Treasure of the Fort Snelling Prison Camp," p. 9.

96. Ibid.

97. Hansen, "A Roll of Sioux Mixed-Bloods, 1855–56." See also Transcription, entry 529, box 358, Miscellaneous Reserve Papers, 1825–1907, Record Group 75, National Archives, https://www.ancestry.com/mediaui-viewer/tree/2518810/person/-1810261836/media/6022fc12-66b7-4e6a-be35-9b50d29ee0a5, accessed 4 Oct. 2020.

98. *Minnesota Genealogical Journal*, vol. 6 (Nov. 1986) p. 524; and *Minnesota Genealogical Journal*, vol. 7 (Nov. 1987) p. 613.

99. Pauline Turner Strong and Barrike Van Winkle, "'Indian Blood': Reflections on the Reckoning and Refiguring of Native North American Identity," *Cultural Anthropology* 11, no. 4 (Nov. 1996): 560.

100. Sweet, "Native Suffrage: Race, Citizenship, and Dakota Indians in the Upper Midwest," p. 101.

101. Hämäläinen, *Lakota America*, p. 17.

102. Raymond DeMaillie and Gilles Havard, "Writing the History of North America from Indian Country," *Journal de la Société des Américanistes* 105:1 (2019): 33.

103. Sweet, "Native Suffrage: Race, Citizenship, and Dakota Indians in the Upper Midwest," p. 109.

104. Kimberly TallBear, "DNA, Blood, and Racializing the Tribe," *Wicazo Sa Review* 18, no. 1 (Spring 2003): 92.

105. DeMaillie and Havard, "Writing the History of North America from Indian Country," p. 34.

106. Ibid.

107. David Greene to Thomas Williamson, ABCFM Indians, vol. 9, p. 312, ABCFM Papers.

108. Charles M. Gates, "The Lac qui Parle Indian Mission," *Minnesota History* 16, no. 2 (June 1935): 133.

109. For information on Eatonville, see Gary Clayton Anderson, "The Removal of the Mdewakanton Dakota in 1837," *South Dakota History* 10, no. 4 (Fall 1980): 316; 318; and Meyer, *History of the Santee Sioux*, pp. 49–50, 52. For information on Lawrence Taliaferro, see Willoughby M. Babcock, "Major Lawrence Taliaferro, Indian Agent," *Mississippi Valley Historical Review*, 11, no. 3 (Dec. 1924): 358–75.

110. Thomas Williamson to Selah Treat, Sept. 1851, mss. 244, no. 15, ABCFM Papers.

111. When they first arrived at Lac qui Parle in 1835, Joseph Renville provided the Huggins family with a home until they could build their own log cabin; the Williamson family lived in another of Mr. Renville's homes "till spring." See Frances Huggins Pettijohn, "A Family History," (1888), Alexander G. Huggins and Family Papers, MNHS, http://www2.mnhs.org/library/findaids/00679/pdfa/00679-00005-1.pdf.

112. Thomas Williamson to David Greene, "Obituary of Joseph Renville Sr., mss. 244, no. 370, ABCFM Papers.

113. Thomas Williamson to David Greene, 1 Oct. 1836, mss. 74, no. 29, ABCFM Papers.

114. Thomas Williamson to David Greene, 13 July 1837, mss. 141, no. 1, ABCFM Papers.

115. Mary Riggs to her mother, 9 Sept. 1837, Stephen Return Riggs Papers, PHS.

116. Stephen Riggs to David Greene, 26 Mar. 1839, mss. 141, no. 49, ABCFM Papers.

117. Thomas Williamson, 28 May 1840, mss. 141, no. 14, ABCFM Papers.

118. Riggs, *Mary and I*, p. 100.

119. For example, the "Ninth Annual Report of Lac qui Parle Mission School for the Year ending June 30th A.D. 1844" lists Magdeleine and Marguerite Renville as teachers and as students; at least eight other Renvilles are on the class lists as students. Thomas Williamson to David Greene, mss. 244, no. 360, ABCFM Papers. See also, "Eleventh Annual Report of the Lac qui Parle Mission School for the Year ending June 20, 1846," Thomas Williamson to David Greene, mss. 244, no. 371, ABCFM Papers.

120. Thomas Williamson to Samuel Pond, 16 Nov. 1843, Pond Family Papers.

121. Thomas Williamson to David Greene, 29 Mar. 1844, mss. 141: no. 30, ABCFM Papers. See also Thomas Williamson to David Greene, 3 Apr. 1844, mss. 141: no. 29, ABCFM Papers.

122. "Ninth Annual Report of Lac qui Parle Mission School for the Year ending June 30th A.D. 1844," Thomas Williamson to David Greene, mss. 244, no. 360, ABCFM Papers.

123. Samuel Pond to David Greene, 4 Feb. 1840, mss. 141, no, 92, ABCFM Papers.

124. Thomas Williamson to David Greene, 13 July 1837, mss. 141, no. 1, ABCFM Papers; and Thomas Williamson to David Greene, 10 May 1837, mss. 74, no. 32, ABCFM Papers.

125. Stephen Riggs to David Greene, 10 Sept. 1839, mss. 141, no. 56, ABCFM Papers.

126. Thomas Williamson to David Greene, "Obituary of Joseph Renville Sr., mss. 244, no. 370, ABCFM Papers.

127. Mary Riggs to Mr. and Mrs. Longley, 9 Feb. 1839, Stephen R. Riggs and Family Papers; and Maida Leonard Riggs, *A Small Bit of Bread and Butter: Letters from Dakota Territory* (South Deerfield, MA: Ash Grove Press, 1996), pp. 89–90.

128. Mary Riggs to Mr. and Mrs. Longley, 9 Feb. 1839, Stephen R. Riggs and Family Papers. For information on Dakota burial practices, see Pond, *The Dakota or Sioux in Minnesota*, pp. 162–69.

129. Mary Riggs to Mr. and Mrs. Longley, 9 Feb. 1839, Stephen R. Riggs and Family Papers; and Riggs, *A Small Bit of Bread and Butter*, pp. 89–90.

130. Stephen Riggs to David Greene, 29 Apr. 1846, mss. 244, no. 223, ABCFM Papers.

131. Royal B. Hassrick, *The Sioux: Life and Customs of a Warrior Society* (Norman: University of Oklahoma Press, 1988), pp. 132–33.

132. Stephen Riggs, "The Dakota Mission," *Collections of the Minnesota Historical Society* 3 (1870–1880): 120.

133. Pond, *The Dakota or Sioux in Minnesota*, p. 139.

134. Thomas Williamson to David Greene, 14 Aug. 1837, mss. 141: no. 2, ABCFM Papers.

135. In the early years of the Dakota mission, Thomas Williamson was conflicted about dissolving all polygamous marriages, as he argued that it would break up families. However, in the post-war period, no evidence could be found that Williamson continued to oppose breaking up polygamous marriages; indeed, he urged those who remained in polygamous marriages to choose only one spouse. Stephen Riggs always took a much harder line and demanded that all male converts "put away" all wives but one before the marriage would be recognized by the church. See Linda Clemmons, *Dakota in Exile: Untold Stories of Captives in the Aftermath of the U.S-Dakota War* (Iowa City: University of Iowa Press, 2019), pp. 123–24, 163–64, 218.

136. Moses Adams to Selah Treat, 1 Aug. 1853, mss. 244: no, 81, ABCFM Papers.

137. Riggs, *Taḣ-Koo Wah-Kań*, p. xxix.

138. Thomas Williamson to David Greene, 15 June 1847, mss. 244: no. 378, ABCFM Papers.

139. See Riggs, *Mary and I*, p. 71.

140. Thomas Williamson to David Greene, 10 Apr. 1848, mss. 244, no. 368, ABCFM Papers.

141. Thomas Williamson to David Greene, "Obituary of Joseph Renville Sr.," mss. 244, no. 370, ABCFM Papers.

142. Stephen Riggs, "My Dear Times," *Minnesota Weekly Times*, 8 Mar. 1856, p. 2.

143. *Minnesotian*, 21 Feb. 1852.

144. "Polygamy," *Minnesota Pioneer*, 4 Mar. 1852.

145. See Riggs, *Mary and I*, pp. 105; 128.

146. "Review of the Third Session of the Legislative Assembly of Minnesota Territory," *Minnesota Pioneer*, 11 Mar. 1852.

147. Lawrence Taliaferro to Samuel Pond, 26 Aug. 1839, Pond Family Papers.

148. Stephen Riggs to David Greene, Dec. 1838–May 1839, mss. 141, no. 52, ABCFM Papers.

149. Stephen Riggs to Selah Treat, 15 Oct. 1852, mss. 244, no. 285, ABCFM Papers.

150. Robert Hopkins and Alexander Huggins to David Greene, 22 June 22 1848, mss. 244, no. 34, ABCFM Papers.

151. Samuel Pond to Selah Treat, 12 Sept. 1849, mss. 244, no. 12, ABCFM Papers.

152. Thomas Williamson to David Greene, 5 May 1843, mss. 141, no. 24, ABCFM Papers.

153. David Greene to Stephen Riggs, 28 Apr. 1837, ABCFM Indians, Letter Books, vol. 2, p. 158, ABCFM Papers.

154. Samuel Pond to Selah Treat, 12 Sept. 1849, mss. 244, no. 12, ABCFM Papers.

155. Stephen Riggs to Selah Treat, 16 Feb. 1853, mss. 244, no. 290, ABCFM Papers; and Thomas Williamson to David Greene, 13 July 1837, mss. 141, no. 1, ABCFM Papers.

156. Samuel Pond to Selah Treat, 12 Sept. 1849, mss. 244, no. 12, ABCFM Papers.

157. Stephen Riggs to Selah Treat, 12 Jan. 1850, mss. 244, no. 250, ABCFM Papers; and Stephen Riggs, "My Dear Times," *Minnesota Weekly Times*, 8 Mar. 1856, p. 2.

158. Gideon Pond to Selah Treat, 25 Sept.1849, mss. 244, no. 174, ABCFM Papers.

159. Thomas Williamson to David Greene, 13 July 13 1837, mss. 141: no. 1, ABCFM Papers; and Riggs, *Taḣ-Koo Wah-Kań*, pp. 157–58.

160. Thomas Williamson to David Greene, 19 Dec. 1843, mss. 141, no. 29, ABCFM Papers.

161. Riggs, *Taȟ-Koo Wah-Kań*, p. 167.

162. Historian Pekka Hämäläinen, in *Lakota America*, stresses that the Lakota—and Dakota as well—had a "stunning ability and willingness to change" (p. 9).

CHAPTER 2

1. Portions of this chapter were previously published. See Linda Clemmons, "We Find It a Difficult Work": Educating Dakota Children in Missionary Homes, 1835–1862," *American Indian Quarterly* 24, no. 4 (Autumn 2000): 570–600.

2. This information comes from Stephen Riggs, who wrote short biographies of most of the children who were taken into mission homes or resided at the boarding school. Rosalie, Angelique, Agnes, and Thomas appear in his handwritten record book. This book does not have page numbers for the portion listing Dakota children who boarded with the missionaries. See Stephen Riggs and Martha Riggs, *A Tableau of the families, and single persons, connected with the American Board of Commissioners for Foreign Mission in the Dakota Mission, during the quarter of a century 1835–1860*, Sept. 1861, http://www2.mnhs.org/library/findaids/00797/pdfa/00797-00033.pdf (Hereafter *A Tableau of the families*). Backing up Riggs's handwritten notes in his *Tableau*, Martha Riggs wrote in December 1855, "Angelique's sister Agnes is living with us now." Martha Riggs to Lucy Spooner, 5 Dec. 1855, Stephen R. Riggs and Family Papers, MNHS.

3. Carroll, "Naginowenah, Lucy Prescott, and the Wizard of Cereal Foods," p. 65; Carroll, "'Who was Jane Lamont?'," p. 187; Carroll, "'This Higgledy-Piggledy Assembly'," p. 227.

4. Joseph Laframboise to Henry Sibley, 10 May 1850, reel 32, Henry Hastings Sibley Papers, MNHS.

5. Joseph Laframboise to Henry Sibley, 10 July 1854, reel 32, Henry Hastings Sibley Papers.

6. Unfortunately, Riggs was inconsistent in recording arrival dates for all the children who boarded at the mission. Although Riggs's records do not appear to be strictly chronological, Alex Laframboise's name appears near those children whom Riggs noted as arriving in at the mission in 1854. See Riggs, *A Tableau of the families*.

7. Anderson, "Joseph Renville and the Ethos of Biculturalism," p. 78.

8. Gideon Pond to Moses Titus, 18 Aug. 1837, Pond Family Papers.

9. Robert Hopkins to Selah Treat, 8 Oct. 1850, mss. 244, no. 148, ABCFM Papers.

10. Joseph Hancock to Selah Treat, 2 May 1854, mss. 244, no. 119, ABCFM Papers.

11. Stephen Riggs to Selah Treat, 10 Oct. 1852, mss. 244, no. 285, ABCFM Papers.

12. David Green to Thomas Williamson 14 Aug. 1837, mss. 141, no. 2, ABCFM Papers.

13. Morris, "Angelique Renville Crawford," p. 32.

14. Brenda Child, "The Boarding School as Metaphor," *Journal of American Indian Education* 57, no. 1 (Spring 2018): 38.

15. Waziyatawin Angela Wilson, ed., *In the Footsteps of Our Ancestors: The Dakota Commemorative Marches of the 21st Century* (St. Paul, Minn.: Living Justice Press, 2006), p. 45.

16. *South Dakota Historical Collections*, vol. 13 (Pierre: Hipple Printing Co., 1926), pp. 327–28.

17. Moses Adams, like all the ABCFM missionaries, hoped that "the day is not far distant when we shall have one or more Boarding Schools established in this Mission." Moses Adams to Selah Treat, 7 June 1852, mss. 244, no. 72, ABCFM Papers.

18. In 1839, when Jedidiah Stevens asked for increased funding, David Green, the corresponding secretary assigned to the Dakota mission, informed him, "In view of the Committee, your station must continue to be conducted on a small scale and at a small expense, until the prospect of exerting a wide influence among the Indians shall be fairer than it at present seems to them." David Greene to Jedidiah Stevens, 18 Mar. 1839, ABCFM Indians, vol. 4, p. 250, ABCFM Papers.

19. Lucius Frederick Hubbard, William Pitt Murray, et al., *Minnesota In Three Centuries, 1655-1908: Early History*, vol. 2 (Publishing Society of Minnesota, 1908), p. 254.

20. Nancy McClure noted that when she boarded with the Williamson family, "quite a number of the other Indian children attended the school during the day, but they went home to their parents at night." Nancy McClure, "The Story of Nancy McClure. Captivity Among the Sioux," *Minnesota Historical Society Collections* 6 (1894): 442.

21. Samuel Pond to Selah Treat, 12 Sept. 1849, mss. 244, no. 12, ABCFM Papers.

22. Ibid.

23. Kerlinger, "Reminiscences of Missionaries Among the Dakotas," part 5, p. 131.

24. Jacobs, *White Mothers to a Dark Race*, p. xxxi. For further information on "adoptions" of children into mission families, see Lisa Joy Pruitt, *A Looking Glass for Ladies: American Protestant Women and the Orient in the Nineteenth Century* (Macon, Ga.: Mercer University Press, 2005), pp. 68–86.

25. Mary Riggs to her mother, 1 Aug. 1839, Stephen R. Riggs Family Correspondence, Concerning Lac qui Parle and Other Matters, 1832-1869, typescript, MNHS (hereafter Stephen R. Riggs Family Correspondence); Mary Riggs to her parents, 11 Nov. 1842, *Stephen R. Riggs Family Correspondence*; and Mary Riggs to Mrs. Drake, 17 Feb. 1858, *Stephen R. Riggs Family Correspondence*.

26. Riggs, *A Small Bit of Bread and Butter*, 98; Mary Riggs to her parents, 4 June 1838, Stephen Return Riggs Papers, PHS.

27. Kerlinger, "Reminiscences of Missionaries Among the Dakotas," part 5, pp. 126, 131.

28. Ibid., p. 146.

29. Mary Riggs to her mother, 1 Aug. 1839, *Stephen R. Riggs Family Correspondence.*

30. Stephen Riggs to Mrs. Drake, 3 Feb. 1863, *Stephen R. Riggs Family Correspondence.*

31. Peterson, *Indians in the Family*, p. 17.

32. Cassandra Berman, "Motherhood on a Mission: Missionaries, 'Heathens,' and the Maternal Ideal in the Early American Republic," *Early American Studies* 17, no. 4 (Fall 2019): 477.

33. Jacobs, "Breaking and Remaking Families," p. 35.

34. Morris, "Angelique Renville Crawford," p. 32.

35. Kerlinger, "Reminiscences of Missionaries Among the Dakotas," part 5, p. 125.

36. Alexander Huggins to Selah Treat, 6 Jan. 1852, mss. 244, no 164, ABCFM Papers.

37. Stephen Riggs to Selah Treat, 15 Oct. 1852, mss. 244, no. 285, ABCFM Papers.

38. Thomas Williamson to Selah Treat, 24 Oct. 1855, mss. 244, no. 432, ABCFM Papers. See also, Thomas Williamson to Selah Treat, 10 July 1858, mss. 255, no. 439, ABCFM Papers.

39. Robert Hopkins to S. Pomroy, 18 Dec. 1850, mss. 244, no. 156, ABCFM Papers.

40. Samuel Pond to David Greene, Jan. 1841, mss. 141, no. 94, ABCFM Papers.

41. Selah Treat to Stephen Riggs, 13 July 1854, ABCFM Indians, vol. 18, p. 367, ABCFM Papers.

42. Thomas Williamson to Selah Treat, 18 Nov. 1858, mss. 244, no. 448, ABCFM Papers. Many donations came from Ohio, the home state of several missionaries including Thomas Williamson and Stephen Riggs. Williamson noted, "we received considerable donations of clothing and some of provisions, from friends in Ohio." Thomas Williamson, "Opening Discourses," *St. Paul Weekly Minnesotian*, 18 Sept. 1858, p. 5.

43. Mary Riggs to her mother and father, 5 Apr. 1838, Stephen Return Riggs Papers, PHS.

44. Moses Adams to Selah Treat, 2 July 1849, mss. 244, no. 54, ABCFM Papers.

45. For notice about the forty-dollar increase, see Stephen Riggs to Selah Treat, 27 Oct. 1854, mss. 244, no. 315, ABCFM Papers. See also Thomas Williamson to Selah Treat, 14 Oct. 1855, mss. 244, no. 432, ABCFM Papers; and Thomas Williamson to Selah Treat, 10 July 1858, mss. 244, no. 439, ABCFM Papers.

46. Thomas Williamson to Selah Treat, 24 Dec. 1849, mss. 244, no. 392, ABCFM Papers.

47. James L. Hansen, "A Roll of Sioux Mixed-Bloods, 1855–56," *Minnesota Genealogical Journal* 7 (1976): 613.

48. Stephen Riggs to Martin McLeod, 27 Feb. 1857, box 2, Martin McLeod Papers, MNHS.

49. Ibid.

50. *The Revised Statutes of the Territory of Minnesota*, passed at the second session of the Legislative Assembly, 1 Jan. 1851 (St. Paul: James M. Goodhue, 1851), pp. 277–78. https://www.revisor.mn.gov/statutes/1851/document/misc/Preface/, accessed 28 Dec. 2021. According to the statute, "The father of the minor if living, and in the case of his decease, the mother while she remains unmarried, being themselves respectfully competent . . . shall be entitled to the custody of the person of the minor. . . . If the minor have no father or mother competent to have the custody and care of the education of such minor, the guardian so appointed shall have full custody and tuition of his ward."

51. *The Revised Statutes of the Territory of Minnesota*, 1851, p. 278; and *General Statutes of the State of Minnesota*, 17 Feb. 1863 (St. Paul: Frederick Driscoll, 1865), pp. 475, 480. https://www.revisor.mn.gov/statutes/1863/cite/63/pdf, accessed 28 Dec. 2021.

52. Ibid., pp. 224–27.

53. Riggs, *Taḣ-Koo Wah-Kaṅ*, p. 328.

54. Agnes Renville, U.S. Wills and Probate Records, 1801–1925, Nicollet County, Probate Case File, no. 74–122, p. 315, https://www.ancestry.com/imageviewer/collections/9070/images/007667805_00315?usePUB=true&_phsrc=Ehz17&_phstart=successSource&usePUBJs=true&pId=3738522, accessed 28 Dec. 2021. According to historian Katrina Jagodinsky, guardianship statutes almost universally described Indian women as "'wholly unqualified and incompetent to the care, maintenance, and education' of her progeny."

55. Jacobs, "Breaking and Remaking Families," p. 35.

56. Minnesota, Wills and Probate Records, ca. 1857–1881, Brown County, p. 589. https://www.ancestry.com/imageviewer/collections/9070/images/007668306_00574?usePUB=true&_phsrc=Ehz187&_phstart=successSource&usePUBJs=true&pId=804738, accessed 28 Dec. 2021.

57. Minnesota, Wills and Probate Records, p. 574.

58. Minnesota, Wills and Probate Records, p. 581.

59. Stephen Riggs to Martin McLeod, 6 June 1857, box 2, Martin McLeod Papers.

60. "Account for Angelique Renville with S. R. Riggs, guardian," Joseph R. and Samuel J. Brown and Family Papers, reel 4, MNHS. Riggs listed her expenses and interest from July 1857 until June 1866.

61. Stephen Riggs to Martin McLeod, 22 Feb. 1858, box 1, Martin McLeod Papers.

62. Minnesota, Wills and Probate Records, p. 581.

63. John Rudolph to Stephen Riggs, 24 Dec. 1861, Stephen R. Riggs and Family Papers.

64. John Rudolph to Stephen Riggs, 24 Dec. 1861, Stephen R. Riggs and Family Papers.

65. Stephen Riggs to the ABCFM, 22 July 1862, mss. 309, no. 167, ABCFM Papers

66. Stephen Riggs to Selah Treat, 21 Jan. 1863, mss. 310, no. 25, ABCFM Papers.

67. "Account for Angelique Renville with S. R. Riggs, guardian," Joseph R. and Samuel J. Brown and Family Papers, reel 4. Minnesota statutes did not specifically state whether or not Riggs could charge his wards six percent yearly interest. Minnesota guardianship law at the time stated that "Every guardian shall be allowed his reasonable expenses, incurred in the execution of his trust, and such compensation for his services, as the court in which his accounts are settled and deems just and reasonable." Riggs submitted his expenses to the court, and no existing documents indicate that this expense was rejected. See "The Statutes at Large of the State of Minnesota, Comprising the General Statutes of 1866," vol. 1 (Chicago: Callaghan and Co., 1873), p. 708.

68. Stephen Riggs to Martin McLeod, 22 Feb. 1858, box 2, Martin McLeod Papers.

69. Historian Katrina Jagodinsky argues that guardianship laws stripped American Indian children of their "dignity, family, and property" and were a transitional "system between coercive indenture and covert adoption." "Guarding Indigenous Women's Children," pp. 161, 163.

70. Thomas Williamson to David Greene, 10 May 1842, Indian Letters, 18.3.7, vol.2, no. 21, ABCFM Papers.

71. Thomas Williamson to Selah Treat, "Dakota Mission," June 1850, mss. 244, no. 13, ABCFM Papers.

72. Thomas Williamson to Selah Treat, Sept. 1851, mss. 244, no. 15, ABCFM Papers.

73. Moses Adams to Selah Treat, 7 June 1852, 18.3.7, vol. 3, no. 72, ABCFM Papers.

74. Kerlinger, "Reminiscences of Missionaries Among the Dakotas," part 5, p. 126.

75. Stephen Riggs to Selah Treat, 12 July 1860, mss. 310, no. 4, ABCFM Papers.

76. Jacqueline Fear-Segal, *White Man's Club: Schools, Race, and the Struggle of Indian Acculturation* (Lincoln: University of Nebraska Press, 2009), p. 79.

77. Stephen Riggs, "Biography of Men Connected with the Dakota Mission, 1835–1860," Stephen R. Riggs and Family Papers.

78. Mary Riggs to her mother, 1 Aug. 1839, *Stephen R. Riggs Family Correspondence.*

79. Morris, "Angelique Renville Crawford," p. 32.

80. Martha Riggs to Miss Spooner, 20 June 1854, Stephen R. Riggs and Family Papers.

81. Martha Riggs to Lucy Drake, 19 Sept. 1860, Stephen R. Riggs and Family Papers.

82. Mary Riggs to her mother, 19 June 1839, *Stephen R. Riggs Family Correspondence.*

83. Riggs, "Biography of Men Connected with the Dakota Mission, 1835-1860."

84. Moses Adams to Selah Treat, 26 Nov. 1852, 18.3.7, 3: 71, ABCFM Papers.

85. Mary Riggs to her brother and sister, 30 Jan. 1837, *Stephen R. Riggs Family Correspondence.*

86. Samuel Pond to Rebecca Hine, 10 Dec. 1840, Pond Family Papers.

87. Mary Riggs to Henrietta Longley, 28 Dec. 1839, *Stephen R. Riggs Family Correspondence.*

88. Stephen Riggs to Selah Treat, 20 May 1852, mss. 244, no. 276, ABCFM Papers.

89. Stephen Riggs to Selah Treat, August 13, 1857, mss. 244, 341, ABCFM Papers.

90. Morris, "Angelique Renville Crawford," p. 32.

91. Frank Blackwell Mayer, *With Pen and Pencil on the Frontier in 1851* (St. Paul: Minnesota Historical Society Press, 1986), p. 168.

92. Riggs, *A Tableau of the families.*

93. Moses Adams to Selah Treat, 2 July 1849, mss. 244, no. 54, ABCFM Papers.

94. Stephen Riggs to David Greene, 10 Sept. 1839, mss. 141, no. 56, ABCFM Papers.

95. Riggs, *A Tableau of the families.*

96. Morris, "Angelique Renville Crawford," p. 32.

97. Mary Riggs to her mother, 4 Apr. 1839, *Stephen R. Riggs Family Correspondence.*

98. Mary Riggs to Thomas and Henrietta Longley, 30 Jan. 1837, *Stephen R. Riggs Family Correspondence.*

99. Mary Riggs to her mother, 9 Sept. 1837, Stephen Return Riggs Papers, PHS. For additional commentary by Mary Riggs about Dakota children's clothing, see Riggs, *Mary and I*, pp. 68–69.

100. Riggs, *Mary and I*, p. 280.

101. Riggs, *Tah́-Koo Wah-Kań*, p. 459.

102. "Method of Clothing Indians," *Iapi Oaye: The Word Carrier*, 1 May 1878, p. 20.

103. Riggs, *Mary and I*, p. 157.

104. Mary Riggs to her mother, 1 Aug. 1839, *Stephen R. Riggs Family Correspondence.*

105. Riggs, *Mary and I*, p. 80.

106. Martha Riggs to Lucy Spooner, Dec. 1855, Stephen R. Riggs and Family Papers.

107. Angelique Renville to Stephen Riggs, 4 Mar. 1862, Stephen R. Riggs and Family Papers.

108. Riggs, *A Tableau of the families.*

109. Mary Riggs to her parents, 9 Feb. 1839, *Stephen R. Riggs Family Correspondence.* For notice of the $500 bequeathment to the mission, see Mary Riggs to her mother, 25 Mar. 1840, *Stephen R. Riggs Family Correspondence.*

110. Kerlinger, "Reminiscences of Missionaries Among the Dakotas," part 5, p. 142. In fairness, the female children of missionaries also received the names of other female Dakota missionaries. For example, the daughter of Alexander Huggins and Lydia Pettijohn Huggins, Mary Ann Longley Huggins, was named after the missionary Mary Ann Longley Riggs. See Frances Huggins Pettijohn, "A Family History" (1888), http://www2.mnhs.org/library/findaids/00679/pdfa/00679-00005-1.pdf, MNHS. The Riggs family named their daughter Isabella Burgess Riggs after their friend and donor to the mission. All information on the missionary children and Dakota boarders' names was taken from Riggs, *A Tableau of the families.*

111. Stephen Riggs wrote, "Like all primitive peoples, they have no family names; and their proper names, or names given to persons, all have meanings." For Dakota naming practices, see Riggs, *Taȟ-Koo Wah-Kaŋ́*, pp. 11–12.

112. Stephen Riggs to Selah Treat, 10 Dec. 1855, mss. 244, no. 332, ABCFM Papers.

113. Taylor Spence, "Naming Violence in United States Colonialism," *Journal of Social History* 53, no. 1 (Fall 2019): 174.

114. Martha Riggs to Alfred Riggs, 11 Sept. 1860, Alfred L. Riggs Papers, the Center for Western Studies, Augustana University, Sioux Falls, S.Dak. (Hereafter CWS).

115. Stephen Riggs to Selah Treat, 28 Aug. 1852, mss. 244, no. 283, ABCFM Papers. Mary Riggs described their home at Lac qui Parle as a "plain snug one story house with a sitting room kitchen and two bed rooms on the lower floor, and two rooms above." Mary Riggs to her parents, 23 May 1848, Stephen Return Riggs Papers, PHS.

116. Kerlinger, "Reminiscences of Missionaries Among the Dakotas," part 5, p. 126.

117. "Fire at Lac qui Parle, March 3, 1854," mss. 244, no. 303, ABCFM Papers.

118. Angelique to Miss Spooner, 8 June 1853, Stephen R. Riggs Papers, CWS.

119. Every few years a young, single woman from the east arrived at the mission to spend a year or two teaching the missionary children before returning home to marry, as had Lucy Spooner Drake. Although most of the young women lost touch with their former students after they left the mission, Drake would continue to play a role in Angelique's life. Carrie Reber Zeman and Kathryn Zabelle Derounian-Stodola, eds., *Mary Butler Renville, Dispatches from the*

Dakota War: A Thrilling Narrative from Indian Captivity (Lincoln: University of Nebraska Press, 2012), p. 31.

120. James K. Beatty, "Interpreting the Shawnee Sun: Literacy and Cultural Persistence in Indian Country, 1833–1841," *Kansas History* 31, no. 4 (Winter 2008–2009): 248.

121. Riggs, *Taḣ-Koo Wah-Kań*, p. 409.

122. *Annual Report of the Commissioner of Indian Affairs* (1871), p. 268.

123. For information on the translation of the Dakota language into written form, see Samuel Pond to Preston Hollister, 28 Mar. 1835, Pond Family Papers; Riggs, *Taḣ-Koo Wah-Kań*, p. 414; and Riggs, *Mary and I*, pp. 59–60.

124. For a bibliography of the Dakota missionaries' religious translations, see "Dakota Bibliography," *Minnesota Historical Collections* 3 (1870–1880): 37–42.

125. Martha Riggs to Lucy Spooner Drake, 5 Dec. 1855, Stephen R. Riggs Papers.

126. Eliza Huggins, "Report of the Hazelwood Mission School taught by Miss Eliza M. Huggins," 31 Dec. 1861, mss. 309, no. 168, ABCFM Papers.

127. Ibid.

128. Ibid. Jane Williamson, another mission teacher, reported, "Thus far I have not been successful in teaching [mathematics] to them; though, when taken into their family, they are as ready in computing numbers as other children." Jane S. Williamson to ABCFM, 31 Dec. 1861, mss. 309, no. 163, ABCFM Papers.

129. Martha Riggs to Jane Huggins, 5 Mar. 1852, Alexander G. Huggins and Family Papers, MNHS.

130. Stephen Riggs to Selah Treat, 30 Jan. 1854, mss. 244, no. 302, ABCFM Papers.

131. Stephen Riggs to Selah Treat, 12 Apr. 1855, mss. 244, no. 326, ABCFM Papers.

132. Martha Riggs to Lucy Spooner Drake, 8 Nov. 1854, Stephen R. Riggs Papers.

133. Ibid.

134. Ibid.

135. Anna Jane Riggs to Rebecca Pond, 16 May 1859, box 4, Pond Family Papers.

136. Stephen Riggs to Selah Treat, 14 Aug. 1861, mss. 310, no. 12, ABCFM Papers.

137. Martha Riggs to Lucy Spooner Drake, 5 Dec. 1855, Stephen R. Riggs Papers.

138. Martha Riggs to Lucy Spooner Drake, 5 Dec. 1855, Stephen R. Riggs Papers.

139. Stephen Riggs to Selah Treat, 15 Oct. 1852, mss. 244, no. 285, ABCFM Papers.

140. Martha Riggs to Lucy Spooner Drake, 5 Dec. 1855, Stephen R. Riggs Papers.

141. Mary Riggs wrote, "Indian women are too much the slaves of their husbands and brothers, and they seem peculiarly so among this tribe." Mary Riggs to Miss Hallock, 24 Apr. 1840, *Stephen R. Riggs Family Correspondence.*

142. David Greene to Abel Itewawinehangan, 31 Mar. 1843, ABCFM Indians, vol. 7, p. 45, ABCFM Papers.

143. Stephen Riggs to David Green, 26 Mar. 1839, mss. 141, no. 49, ABCFM Papers.

144. Stephen Riggs to the ABCFM, mss. 309, no. 169, ABCFM Papers.

145. Thomas Williamson to David Greene, 24 May 1841, mss. 141, no. 17, ABCFM Papers.

146. Mary Riggs to her mother, 19 June 1839, *Stephen R. Riggs Family Correspondence.*

147. Martha Riggs to Lucy Spooner Drake, 5 Dec. 1855, Stephen R. Riggs Papers.

148. Mary Riggs to Lucy Spooner Drake, 16 Feb. 1856, *Stephen R. Riggs Family Correspondence.*

149. Historians have criticized domestic and vocational labor in the late nineteenth-century boarding schools. For example, see K. Tsianina Lomawaima, *They Called it Prairie Light: The Story of Chilocco Indian School* (Lincoln: University of Nebraska Press, 1995). Lomawaima harshly criticizes the boarding schools' vocational programs as exploiting the children's labor and attempting to produce "docile, efficient workers" (p. 65). See also Margaret D. Jacobs, "Diverted Mothering among American Indian Domestic Servants, 1920–1940," in Carol Williams, ed., *Indigenous Women and Work: From Labor to Activism* (Urbana: University of Illinois Press, 2012).

150. Much of the labor centered around the many children within the mission homes. Stephen Riggs stated, "The feeding and clothing of these [boarding children] . . . make a good deal of work." The missionaries also had large families of their own. See Stephen Riggs to Selah Treat, 14 Feb. 1859, mss. 244, no. 349, ABCFM Papers.

151. Martha Riggs to Lucy Spooner Drake, 4 May 1858, Stephen R. Riggs Papers.

152. Stephen Riggs to Selah Treat, 14 Feb. 1859, mss. 244, no. 349, ABCFM Papers.

153. Riggs, *Mary and I*, p. 406.

154. Morris, "Angelique Renville Crawford," p. 32.

155. Berman, "Motherhood on a Mission," p. 489.

156. Kerlinger, "Reminiscences of Missionaries Among the Dakotas," part 5, p. 148.

157. Marth Riggs to Lucy Spooner Drake, 22 Mar. 1855, Stephen R. Riggs Papers.

158. Martha Riggs to Alfred Riggs, 4 Aug. 1860, Alfred L. Riggs Papers, CWS.

159. Martha Riggs to Alfred Riggs, 20 Nov. 1860, Alfred L. Riggs Papers.

160. Anna Riggs to Alfred Riggs, 1 Mar. 1860, Alfred L. Riggs Papers.

161. Kerlinger, "Reminiscences of Missionaries Among the Dakotas," part 4, p. 99.

162. Nancy Jane Williamson to Mrs. Aiton, 11 Oct. 1858, Thomas S. Williamson Papers, MNHS.

163. Kerlinger, "Reminiscences of Missionaries Among the Dakotas," part 6, pp. 162–63.

164. *Annual Report of the Commissioner of Indian Affairs* (1854), p. 275.

165. Gideon Pond to Selah Treat, 20 Feb. 1852, 18.3.7, vol. 3, no. 178, ABCFM Papers.

166. Thomas Williamson to Selah Treat, 18 Jan. 1858, mss. 244, no. 442, ABCFM Papers.

167. Riggs, "Biography of Men Connected with the Dakota Mission."

168. *Annual Report of the ABCFM* 48 (1858): 131.

169. The yearly statistics compiled for the ABCFM and the commissioner of Indian Affairs illustrate that few Dakotas chose to join the mission church. In 1841, for example, two missions staffed by ten missionaries reported only 41 Dakota members out of a population of approximately 6,000. By 1861, the number had increased only to 72, despite the work of more than 31 missionaries. In some years, the number of church members actually decreased from the previous year. In 1851, 32 Dakotas had joined the church, while in 1854, only 27 appeared in the census. For statistics on Dakota conversions, see *Annual Report of the ABCFM* 31 (1841), 123; *Annual Report of the ABCFM* 51 (1861), 123; and *Missionary Herald* 50, no. 6 (June 1854): 185.

170. *Missionary Herald* 50, no. 8 (July 1854): 220; and Stephen Riggs to Selah Treat, 6 May 1854, 18.3.7, 3:388, ABCFM Papers.

171. *Missionary Herald* 42, no. 2 (Feb. 1846): 51.

172. Riggs, "Biography of Men Connected with the Dakota Mission."

173. Riggs, "Biography of Men Connected with the Dakota Mission"; and *Missionary Herald* 49, no. 8 (July 1853): 212.

174. Kerlinger, "Reminiscences of Missionaries Among the Dakotas," part 6, p. 163.

175. Thomas Williamson to Selah Treat, 11 Feb. 1861, mss. 310, no. 215, ABCFM Papers. See also Stephen Riggs to Selah Treat, 22 Feb. 1861, mss. 310, no. 10, ABCFM Papers.

176. Stephen Riggs to Selah Treat, 12 June 1858, mss. 244, no. 346, ABCFM Papers.

177. Martha Riggs to Lucy Spooner Drake, 5 Dec. 1855, Stephen R. Riggs Papers.

178. Riggs, "Biography of Men Connected with the Dakota Mission."

179. Thomas Williamson, "Opening Discourses," *St. Paul Weekly Minnesotian*, 18 Sept. 1858, p. 5.

180. For information on Dakota child-rearing practices, see Pond, *The Dakota or Sioux in Minnesota*, pp. 144–45.

181. Martha Riggs to Lucy Spooner Drake, 5 Dec. 1855, Stephen R. Riggs Papers.

182. E. W. Huggins to Selah Treat, 12 Feb. 1862, ABCFM Papers.

183. Bysiewicz and Van de Mark, "The Legal Status of the Dakota Indian Woman," p. 257.

184. Sioux Missionaries to Selah Treat, mss. 244, no. 11, ABCFM Papers.

185. Stephen Riggs to Selah Treat, 11 July 1856, mss. 244, no. 336, ABCFM Papers.

186. Ibid.

187. Martha Riggs to Lucy Spooner Drake, 3 Dec. 1855, Stephen R. Riggs Papers.

188. Jane S. Williamson to ABCFM, 30 June 1862, mss. 309, no. 166, ABCFM Papers.

189. Gideon Pond to Rebecca Hine, 1 Mar. 1837, Pond Family Papers

190. Thomas Williamson, "Opening Discourses," *St. Paul Weekly Minnesotian*, 18 Sept. 1858, p. 5.

191. Martha Riggs to Lucy Spooner Drake, 22 Mar. 1855, Stephen R. Riggs Papers.

192. Jane S. Williamson to ABCFM, 31 Mar. 1862, mss. 309, no. 164, ABCFM Papers.

193. Riggs, *A Tableau of the families*.

194. On the 1860 United States Federal Census, Therese is listed as living at Yellow Medicine (located close to the Hazelwood mission). She is listed as the head of her family, along with David (age twenty), Angelique (fifteen), Agnes (thirteen), and Thomas (nine) as her children. The three younger children are recorded as attending school and owning 600 acres of land each (it actually would have been 640 acres). https://www.ancestry.com/imageviewer/collections/7667/images/4232720_00239?treeid=&personid=&rc=&usePUB=true&_phsrc=Ehz21&_phstart=successSource&pId=45442206.

195. Anna Jane Riggs to Rebecca Pond, 16 May 1859, box 4, Pond Family Papers.

196. Quoted in Richard E. Berg and James E. Myster, "Archaeological Remains of Two Mid-Century Dakota Homes Associated with the Riggs Hazelwood Mission Site," *Minnesota Archaeologist* 65 (2006): 170.

197. Anna Jane wrote: "Last Tuesday, Mr. Antoine Renville and his wife and children, Mr. Baptiste Campbell and his wife and her sister Madalien Renville and Mrs. Therese Renville and all her children, and Mr. John Baptiste Renville and another man went on a buffalo hunt. The Indians say that the buffalo are very near. The party that went out are going to come back this week if they do not find buffalo. Angelique and Agnes Renville went with their mother." Anna Jane Riggs to Rebecca Pond, 10 May 1858, box 4, Pond Family Papers.

198. Martha Riggs to Alfred Riggs, 4 Aug. 1860, Alfred L. Riggs Papers.

199. Riggs, "Biography of Men Connected with the Dakota Mission, 1835–1860."

200. Both Stephen Riggs and his daughter Anna Jane wrote lengthy descriptions of the "abduction" of little Mary Cloud. All quotations in this paragraph come from one of these two letters. See Anna Riggs to Alfred Riggs, 1 Mar. 1860, Alfred L. Riggs Papers; and Stephen Riggs to Alfred Riggs, 20 Feb. 1860, Alfred L. Riggs Papers. Stephen was much harsher in his evaluation of the actions of Mary's mother than Anna Jane was.

201. Stephen Riggs to Alfred Riggs, 20 Feb. 1860, United Church of Christ South Dakota Conference Collections, digital letters, https://np3.augie.edu/digital/collection/p16078coll14/id/42/.

202. Robert Hopkins to Selah Treat, 19 May 1851, 18.3.7, vol. 3, no. 3:152, ABCFM Papers.

203. Anna Jane Riggs to Rebecca Pond, 10 May 1858, Pond Family Papers.

204. Riggs, *Mary and I*, p. 134.

205. "Reminiscences" (1895), Lorenzo Lawrence Papers, p. 3, MNHS.

206. Stephen Riggs, "My Dear Times," *Minnesota Weekly Times*, 7 Mar. 1856, p. 2.

207. Riggs, "My Dear Times."

208. Ibid.

CHAPTER 3

1. Martha Riggs to Lucy Spooner Drake, 24 Oct. 1857, Stephen R. Riggs and Family Papers. Julia attended the Western Female Seminary for only one year and then switched for several months to another female seminary. She later attended the Rockford Female Seminary in Rockford, Illinois. Julia Laframboise and Anna Jane Riggs attended Rockford at the same time, both graduating in 1864 and focusing their studies on music.

2. Mary Riggs to Lucy Spooner Drake, 17 Feb. 1858, Stephen R. Riggs Papers, CWS.

3. Jacqueline Johnson, *Western College for Women* (Mount Pleasant, S.C.: Arcadia Publishing, 2014), p. 7.

4. Eliza Huggins, "Report of the Hazelwood Mission School taught by Miss Eliza M. Huggins," 31 Dec. 1861, mss. 309, no. 168, ABCFM Papers.

5. "Mary Ann Huggins souvenir autograph book, 1858-1860s," p. 37, in Alexander G. Huggins and Family Papers, http://www2.mnhs.org/library/findaids/00679/pdfa/00679-00012-4.pdf, accessed 1 Jan. 2022.

6. Morris, "Angelique Renville Crawford," p. 32.

7. Coleman, "Not Race, but Grace."

8. Mary Riggs to Lucy Spooner Drake, 8 Nov. 1862, *Stephen R. Riggs Family Correspondence*.

9. The female seminaries following the Revolutionary War had "a clearly articulated mission, a faculty that offered inspiring role models, and a cur-

riculum that introduced them to female exemplars. In educational practices ranging from classroom instruction to literary societies to reading protocols to emulation of intellectually accomplished women, students were schooled in a curriculum that matched the course of study at male colleges." Mary C. Kelley, "'The Need of Their Genius': A Women's Revolution in Early America," in Thomas A. Foster, ed., *Women in Early America* (New York: New York University Press, 2015), pp. 246, 253–56.

10. Mary Riggs to Alfred Longley, 24 Nov. 1834, *Stephen R. Riggs Family Correspondence.*

11. Porterfield, *Mary Lyon and the Mount Holyoke Mission*, p. 32.

12. Ibid.

13. Leonard I. Sweet, "The Female Seminary Movement and Woman's Mission in Antebellum America," *Church History* 54, no. 1 (Mar. 1985): 43.

14. Sweet, "The Female Seminary Movement and Woman's Mission in Antebellum America," p. 44.

15. Porterfield, *Mary Lyon and the Mount Holyoke Mission*, p. 16.

16. Margaret A. Nash, "'A Salutary Rivalry': The Growth of Higher Education for Women in Oxford, Ohio, 1855–1867," in Roger L. Geiger, ed., *The American College in the Nineteenth Century* (Nashville: Vanderbilt University Press, 2000), p. 171.

17. Patricia Hart Mangan, "Instantiating Vision at the Mount Holyoke Female Seminary," *Journal of Religious History* 40, no. 1 (Mar. 2016): 111. See also Porterfield, *Mary Lyon and the Mount Holyoke Missionaries.*

18. Porterfield, *Mary Lyon and the Mount Holyoke Mission*, p. 40.

19. Nash, "'A Salutary Rivalry'," p. 175.

20. Porterfield, *Mary Lyon and the Mount Holyoke Mission*, p. 6.

21. Pruitt, *A Looking Glass for Ladies*, p. 53.

22. Riggs, *Mary and I*, p. 3.

23. Mary Riggs to Alfred Longley, 24 Nov. 1834, *Stephen R. Riggs Family Correspondence.*

24. Riggs, *Mary and I*, p. 364.

25. 26. Martha Riggs to Lucy Spooner Drake, 23 May 1859, Stephen R. Riggs and Family Papers.

27. Anna Jane Riggs to Lucy Spooner Drake, 7 Jan. 1860, Stephen R. Riggs and Family Papers.

28. The Western Female Seminary was founded by the Reverend Daniel Tenney, pastor of the Second Presbyterian Church in Oxford, Ohio. He promised to "check the frivolity and wrecklessness [*sic*] of our young ladies" through both secular and religious education. Johnson, *Western College for Women*, p. 7. See also Nash, "'A Salutary Rivalry'," p. 175.

29. Johnson, *Western College for Women*, p. 19.

30. Ibid., p. 16.

31. Nash, "'A Salutary Rivalry'," p. 171.

32. Stephen Riggs to Selah Treat, 14 Jan. 1856, mss. 244, no. 333, ABCFM Paper; Stephen Riggs to Selah Treat, 12 June 1858, mss. 244, no. 346, ABCFM Papers.

33. Stephen Riggs to Selah Treat, 16 Mar. 1859, mss. 244, no. 351, ABCFM Papers.

34. Martha Riggs to Lucy Spooner Drake, 18 July 1860, Stephen R. Riggs and Family Papers.

35. Riggs, *Mary and I*, p. 172.

36. Johnson, *Western College for Women*, p. 7; and Nash, "'A Salutary Rivalry'," p. 171.

37. *Ohio Female College at College Hill, Hamilton Co., Ohio with the Plan, Reasons, and Encouragement for its Permanent Endowment as a First-Class Female Seminary* (New York: Edward O. Jenkins, 1862), p. 4. (Hereafter, *Ohio Female College at College Hill*)

38. Sweet, "The Female Seminary Movement and Woman's Mission in Antebellum America," p. 54.

39. *Ohio Female College at College Hill*, p. 5.

40. Ibid.

41. Ibid., p. 7.

42. Martha Riggs to Albert Riggs, 8 Oct. 1861, Alfred L. Riggs Papers.

43. Miami University Special Collections and Libraries, "Western College: Photographs of Classes," https://spec.lib.miamioh.edu/home/western-college-photographs-of-classes/.

44. *The Thirteenth Annual Catalogue and Prospectus of the Ohio Female College, at College Hill, Hamilton Co., Ohio, for 1862* (Cincinnati: Spiller and Brother, Book and Job Printer, 1862), p. 6. (Hereafter, *Thirteenth Annual Catalogue and Prospectus of the Ohio Female College*)

45. Eliza Huggins, "Report of the Hazelwood Mission School taught by Miss Eliza M. Huggins," 31 Dec. 1861, mss. 309, no. 168, ABCFM Papers.

46. Martha Riggs to Alfred Riggs, 20 Nov. 1860, Alfred L. Riggs Papers.

47. Martha Riggs to Alfred Riggs, 4 Aug. 1860, Alfred L. Riggs Papers.

48. In August 1851, Daniel Renville is recorded as attending Miss Jane S. Williamson's school at Kaposia. He took classes with the Williamson and Huggins children. *Annual Report of the Commissioner of Indian Affairs* (1851), p. 439.

49. Mary Butler Renville, *A Thrilling Narrative of Indian Captivity: Dispatches from the Dakota War*, eds. Carrie Reber Zeman and Kathryn Zabelle Derounian-Stodola (Lincoln: University of Nebraska Press, 2021), p. 15.

50. Renville, *A Thrilling Narrative of Indian Captivity*, p. 25.

51. George E. Day, *The Theological Eclectic*, vol. 1 (Cincinnati: William Scott, 1864), p. 18.

52. *Thirteenth Annual Catalogue and Prospectus of the Ohio Female College*, p. 9.

53. Nash, "'A Salutary Rivalry'," p. 177.

54. *Thirteenth Annual Catalogue and Prospectus of the Ohio Female College*, p. 9.

55. Ibid., p. 10.

56. Martha Riggs to Lucy Spooner Drake, 18 Feb. 1860, Stephen R. Riggs and Family Papers.

57. Martha Riggs to Alfred Riggs, 8 Oct. 1861, Alfred L. Riggs Papers.

58. Riggs, *Mary and I*, p. 135.

59. Ibid.

60. Mary Riggs to Alfred Riggs, 11 Jan. 1861, *Stephen R. Riggs Family Correspondence*.

61. Riggs, *Mary and I*, p. 135.

62. Martha Riggs to Lucy Spooner Drake, 19 Sept. 1860, Stephen R. Riggs and Family Papers. In the nineteenth century, agents of colleges coordinated a wide variety of fundraising activities. For a list of fundraising activities in this era, see James Findlay, "Agency, Denominations, and the Western Colleges, 1830-60," in Geiger, ed., *The American College in the Nineteenth Century*, p. 123.

63. Martha Riggs to Lucy Spooner Drake, 19 Sept. 1860, Stephen R. Riggs and Family Papers.

64. Martha Riggs to Alfred Riggs, 31 Jan. 1860, Alfred L. Riggs Papers.

65. Martha Riggs to Alfred Riggs, 9 Dec. 1861, Alfred L. Riggs Papers.

66. Martha Riggs to Alfred Riggs, 31 Jan. 1860, Alfred L. Riggs Papers.

67. Martha Riggs to Alfred Riggs, 8 Oct. 1861, Alfred L. Riggs Papers.

68. Martha Riggs to Alfred Riggs, 3 Sept. 1860, Alfred L. Riggs Papers.

69. *Thirteenth Annual Catalogue and Prospectus of the Ohio Female College*, p. 10.

70. *Ohio Female College at College Hill*, pp. 27–28.

71. Ibid., p. 28.

72. Ibid.

73. "Account for Angelique Renville with S. R. Riggs, guardian," reel 4, Joseph R. and Samuel J. Brown and Family Papers.

74. Stephen Riggs to ABCFM, 22 July 1862, mss. 309, no. 167, ABCFM Papers.

75. Minnesota, Wills and Probate Records, Brown County, p. 581.

76. *The Revised Statutes of the Territory of Minnesota*, 1851, p. 225.

77. The land records for Nicollet County indicate that "S. R. Riggs Guardian" sold the lands of "Angilie Renville to T. Y. Vail of College Hill" for $150. Mary, Stephen, and Isabella Riggs were listed as the witnesses for the sale. The "General Index to Deeds" summarizes the main facts of the sale and lists the volume and page number. For the general information of this sale, see General Index to Deeds, 1853–1976, misc. index, 1905–1966, deed record, 1853–1966, image 109, https://www.familysearch.org/ark:/61903/3:1:3Q9M-C3WM-SJTR?i=108&cat=447348. For the more detailed record, see General Index to Deeds, vol. E–F, image 583, https://www.familysearch.org/ark:/61903/3:1:3Q9M

-C371-B6BF?i=582&cat=447348. All land records cited hereafter come from FamilySearch.org deed records.

78. F. A. Renz to Stephen Riggs, 29 Jan. 1862, Stephen R. Riggs and Family Papers. For information on how the federal government recorded land sales and patents, see https://www.archives.gov/files/dc-metro/know-your-records/genealogy-fair/2011/handouts/bettag-land-entry-papers-federal-land-records.pdf.

79. J. W. Holtsclaw to Stephen Riggs, 22 Mar. 1862, Stephen R. Riggs and Family Papers.

80. Stephen Riggs to Mrs. Drake, 3 Feb. 1863, *Stephen R. Riggs Family Correspondence.*

81. "Account for Angelique Renville with S. R. Riggs, guardian," reel 4, Joseph R. and Samuel J. Brown and Family Papers.

82. Stephen Riggs to Mrs. Drake, 3 Feb. 1863, *Stephen R. Riggs Family Correspondence.*

83. He wrote, "Last year I sold 120 acres to Mr. Vail." Stephen Riggs to Mrs. Drake, 2 Feb. 1863, *Stephen R. Riggs Family Correspondence.*

84. Anna Sill to Stephen Riggs, 25 June 1862, Stephen R. Riggs and Family Papers.

85. "Account for Angelique Renville with S. R. Riggs, guardian," reel 4, Joseph R. and Samuel J. Brown and Family Papers.

86. According to a historical survey, in 1860, counties where the "Half-Breed Tract" was located sold for between six and nine dollars per acre, much more than Riggs reported making off the land. See Charles H. Barnard and John Jones, *Farm real estate values in the United States by counties, 1850–1982* (Washington, D.C.: U.S. Dept. of Agriculture, Economic Research Service, 1987), http://hdl.handle.net/2027/uiug.30112046854219.

87. Stephen Riggs to Mrs. Drake, 3 Feb. 1863, *Stephen R. Riggs Family Correspondence.*

88. For example, when the Riggs family traveled to Massachusetts, by way of Illinois, Michigan, and Ohio, they "took a steamer to Galena, where we took passage in the freight wagons that were going to Elgin, the terminus of the railroad that was then being made west from Chicago . . . we crossed Lake Michigan, and by the Michigan Central of Detroit and then took a lake boat to Cleveland." Riggs, *Mary and I*, p. 120.

89. Martha Riggs to Lucy Spooner Drake, 19 Sept. 1860, Stephen R. Riggs and Family Papers.

90. Martha Riggs to Alfred Riggs, 8 Oct. 1861, Alfred L. Riggs Papers.

91. Martha Riggs to Alfred Riggs, 1 Oct. 1861, Alfred L. Riggs Papers.

92. *Thirteenth Annual Catalogue and Prospectus of the Ohio Female College*, p. 3.

93. Ibid.

94. Ibid.

95. Anna Riggs to Alfred Riggs, 24 Oct. 1860, Alfred L. Riggs Papers.

96. Nash, "'A Salutary Rivalry'," p. 177.

97. *Thirteenth Annual Catalogue and Prospectus of the Ohio Female College*, p. 3.

98. *Thirteenth Annual Catalogue and Prospectus of the Ohio Female College*, p. 4. See also Nash, "'A Salutary Rivalry'," p. 177.

99. *Thirteenth Annual Catalogue and Prospectus of the Ohio Female College*, p. 4.

100. Ibid.

101. Angelique Renville to Alfred Riggs, 12 Apr. 1862, Alfred L. Riggs Papers.

102. Nash, "'A Salutary Rivalry'," p. 180.

103. Martha Riggs to Alfred Riggs, 8 Oct. 1861, Alfred L. Riggs Papers.

104. Angelique Renville to Stephen Riggs, 20 Jan. 1862, Stephen R. Riggs and Family Papers.

105. *Thirteenth Annual Catalogue and Prospectus of the Ohio Female College*, p. 9.

106. The majority of students came from Ohio, with Indiana second and Kentucky third. Martha and Angelique actually were not from the farthest location; three girls at the Ohio Female College hailed from San Francisco. Several other girls also travelled from Iowa, Missouri, New York, and Virginia. See *Thirteenth Annual Catalogue and Prospectus of the Ohio Female College*, pp. 6, 12–16.

107. Angelique Renville to Alfred Riggs, 12 Apr. 1862, Alfred L. Riggs Papers.

108. Angelique Renville to Stephen Riggs, 24 Mar. 1862, Stephen R. Riggs and Family Papers.

109. Angelique Renville to Stephen Riggs, 20 Mar. 1863, Stephen R. Riggs and Family Papers.

110. Angelique Renville to Stephen Riggs, 20 Jan. 1862, Stephen R. Riggs and Family Papers.

111. Angelique Renville to Stephen Riggs, 20 Mar. 1863, Stephen R. Riggs and Family Papers.

112. Mary Riggs to Alfred Riggs, 14 Nov. 1861, *Stephen R. Riggs Family Correspondence*.

113. Angelique Renville to Stephen Riggs, 1 Feb. 1862, Stephen R. Riggs and Family Papers.

114. *Thirteenth Annual Catalogue and Prospectus of the Ohio Female College*, p. 6.

115. Ibid., p. 8.

116. Nash, "'A Salutary Rivalry'," p. 179.

117. Lucy Spooner Drake to Mary Riggs, 11 Nov. 1862, Stephen R. Riggs and Family Papers.

118. Mary Riggs to Lucy Spooner Drake, 8 Nov. 1862, *Stephen R. Riggs Family Correspondence*.

119. Angelique Renville to Stephen Riggs, 24 Mar. 1862, Stephen R. Riggs and Family Papers.

120. Angelique Renville to Alfred Riggs, 12 Apr. 1862, Alfred L. Riggs Papers.

121. Martha Riggs to Alfred Riggs, 22 Mar. 1862, Alfred L. Riggs Papers.

122. Angelique Renville to Stephen Riggs, 20 Jan. 1862, Stephen R. Riggs and Family Papers.

123. Angelique Renville to Alfred Riggs, 12 Apr. 1862, Alfred L. Riggs Papers.

124. Angelique Renville to Stephen Riggs, 1 Feb. 1862, Stephen R. Riggs and Family Papers.

125. Lucy Spooner Drake to Mary Riggs, 11 Nov. 1862, Stephen R. Riggs and Family Papers.

126. Angelique Renville to Stephen Riggs, 24 Mar. 1862, Stephen R. Riggs and Family Papers.

127. Martha Riggs to Albert Riggs, 8 Oct. 1861, Alfred L. Riggs Papers.

128. Beatrice Sarlos, "Noble Savage to Indian Fairy: An Analysis of 19th Century Schoolbook Illustrations of Native Americans," *Internationale Schulbuchforschung* 16, no. 4 (1994): 420.

129. John M. Coward, *Indians Illustrated: The Image of Native Americans in the Pictorial Press* (Urbana: University of Illinois Press, 2016), pp. 3, 5.

130. "Destruction of the Pequod Indians," *McGuffey's Alternate Sixth Reader* (Cincinnati: Van Antwerp, Bragg, and Company, 1889): 229–38. McGuffey's readers were first published in the early nineteenth century and remained common in classrooms across the United States until into the twentieth century. Interestingly, several homeschool websites today advocate using these readers.

131. "The Captive," *The New McGuffey Fourth Reader* (New York: American Book Company, 1901), p. 123.

132. Anna Riggs to Alfred Riggs, 17 Nov. 1860, Alfred L. Riggs Papers.

133. Angelique Renville to Stephen Riggs, 1 Feb. 1862, Stephen R. Riggs and Family Papers.

134. Martha Riggs to Alfred Riggs, 9 Dec. 1861, Alfred L. Riggs Papers.

135. *Thirteenth Annual Catalogue and Prospectus of the Ohio Female College*, p. 9.

136. Angelique Renville to Stephen Riggs, 24 Mar. 1862, Stephen R. Riggs and Family Papers.

137. Angelique Renville to Stephen Riggs, 1 Feb. 1862, Stephen R. Riggs and Family Papers.

138. Angelique Renville to Stephen Riggs, 24 Mar. 1862, Stephen R. Riggs and Family Papers.

139. Ibid.

140. Angelique Renville to Alfred Riggs, 12 Apr. 1862, Alfred L. Riggs Papers.

141. Ibid

142. Pond, *The Dakota or Sioux in Minnesota*, p. 150.

143. Angelique Renville to Stephen Riggs, 1 Feb. 1862, Stephen R. Riggs and Family Papers.

144. Catharine Wood, from Denton, Ohio, was in the four-year college preparatory level as a "janitor," the fourth and lowest level of the college course. *Thirteenth Annual Catalogue and Prospectus of the Ohio Female College*, p. 14.

145. Angelique Renville to Stephen Riggs, 1 Feb. 1862, Stephen R. Riggs and Family Papers.

146. Angelique Renville to Stephen Riggs, 24 Mar. 1862, Stephen R. Riggs and Family Papers.

147. Angelique Renville to Alfred Riggs, 12 Apr. 1862, Alfred L. Riggs Papers.

148. Ibid.

149. Ibid.

150. Martha Riggs to Albert Riggs, 8 Oct. 1861, Alfred L. Riggs Papers.

151. Martha Riggs to Alfred Riggs, 9 Dec. 1861, Alfred L. Riggs Papers.

152. Angelique Renville to Stephen Riggs, 20 Jan. 1862, Stephen R. Riggs and Family Papers.

153. Ibid.

154. Anna Riggs to Alfred Riggs, 20 Sept. 1862, Alfred L. Riggs Papers.

155. Angelique Renville to Stephen Riggs, 20 Jan. 1862, Stephen R. Riggs and Family Papers.

156. Ibid.

157. Angelique Renville to Stephen Riggs, 1 Feb. 1862, Stephen R. Riggs and Family Papers.

158. Angelique Renville to Stephen Riggs, 24 Mar. 1862, Stephen R. Riggs and Family Papers.

159. Martha Riggs to Alfred Riggs, 7 Feb. 1862, Alfred L. Riggs Papers.

160. Martha Riggs to Alfred Riggs, 9 Dec. 1861, Alfred L. Riggs Papers.

161. Angelique Renville to Stephen Riggs, 24 Mar. 1862, Stephen R. Riggs and Family Papers.

162. Angelique Renville to Stephen Riggs, 1 Feb. 1862, Stephen R. Riggs and Family Papers.

163. Angelique Renville to Stephen Riggs, 24 Mar. 1862, Stephen R. Riggs and Family Papers.

164. Martha Riggs to Alfred Riggs, 9 Dec. 1861, Alfred L. Riggs Papers.

165. Ibid.

166. Martha Riggs to Albert Riggs, 8 Oct. 1861, Alfred L. Riggs Papers.

167. Spooner wrote of the missing letters: "I presume [the letter] was lost as it was mailed about ten days before the Indian trouble began." Angelique mailed a letter at the same time giving particulars. Neither of these letters were acknowledged as received. See Lucy Spooner Drake to Mary Riggs, 11 Nov. 1862, Stephen R. Riggs and Family Papers.

168. Eliza McCabe to Mary Riggs, 23 July 1862, Stephen R. Riggs and Family Papers.

169. Mary Riggs to Mrs. Drake, 8 Nov. 1862, *Stephen R. Riggs Family Correspondence.*

170. Angelique Renville to Stephen Riggs, 24 Mar. 1862, Stephen R. Riggs and Family Papers.

171. Lucy Spooner Drake to Mary Riggs, 11 Nov. 1862, Stephen R. Riggs and Family Papers.

CHAPTER 4

1. Martha Riggs to Alfred Riggs, 7 Feb. 1862, Alfred L. Riggs Papers.

2. Martha Riggs to Alfred Riggs, 16 Apr. 1862, Alfred L. Riggs Papers.

3. Mary Riggs to Alfred Riggs, 29 June 1862, *Stephen R. Riggs Family Correspondence.*

4. Ibid.

5. Riggs, *A Tableau of the families.*

6. Mary Riggs to Stephen Riggs, 5 May 1862, *Stephen R. Riggs Family Correspondence.*

7. Mary Riggs to Lucy Spooner Drake, 8 Nov. 1862, *Stephen R. Riggs Family Correspondence.*

8. Lucy Spooner Drake to Mary Riggs, 11 Nov. 1862, Stephen R. Riggs and Family Papers.

9. Ibid.

10. Martha Riggs to Alfred Riggs, 9 Dec. 1861, Alfred L. Riggs Papers.

11. Angelique Renville to Alfred Riggs, 12 Apr. 1862, Alfred L. Riggs Papers.

12. Lucy Spooner Drake to Mary Riggs, 17 Aug. 1862, Stephen R. Riggs and Family Papers. According to the "Dictionary of Common Civil War Medical Terms," bilious fever was a catch-all term for symptoms including headache, abdominal pain, and constipation. It was often associated with malaria or typhoid. See https://ehistory.osu.edu/exhibitions/cwsurgeon/cwsurgeon/commonterms, accessed 29 Apr. 2021.

13. Lucy Spooner Drake to Mary Riggs, 17 Aug. 1862, Stephen R. Riggs and Family Papers.

14. Ibid.

15. Lucy Spooner Drake to Mary Riggs, 11 Nov. 1862, Stephen R. Riggs and Family Papers.

16. Stephen Riggs to Lucy Spooner Drake, 24 Sept. 1863, Stephen R. Riggs Papers, CWS

17. Lucy Spooner Drake to Stephen Riggs, 17 Aug. 1862, Stephen R. Riggs and Family Papers.

18. Lucy Spooner Drake to Mrs. and Mrs. Riggs, 20 Mar. 1863, Stephen R. Riggs and Family Papers.

19. Angelique Renville to Mary Renville, May 1863, Stephen R. Riggs and Family Papers.

20. Lucy Spooner Drake to Mary Riggs, 14 Dec. 1863, Stephen R. Riggs and Family Papers.

21. Ibid.

22. Angelique Renville to Mary Renville, May 1863, Stephen R. Riggs and Family Papers.

23. Angelique Renville to Mary Riggs, 20 Mar. 1863, Stephen R. Riggs and Family Papers.

24. Angelique Renville to Mary Riggs, May 1863, Stephen R. Riggs and Family Papers.

25. Angelique Renville to Mary Riggs, 20 Mar. 1863, Stephen R. Riggs and Family Papers.

26. Lucy Spooner Drake to Mrs. and Mrs. Riggs, 20 Mar. 1863, Stephen R. Riggs and Family Papers.

27. Lucy Spooner Drake to Mary Riggs, 11 Nov. 1862, Stephen R. Riggs and Family Papers.

28. Ibid.

29. Lucy Spooner Drake to Mr. and Mrs. Riggs, 20 Mar. 1863, Stephen R. Riggs and Family Papers.

30. Ibid.

31. Angelique Renville to Mary Riggs, May 1863, Stephen R. Riggs and Family Papers.

32. Angelique Renville to Mary Riggs, 20 Mar. 1863, Stephen R. Riggs and Family Papers.

33. Angelique Renville to Mary Riggs, May 1863, Stephen R. Riggs and Family Papers.

34. For more information about the war, see Gary Clayton Anderson, *Massacre in Minnesota: The Dakota War of 1862, the Most Violent Ethnic Conflict in American History* (Norman: University of Oklahoma Press, 2019); Kenneth Carley, *The Dakota War of 1862*, 2nd ed. (St. Paul: Minnesota Historical Society Press, 2001); Michael Clodfelter, *The Dakota War: The United States Army Versus the Sioux, 1862–1865* (Jefferson, N.C.: McFarland, 1998); and Meyer, *History of the Santee Sioux*.

35. John Bell, "The Sioux War Panorama and American Mythic History," *Theatre Journal* 48, no. 3 (Oct. 1996): 285.

36. Scott M. Berg, "Lincoln's Choice," *Quarterly Journal of Military History* 26, no. 2 (Winter 2014): 33.

37. "Annual Message of Governor Ramsey to the Legislature of Minnesota, January 9, 1862," p. 18. Available at https://www.leg.state.mn.us/docs/NonMNpub/oclc18189672.pdf, accessed 29 Dec. 2021.

38. Westerman and White, *Mni Sota Makoce*, p. 193.

39. Winifred W. Barton, *John P. Williamson: A Brother to the Sioux* (New York: Fleming H. Revell Co., 1919), p. 48.

40. "A Sioux Story of the War: Chief Big Eagle's Story of the Sioux Outbreak," *Collections of the Minnesota Historical Society*, vol. 6 (1894): 384.

41. John Peacock, "An Account of the Dakota-US War as Sacred Text," *American Indian Culture and Research Journal* 37, no. 2 (2013): 193.

42. The number of settlers who died varies according to the source and remains controversial. The 1862 *Annual Report of Commissioner of Indian Affairs* (hereafter *ARCIA*) reported that 382 settlers were killed during the war (p. 66). In the 1863 *ARCIA*, the Dakotas' agent, Thomas J. Galbraith, listed 644 citizens and 93 soldiers killed, for a total of 737 (p. 294). Thomas Williamson "carefully inquired of persons well acquainted in the counties which suffered the most" and put the number at around 600. Thomas Williamson to Walter Griffith, 10 Apr. 1863, mss. 310, no. 226, ABCFM Papers. Today, most historians mention 500 deaths, but estimates of 400–800 also appear in some sources. Legal scholar Carol Chomsky lists 464 fatalities, including 77 American soldiers, 29 citizen-soldiers, and 358 settlers. See Carol Chomsky, "The United States-Dakota War Trials: A Study in Military Injustice," *Stanford Law Review* 43, no. 1 (Jan. 1990): 1. Most sources focus on the number of settlers killed and rarely mention Dakota deaths. David A. Nichols reminds us that "it was characteristic of the time that few bothered to calculate Indian casualties." In "The Other Civil War: Lincoln and the Indians," *Minnesota History* 44, no. 1 (Spring 1974): 8.

43. Riggs, *Taȟ-Koo Wah-Kaŋ́*, p. 305; and Gary Clayton Anderson and Alan R. Woolworth, eds., *Through Dakota Eyes: Narrative Accounts of the Minnesota Indian War of 1862* (St. Paul: Minnesota Historical Society Press, 1988), p. 1.

44. Riggs, *Mary and I*, p. 154.

45. Ibid.

46. *Annual Report of the Commissioner of Indian Affairs* (1866), p. 238.

47. Mary Riggs to Stephen Riggs, 24 Oct. 1862, Stephen R. Riggs Papers, CWS; and Riggs, *Mary and I*, p. 170.

48. Renville, *Dispatches from the Dakota War*, p. 2.

49. H. H. Sibley to John Pope, 30 Oct. 1862, in United States War Department, *The War of the Rebellion: A Compilation of the Official Records of the Union and Confederate Armies*, series 1, vol. 13 (Washington: Government Printing Office, 1885): 708.

50. H. H. Sibley to "those of Half-Breeds and Sioux Indians who have not been concerned in the murder and outrages upon the white settlers," 13 Sept. 1863, in *The War of the Rebellion*, p. 632.

51. H. H. Sibley to Ma-za-ka-tame and Wa-ke-nan-nan-te," 24 Sept. 1862, in *The War of the Rebellion*, p. 667.

52. Barton, *John P. Williamson*, p. 58.

53. Meyer, *History of the Santee Sioux*, p. 136; and Barton, *John P. Williamson*, p. 59.

54. Colette Routel, "Minnesota Bounties on Dakota Men During the U.S.-Dakota War," *William Mitchell Law Review* 1 (2013): 9.

55. Maeve Herbert, "Explaining the Sioux Military Commission of 1862," *Columbia Human Rights Law Review* 40, no. 743 (2009): 771.

56. H. H. Sibley to John Pope, 28 Sept. 1862, in *The War of the Rebellion*, p. 687.

57. H. H. Sibley to Charles E. Flandreau, 28 Sept. 1862, in *The War of the Rebellion*, p. 688.

58. John Isch, *The Dakota Trials: Including the Complete Transcripts and Explanatory Notes on the Military Commission Trials in Minnesota, 1862–1864* (New Ulm, Minn.: Brown County Historical Society, 2013), p. 265. Gabriel, Joseph, Daniel, Antoine, Michel, and Isaac Renville all testified, both for and against the defendants, at the trials. Gabriel Renville mostly testified against the defendants, which helped lead to their convictions. Antoine and Isaac Renville, in the case of Happan, testified that he stole a horse; he was found not guilty. For references to Renville participation in the trials, see pp. 68–69, 94–95, 97–98, 180, 184, and 204–05.

59. Peacock, "An Account of the Dakota-US War of 1862 as Sacred Text," p. 194. See also Chomsky, "The United States-Dakota War Trials," p. 7. For a list of the Dakota prisoners and their sentences, see "Names of the Condemned Dakota Men," *American Indian Quarterly* 28, no. 1–2 (Winter–Spring 2004): 175–183. Fourteen Ho-Chunk men were also tried; thirteen were acquitted, and one was sent to Camp Kearney in Davenport, Iowa.

60. Waziyatawin, "*Colonial Calibrations*: The Expendability of Minnesota's Original People," *William Mitchell Law Review* 39, no. 2 (2013): 464.

61. H. H. Sibley to Charles Flandreau, 28 Sept. 1862, in *The War of the Rebellion*, p. 688.

62. Mary Renville to Stephen Riggs, 10 Jan. 1863, Stephen R. Riggs and Family Papers.

63. Stephen Riggs, "October 1862—at Camp Release," Stephen R. Riggs and Family Papers.

64. Millikan, "The Great Treasure of the Fort Snelling Prison Camp," p. 10.

65. *Annual Report of the ABCFM* (1863), p. 148. See also Stephen Riggs to Selah Treat, 21 Jan. 1863, mss. 310, no. 25, ABCFM Papers.

66. Folwell, *A History of Minnesota, Volume 2*, p. 252. The missionaries estimated that 1,600 Dakotas were imprisoned at Fort Snelling. *Annual Report of the ABCFM* (1863), p. 148. R. J. Creswell reported that 1,500 Dakotas were held at Fort Snelling; Creswell, *Among the Sioux: A Story of the Twin Cities and the Two Dakotas* (Minneapolis: The University Press, 1906), p. 35.

67. Stephen Riggs to Selah Treat, 21 Jan. 1863, mss. 310, no. 25, ABCFM Papers.

68. Thomas Williamson to Selah Treat, 1 Dec. 1862, mss. 310, no. 226, ABCFM Papers.

69. Stephen Riggs to Selah Treat, 21 Jan. 1863, mss. 310, no. 25, ABCFM Papers.

70. D. Frenier to SRR, 14 Jan. 1863, Stephen R. Riggs and Family Papers.

71. "Sketches of the Dakota Mission," *Iapi Oaye: The Word Carrier* 2, no. 5 (May 1873): 24.

72. *Missionary Herald* 58 (1862): 204.

73. In March 1863, Lucy Spooner Drake noted that she would have Angelique

"write to her mother and have Mr. Riggs read it for her." Lucy Spooner Drake to Mr. and Mrs. Riggs, 20 Mar. 1863, Stephen R. Riggs and Family Papers.

74. Lucy Spooner Drake to Mary Riggs, 11 Nov. 1862, Stephen R. Riggs and Family Papers.

75. Lucy Spooner Drake to Mr. and Mrs. Riggs, 20 Mar. 1863, Stephen R. Riggs and Family Papers; and Jane Williamson to Mary Riggs, 22 Feb. 1864, Stephen R. Riggs and Family Papers. Sophia Renville was the daughter of Angelique's uncle, Antoine Renville. In 1851, the same year Angelique was "adopted" by the Riggs family, Sophia also was taken in by the Adams family at the Lac qui Parle mission. When the war broke out, Sophia lived with another uncle, John B. Renville, and his wife Mary. See Riggs, *A Tableau of the families.*

76. Lucy Spooner Drake to Mary Riggs, 14 Dec. 1863, Stephen R. Riggs and Family Papers.

77. Ibid.

78. Angelique Renville to Mary Riggs, 20 Mar. 1863, Stephen R. Riggs and Family Papers.

79. Anderson, *Through Dakota Eyes*, p. 181.

80. H. H. Sibley, "Sketch of John Other Day," *Collections of the Minnesota State Historical Society* 3 (1870–1880): 99.

81. Anderson, *Through Dakota Eyes*, p. 181; and Sibley, "Sketch of John Other Day," p. 100.

82. Anderson, *Through Dakota Eyes*, p. 120.

83. Ibid. For Other Day's statement about his actions during the first days of the war, see "Statement of John Other Day" in Henry Benjamin Whipple, *Light and Shadows of a Long Episcopate* (New York: Macmillan Co., 1902), pp. 119–21.

84. Otherday, "Highly Interesting Narrative of the Outbreak of Indian Hostilities," *Saint Paul Daily Press*, 8 Aug. 1862, p. 2; *Shakopee Weekly Argus*, 25 Nov. 1869; and James Hinds to his mother, 21 May 1863, James Hinds Papers, MNHS; and *Saint Paul Press*, 18 Nov. 1862, p. 4.

85. "From the Red Woods Falls Mail," 19 Nov. 1869, reel 14, Henry Hastings Sibley Papers.

86. Curt Brown, "Unusual couple went from heroism to poverty," *Star Tribune*, 20 May 2017. Brown writes that Other Day died "with Roxana by his bedside."

87. Renville, *Dispatches from the Dakota War*, p. 30. All the documents that I located mentioning John Other Day's death indicate that his "wife" was with him, but they do not provide her name. As already noted, several historians have assumed that this meant Roxanne, but it could have been Therese. For descriptions of Other Day's death, see Cocker to Stephen Riggs, 31 Oct. 1869, Stephen R. Riggs and Family Papers; and Sibley, "Sketch of John Other Day," p. 102.

88. During a visit to the men's prison at Mankato, Stephen Riggs made the men renounce all wives but one before they could join his church. He even made a list recording which wife (or wives) each man should "put away" and

which to keep. For a transcript of the "polygamy problem" list, see Corinne L. Monjeau-Marz, *The Dakota Indian Internment at Fort Snelling, 1862–1864* (St. Paul, Minn.: Prairie Smoke Press, 2005), p. 143.

89. Mary Renville to Stephen Riggs, 23 Jan. 1863, Stephen R. Riggs and Family Papers.

90. Monjeau-Marz, *The Dakota Indian Internment at Fort Snelling*, p. 153. The appendix to the book includes a transcribed list of all the Dakotas baptized by Catholic priests at Fort Snelling.

91. Monjeau-Marz, *The Dakota Indian Internment at Fort Snelling*, p. 153.

92. John B. Renville to Stephen Riggs, 22 Jan. 1863, translation in Renville, *Dispatches from the Dakota War*, p. 227.

93. Stephen Riggs to Martha Riggs, 27 Oct. 1862, Stephen R. Riggs and Family Papers.

94. Mary Riggs to Lucy Spooner Drake, 8 Nov. 1862, *Stephen R. Riggs Family Correspondence.*

95. Stephen Riggs to Selah Treat, 21 Jan. 1863, mss. 310, no. 25, ABCFM Papers.

96. Mary Riggs to Alfred Riggs, 1 Jan. 1863, Alfred L. Riggs Papers.

97. Jane Williamson to Mary Riggs, 25 Dec. 1862, Stephen R. Riggs and Family Papers.

98. Mary Riggs to Alfred Riggs, 1 Jan. 1863, Alfred L. Riggs Papers.

99. Ibid.

100. Jane Williamson wrote in November that she "would gladly have nursed Agnes though [*sic*] the measles but we were very scarce of bedding and the weather might turn cold." Jane Williamson to Mary Riggs, 23 Nov. 1862, Stephen R. Riggs and Family Papers.

101. D. Frenier to Stephen Riggs, 14 Jan. Stephen R. Riggs and Family Papers. Dr. John Wakefield was later investigated for charges of negligence in his role as the government appointed physician at Fort Snelling. Renville, *Dispatches from the Dakota War*, p. 318.

102. D. Frenier to Stephen Riggs, 14 Jan. 1863, Stephen R. Riggs and Family Papers.

103. Stephen Riggs noted on 21 Jan. 1863 that Agnes died the previous week. Stephen Riggs to Selah Treat, 21 Jan. 1863, mss. 310, no. 25, ABCFM Papers.

104. Mary Renville to Stephen Riggs, 23 Jan. 1863, Stephen R. Riggs and Family Papers.

105. Stephen Riggs to Lucy Spooner Drake, 11 Mar. 1863, Stephen R. Riggs Papers, CWS.

106. Mary A. Renville to Stephen Riggs, 23 Jan. 1863, Stephen R. Riggs and Family Papers.

107. Martha Riggs to Albert Riggs, 12 Feb. 1863, Alfred L. Riggs Papers.

108. Angelique Renville to Mary Riggs, 20 Mar. 1863, Stephen R. Riggs and Family Papers.

109. Millikan, "The Great Treasure of the Fort Snelling Prison Camp," p. 12.

110. Mary Renville to Stephen Riggs, 23 Jan. 1863, Stephen R. Riggs and Family Papers.

111. Millikan, "The Great Treasure of the Fort Snelling Prison Camp," p. 12.

112. It appears that Sibley and Riggs did not give the full amount for the sale of their scrip to the Renvilles. For example, Sibley wrote, "Here is due Antoine Renville on the sale of his remaining scrip, after deducting his draft on me . . . for $300." Henry Sibley to Stephen Riggs, 8 Feb. 1865, Stephen R. Riggs and Family Papers. For additional correspondence over the Renville scrip between Riggs and Sibley, see Henry Sibley to Stephen Riggs, 11 Feb. 1865; and Henry Sibley to Stephen Riggs, 6 Mar. 1863, Stephen R. Riggs and Family Papers.

113. Millikan, "The Great Treasure of the Fort Snelling Prison Camp," p. 12.

114. Ibid., p. 15.

115. Gabriel Renville, "A Sioux Narrative of the Outbreak in 1862, and of Sibley's Expedition in 1863," *Minnesota Historical Society Collections* 10, part 2 (1905), p. 611.

116. Dakota scouts remain an extremely controversial subject. Several contemporary Dakota activists and scholars have called the Dakota scouts "traitors" and "betrayers" of their own people. Other historians have described scouts as "renegades, traitors, and mercenaries." Historian Thomas Dunlay summarized this strain of historiography: scouts "consciously and deliberately betray[ed] their own people to serve their own selfish interests." Thomas W. Dunlay, *Wolves for the Blue Soldiers: Indian Scouts and Auxiliaries with the United States Army, 1860–90* (Lincoln: University of Nebraska Press, 1987), pp. 5, 109. However, independent historian Curtis Dahlin makes the opposite argument, calling the Dakota scouts "heroes rather than traitors to their people." Curtis A. Dahlin, *The Fort Sisseton Dakota Scouts and Their Camps in Eastern Dakota Territory* (Roseville, Minn., 2017), pp. 6, 213–216; and "Dakota Scouts and Camps Focus of BCHS Talk," *The Journal* (New Ulm, Minn.), 17 Aug. 2016. See also Mary Beth Faimon, "Ties that Bind: Remembering, Mourning, and Healing Historical Trauma," *American Indian Quarterly* 28, no. 1–2 (Winter–Spring 2004): 240–41; and Waziyatawin, *What Does Justice Look Like?*, p. 124. For additional information on scouts, see Janne Lahti, "Colonized Labor: Apaches and Pawnees as Army Workers," *Western Historical Quarterly* 39, no. 3 (Autumn 2008): 261–81.

117. Lucy Spooner Drake to Mr. and Mrs. Riggs, 20 Mar. 1863, Stephen R. Riggs and Family Papers.

118. Jane Williamson to Mary Riggs, 20 Feb. 1864, Stephen R. Riggs and Family Papers.

119. *General Statutes of the State of Minnesota*, 17 Feb. 1863, p. 475.

120. Stephen Riggs to Lucy Spooner Drake, 11 Mar. 1863, Stephen R. Riggs Papers, CWS.

121. Jane Williamson to Mary Riggs, 20 Feb. 1864, Stephen R. Riggs and Family Papers.

122. Stephen Riggs to Selah Treat, 21 Jan. 1863, mss. 310, no. 25, ABCFM Papers.

123. Stephen Riggs to Lucy Spooner Drake, 3 Feb. 1863, Stephen R. Riggs Papers, CWS.

124. Stephen Riggs to Lucy Spooner Drake, 11 Mar. 1863, Stephen R. Riggs Papers, CWS

125. Stephen Riggs to Selah Treat, 21 Jan. 1863, mss. 310, no. 25, ABCFM Papers.

126. Lucy Spooner Drake to Mr. and Mrs. Riggs, 20 Mar. 1863, Stephen R. Riggs and Family Papers.

127. Ibid.

128. Ibid.

129. Mary Riggs to Lucy Spooner Drake, 11 Mar. 1863, Stephen R. Riggs Papers, CWS.

130. Lucy Spooner Drake to Mrs. and Mrs. Riggs, 20 Mar. 1863, Stephen R. Riggs and Family Papers.

131. Mary Riggs to Stephen Riggs, 23 July 1863, Stephen R. Riggs Papers, CWS.

132. "Account for Angelique Renville with S. R. Riggs, guardian," reel 4, Joseph R. and Samuel J. Brown and Family Papers. For mention of Angelique's return home, see Stephen Riggs to Selah Treat, 15 Sept. 1863, *Stephen R. Riggs Family Correspondence.*

133. Stephen Riggs to Lucy Spooner Drake, 24 Sept. 1863, Stephen R. Riggs Papers, CWS.

134. Ibid.

135. Lucy Drake to Mary Riggs, 14 Dec. 1863, Stephen R. Riggs and Family Papers.

136. Morris, "Angelique Renville Crawford."

CHAPTER 5

1. Lucy Spooner Drake to Mary Riggs, 14 Dec. 1863, Stephen R. Riggs and Family Papers.

2. Morris, "Angelique Renville Crawford."

3. Victoria Freeman, "Attitudes Toward 'Miscegenation' in Canada, the United States, New Zealand, and Australia," *Native Studies Review* 16, no. 1 (2005): 43.

4. Freeman, "Attitudes Toward 'Miscegenation'," p. 45.

5. The territories or states banning Indian–white intermarriage included Arizona, Georgia, Idaho, Louisiana, Maine, Massachusetts, Nevada, North Carolina, Oklahoma, Oregon, Rhode Island, South Carolina, Tennessee, Virginia, and Washington. See Margaret Jacobs, "The Eastmans and the Luhans: Interracial Marriage between White Women and Native American Men, 1875–1936," *Frontiers: A Journal of Women's Studies* 23, no. 3 (2002): 50, footnote 13.

6. David Smits, "'Squaw Men,' 'Half-Breeds,' and Amalgamators: Late

Nineteenth-Century Anglo-American Attitudes Toward Indian–White Race-Mixing," *American Indian Culture and Research Journal* 15 no. 3 (1991): 29–61; and Freeman, "Attitudes Toward 'Miscegenation'," p. 53.

7. Andrew R. Graybill, *The Red and the White: A Family Saga of The American West* (New York: W. W. Norton and Company, 2013), 48; and Freeman, "Attitudes Toward 'Miscegenation'," p. 53.

8. Jacobs, "The Eastmans and the Luhans," p. 31.

9. Smits, "'Squaw Men,' 'Half-Breeds,' and Amalgamators," p. 47

10. Jacobs, "The Eastman and the Luhans," p. 29.

11. *The Word Carrier*, Vol. 1, no. 1, Mar. 1884, p. 3. Thank you to Dr. Suzanne Lee for sending me the link to this article.

12. Gideon Pond to Rebecca Hine, 1 Mar. 1837, Pond Family Papers

13. Ibid.

14. Riggs, *Taȟ-Koo Wah-Kań*, p. 183.

15. Pond, *Two Volunteer Missionaries*, p. 135.

16. Riggs, *A Tableau of the families*.

17. Riggs, *Taȟ-Koo Wah-Kań*, p. 184.

18. Pond, *Two Volunteer Missionaries*, p. 234.

19. Stephen Riggs and Thomas Williamson to Rev. Rufus Anderson, 1857, mss. 244, no. 40, ABCFM Papers.

20. Riggs, *Taȟ-Koo Wah-Kań*, pp. 404–05.

21. Riggs, *A Tableau of the families*.

22. Ibid.

23. Pond, *Two Volunteer Missionaries*, p. 129.

24. *The Public Statutes of the State of Minnesota, 1849–1858* (Saint Paul: The Pioneer Printing Company, 1859), pp. 460–61.

25. Ibid., 460.

26. Riggs, *Mary and I*, p. 312.

27. Thomas Williamson, "For the Boston Recorder: The Polygamy Question," nd., no. 89, ABCFM Papers.

28. Riggs, *Mary and I*, p. 71.

29. Catherine J. Denial, *Making Marriage: Husbands, Wives, and the American State in Dakota and Ojibwe Country* (St. Paul: Minnesota Historical Society Press, 2013), p. 6.

30. *The Revised Statutes of the Territory of Minnesota*, 1851, pp. 462–66.

31. Denial, *Making Marriage*, p. 69.

32. Ibid., 67.

33. Ella Deloria, *Dakotas Way of Life*, Chapter 6: Courtship and Marriage, Ella Deloria Archive, 121, http://zia.aisri.indiana.edu/deloria_archive/browse.php, accessed 29 Dec. 2021. Elijah Black Thunder et al., *Ehanna Woyakapi: History and Culture of the Sisseton-Wahpeton Sioux Tribe of South Dakota* (Sisseton-Wahpeton Tribe, 1975), p. 99.

34. Amos E. Oneroad, *Being Dakota: Tales and Traditions of the Sisseton and Wahpeton* (St. Paul: Minnesota Historical Society Press, 2005), p. 96.

35. Deloria, *Dakotas Way of Life*, p. 127.

36. Oneroad, *Being Dakota*, p. 96.

37. Sarah Carter, *The Importance of Being Monogamous: Marriage and Nation Building in Western Canada to 1915* (University of Alberta Press, 2008), p. 107.

38. Pond, *Dakotas or Sioux in Minnesota*, p. 138.

39. Deloria, *Dakotas Way of Life*, p. 129.

40. Carter, *The Importance of Being Monogamous*, p. 115.

41. Angela Cavender Wilson, "The Role of Women in Eastern Dakota Society in the Early 1800s," Dakota Mission Culture Park Project, 25, MNHS.

42. Black Thunder, *Ehanna Woyakapi*, 100.

43. Carter, *The Importance of Being Monogamous*, p. 115.

44. Ibid., p. 119.

45. Carroll, *Daybreak Woman*, p. 22.

46. Deloria, *Dakotas Way of Life*, p. 131.

47. Carroll, *Daybreak Woman*, p. 22.

48. Pond, *Dakotas or Sioux in Minnesota*, p. 140.

49. Ibid.

50. Carter, *The Importance of Being Monogamous*, p. 104.

51. Renville, "A Sioux narrative of the outbreak in 1862, and of Sibley's expedition in 1863," pp. 5–6. For references to Charles Crawford's mother and family history, see Doane Robinson Collection, Samuel J. Brown correspondence, Folder 44, pp. 60, 95. South Dakota State Historical Society Collections. https://sddigitalarchives.contentdm.oclc.org/digital/collection/manuscript/id/1858/rec/20.

52. Several primary sources also called him "Charly Brown," mistakenly believing that he had ties to Joseph Brown's family.

53. Stephen Riggs to Selah Treat, 31 July 1856, mss. 244, no. 337, ABCFM Papers; and *Friends' Intelligencer United with the Friends' Journal* 44 (1887): 645.

54. For the constitution and those who signed it, see "The Hazelwood Constitution," 29 July 1856, in Records of the Minnesota Superintendency of Indian Affairs, Record Group 75, Roll 8, National Archives. Thank you to Dr. Jimmy Sweet for graciously sending me a copy of this constitution and sharing with me his extensive collection of primary sources related to Dakota history both before and after the U.S.–Dakota War of 1862.

55. Anderson, *Gabriel Renville*, p. 26.

56. Commissioner of Indian Affairs, *Annual Report* (1859), pp. 452, 454; and Gary Clayton Anderson, *Kinsmen of Another Kind: Dakota- White Relations in the Upper Mississippi Valley, 1650–1862* (St. Paul: Minnesota Historical Society Press, 1997), p. 231.

57. Martha Riggs to Alfred Riggs, 30 Jan. 1861, Alfred L. Riggs Papers.

58. Martha Riggs to Alfred Riggs, 3 June 1861, Alfred L. Riggs Papers.

59. Martha Riggs to Alfred Riggs, 27 Feb. 1861, Alfred L. Riggs Papers.

60. Ibid.

61. Lucy Spooner Drake to Mary Riggs, 14 Dec. 1863, Stephen R. Riggs and Family Papers.

62. Ibid.

63. Ibid.

64. In a letter to Sam Brown, Charles underlined several English words including Treaty, Secretary of the Interior, and commissioner. See Charles Crawford to Sam Brown, 4 Jan. 1871, Joseph R. Brown and Samuel J. Brown and Family Papers, reel 7. Charles was likely fluent in English during his earlier years; he retained some of these skills but lost some fluency over the years. In 1901, Charles testified in court. During his deposition, he stated that he could "speak in English, not plain—broken talk and some things I could not understand the meaning of." The lawyers initially refused to grant him a translator, but later decided that he needed one. Charles did, however, correct a mistranslation; his translator admitted he was correct. See, *In the Court of Claims. The Sisseton and Wahpeton Bands of Sioux Indians vs. The United States*. Original Petition (Washington D.C.: McGill and Wallace, 1901), p. 159.

65. For references to Charles Crawford's interaction with Daniel, Joseph, and Gabriel Renville during the war, see *The Sisseton and Wahpeton Bands of Sioux Indians vs. The United States*, pp. 164–67, 175

66. For an in-depth discussion of the trials, see Chomsky, "The United States–Dakota War Trials: A Study in Military Injustice," 13–98.

67. Isch, *Dakotas Trials,* pp. 47–48.

68. Ibid., pp. 171–172

69. Henry Sibley, "List of Scouts," 28 May 1863, Henry Hastings Sibley Papers, Reel 12.

70. Mary A. L. Riggs to Henry Sibley, 3 Nov. 1863, Henry Hastings Sibley Papers, Reel 12.

71. Ibid.

72. Morris, "Angelique Renville Crawford."

73. Ibid.

74. Lucy Spooner Drake to Mary Riggs, 14 Dec. 1863, Stephen R. Riggs and Family Papers.

75. Morris, "Angelique Renville Crawford."

76. Ibid.

77. Angelique Renville to Stephen Riggs, 8 Feb. 1864, Stephen R. Riggs and Family Papers.

78. Ibid.

79. Angelique Renville to Stephen Riggs, 24 Mar. 1864, Stephen R. Riggs and Family Papers.

80. Ibid.

81. Angelique Renville to Stephen Riggs, Apr. 1864, Stephen R. Riggs and Family Papers.

82. Account for Angelique Renville with S. R. Riggs, guardian," Joseph R. and Samuel J. Brown and Family Papers, Reel 4.

83. Angelique Renville to Stephen Riggs, 8 Feb. 1864, Stephen R. Riggs and Family Papers.

84. Angelique Renville to Stephen Riggs, Apr. 1864, Stephen R. Riggs and Family Papers.

85. Barton, *Brother to the Sioux*, p. 112.

86. Morris, "Angelique Renville Crawford."

87. Ibid.

88. Marriage Certificate, 14 Sept. 1864, Joseph R. and Samuel J. Brown and Family Papers, Reel 3.

89. Mary Riggs to Lucy Spooner Drake, 29 Oct. 1865, Stephen R. Riggs Papers, CWS.

90. Mary Riggs to Thomas Williamson, 30 May 1865, Stephen R. Riggs Papers, CWS.

91. T.S.L. Spink to Stephen Riggs, 21 Oct. 1867, Stephen R. Riggs and Family Papers.

92. Stephen Riggs, "Home Notes," Lake Traverse, DT, 26 June 1866, Stephen R. Riggs Papers, CWS.

93. Stephen Riggs, "Home Notes," 26 June 1866, Stephen R. Riggs Papers, CWS.

94. Mary Riggs to Thomas Williamson, 30 May 1865, Stephen R. Riggs Papers, CWS.

95. Stephen Riggs, "Home Notes," 4 July 1866, Stephen R. Riggs Papers, CWS.

96. Ibid.

97. Stephen Riggs, "Home Notes," July 1866, Stephen R. Riggs Papers, CWS.

98. Thomas Williamson to Selah Treat, 6 July 1866, 310: 255, ABCFM Papers.

99. Stephen Riggs, "Home Notes," 4 July 1866, Stephen R. Riggs Papers, CWS; and Stephen Riggs, "Home Notes," July 1866, Stephen R. Riggs Papers, CWS.

100. Stephen Riggs, "Home Notes," 4 July 1866, Stephen R. Riggs Papers, CWS.

101. John Williamson to Stephen Riggs, 3 Oct. 1864, Stephen R. Riggs and Family Papers.

102. "Census of Lake Traverse Indians taken by Charlie Crawford and Samuel J. Brown, October 3, 1867," Joseph R. and Samuel J. Brown and Family Papers, Reel 5.

103. "List of Indians at Wadsworth, January 1869," Joseph R. and Samuel J. Brown and Family Papers, Reel 5.

104. Mary Riggs to her mother, 28 Aug. 1838, Stephen Return Riggs Papers, PHS.

105. Stephen Riggs, "Home Notes," 4 July 1866, Stephen R. Riggs Papers, CWS.

106. John B. Renville to Stephen Riggs, 1868, Stephen R. Riggs and Family Papers.

107. Deloria, *Dakotas Way of Life*, p. 60.

108. Ibid.

109. Stephen Riggs to Annie Ackley, 8 Nov. 1871, C. E. Van Norman, Jr. Papers, CWS.

110. List of Renville lands in Brown County, 1872, Joseph R. and Samuel J. Brown and Family Papers, Reel 7.

111. All the previous census information on Charles Crawford comes from FamilySearch. See, https://www.familysearch.org/tree/person/sources/GZ76-MJX. Thank you to Misty Heiden, Charles Crawford's great-great granddaughter, who uploaded twenty different census records, several images, and the land allotment certificate for Charles Crawford.

112. Stephen Riggs, "Home Notes," 29 June 1866, Stephen R. Riggs Papers, CWS.

113. Stephen Riggs, "Home Notes," July 1866, Stephen R. Riggs Papers, CWS.

114. Stephen Riggs to Annie Ackley, 8 Nov. 1871, C. E. Van Norman, Jr. Papers, CWS.

115. Angelique A. EagleWoman, "Re-Establishing the Sisseton-Wahpeton Oyate's Reservation Boundaries: Building a Legal Rationale from Current International Law," *American Indian Legal Review* 29, no. 2 (2005): 246.

116. Stephen Riggs to Selah Treat, 2 Sept. 1868, ABCFM Papers, Reel 769, Wheaton College, Il.

117. "Census of Lake Traverse Indians taken by Charlie Crawford and Samuel J. Brown, October 3, 1867," Joseph R. and Samuel J. Brown and Family Papers, Reel 5.

118. Stephen Riggs to Selah Treat, 15 June 1865, ABCFM Papers, Reel 769.

119. *Missionary Herald* 63, no. 4 (1866): 120.

120. Stephen Riggs, "Home Notes," July 1866, Stephen R. Riggs Papers, CWS. See also, *Missionary Herald*, 62, no. 10 (1866): 292.

121. *Missionary Herald* 63, no. 12 (1867): 389.

122. Stephen Riggs, "Home Notes," 29 June 1866, Stephen R. Riggs Papers, CWS.

123. Ibid.

124. Ibid.

125. Stephen Riggs, "Home Notes," 28 Aug. 1867, Stephen R. Riggs Papers, CWS.

126. George D. Crocker to Stephen Riggs, 29 Apr. 1869, Stephen R. Riggs and Family Papers.

127. Stephen Riggs to Robbie and Cornelia Riggs, 19 June 1870, Stephen R. Riggs and Family Papers.

128. Stephen Riggs to Mrs. Ackley, 8 Nov. 1871, Van Norman Collection, CWS.

129. *Iapi Oaye*, 1 Oct. 1875, 4.

130. For a copy of the allotment certificate, see https://www.familysearch.org/tree/person/memories/GZ76-MJX.

131. Moses Adams, "Report on Conditions on the Reservation," August 1872, Box 2, July–Dec. 1872, Moses N. Adams Papers, MNHS.

132. Moses Adams, "Report," 9 Aug. 1872, Box 2, July–Dec. 1872, Moses N. Adams Papers.

133. Moses Adams, "Rules for Reservation," 7 Jan. 1873, Box 3, Jan.–July 1873, Moses N. Adams Papers.

134. Moses Adams, "Report on Conditions on the Reservation," August 1872, Box 2, July–Dec. 1872, Moses N. Adams Papers.

135. Anderson, *Gabriel Renville*, p. 89.

136. Commissioner of Indian Affairs to Moses Adams, 12 Feb. 1873, Box 3, Jan.–July 1873, Moses N. Adams Papers.

137. Commissioner of Indian Affairs to Moses Adams, 24 Mar. 1873, Box 3, Jan.–July 1873, Moses N. Adams Papers.

138. Moses Adams to the Commissioner of Indian Affairs, May 1873, Box 3, Jan.–July 1873, Moses N. Adams Papers.

139. Everett W. Sterling, "Moses N. Adams: A Missionary as Indian Agent," *Minnesota History* 35, no. 4 (Dec. 1956): 173.

140. *Annual Report of the ABCFM* (1873), p. 81.

141. Black Thunder, *Ehanna Woyakapi*, p. 61.

142. *The Annual Report of the ABCFM* (1875), noted that Adams "retired from his post, having performed a valuable service for Dakotas who were placed under his care." (p. 72) See also, Riggs, *Mary and I*, p. 272.

143. Quoted in Anderson, *Gabriel Renville*, p. 97.

144. Moses Adams to the Commissioner of Indian Affairs, 24 Jan. 1873, Box 3, Jan.–July 1873, Moses N. Adams Papers.

145. Quoted in, Sterling, "Moses N. Adams: A Missionary as Indian Agent," 173.

146. Ibid., p. 174.

147. Stephen Riggs to Thomas Williamson, 16 Dec. 1872, Stephen R. Riggs Papers, CWS.

148. While affiliated with the Good Will mission, both Martha and Wyllys received government pay—$35 for Martha and $60 for Wyllys per month—for working in the boarding school. See Department of the Interior, Office of Indian Affairs, 5 Dec. 1873, 11 July–Dec. 1873, Box 4, Moses N. Adams Papers.

149. "Dakota Mission," *Missionary Herald* 67, no. 3 (1871): 71.

150. Stephen Riggs and Martha Riggs Morris wrote hundreds of letters in the 1870s to and from the Good Will mission. These letters are found in the Stephen R. Riggs and Family Papers at the Minnesota Historical Society and the Stephen R. Riggs Papers Center for Western Studies. The ABCFM Papers, located in microfilm at Wheaton College, also contain hundreds of letters from Good Will Mission. Given the extensive nature of this correspondence I did not read every letter. I did, however, skim most of these letters looking for Angelique's name, which I rarely (if ever) found. Given the fact that I did not carefully read every letter, there very well could be some references that I missed.

I can safely say, however, that the number of references to Angelique almost entirely disappeared in this correspondence, especially when compared with references to her earlier years when the Riggs family believed that she had been successfully Christianized and "civilized."

CHAPTER 6

1. Angelique Renville to E. St. Julien Cox, 6 Sept. 1869, Joseph R. and Samuel J. Brown and Family Papers, Reel 6.

2. Mary Riggs to Henrietta Longley, 14 Sept. 1839, Stephen Return Riggs Papers, PHS.

3. Bethany Ruth Berger, "After Pocahontas: Indian Woman and the Law, 1830 to 1834," *American Indian Law Review* 21, no. 1 (1997), 9.

4. Berger, "After Pocahontas," p. 4.

5. Charles Wagner to Stephen Riggs, 23 Feb. 1863, Stephen R. Riggs and Family Papers.

6. Nicollet County, Minnesota, Probate Records 1860–1897, 1856–1859, 118–119; 204–205, https://www.familysearch.org/ark:/61903/3:1:3Q9M-C9RD-H41?mode=g&cat=538439

7. *United States, Wills and Probate Records, 1801–1925*, Minnesota, Nicollet Country, 315. Ancestry.com, https://www.ancestry.com/imageviewer/collections/9070/images/007667805_00309?usePUB=true&_phsrc=IBM244&_phstart=successSource&usePUBJs=true&pId=3738522c

8. The court did not count Agnes's many half-siblings as legal heirs, even though according to Dakota cultural practices children from polygamous marriages were all siblings regardless of whether they had different biological mothers.

9. *U.S., Wills and Probate Records, 1801–1925*, Minnesota, Nicollet Country, 326–28.

10. Jonas Pettijohn to Stephen Riggs, 17 Sept. 1863, 110, Stephen R. Riggs and Family Papers.

11. Ibid.

12. Jonas Pettijohn to Stephen Riggs, 12 May 1865, Stephen R. Riggs and Family Papers.

13. Jonas Pettijohn to Stephen Riggs, 17 Sept. 1863, Stephen R. Riggs and Family Papers.

14. *U.S., Wills and Probate Records, 1801–1925*, Minnesota, Nicollet Country, 309; 318.

15. Ibid., p. 309.

16. Ibid.

17. Jonas Pettijohn to Stephen Riggs, 5 Dec. 1863, Stephen R. Riggs and Family Papers. Land records for Nicollet County, Minnesota (where Agnes's and Angelique's lands were located) have been digitized and are available on the website FamilySearch.Org. Thank you to Dr. Jimmy Sweet for directing me to these records. For the list of Nicollet land records, see https://www

.familysearch.org/search/catalog/447348?availability=Family%20History%20Library, accessed 30 Dec. 2021. All the land records referenced in this chapter's notes come from FamilySearch.Org. For records of Agnes's land sale, see, *General Index to Deeds*, Grantor Vol. 1–4 1853–1913, image 110; and *General Index to Deeds*, vol. G-H, K, 1862–1867, image 660. The first volume contains the brief general information about land sales; the second contains the longer written records of the sale.

18. Jonas Pettijohn to Stephen Riggs, 18 Oct. 1863, Stephen R. Riggs and Family Papers.

19. Jonas Pettijohn to Stephen Riggs, 28 Dec. 1863, 106, Stephen R. Riggs and Family Papers.

20. See, *General Index to Deeds*, Grantor Vol. 1–4 1853–1913, image 110; and *General Index to Deeds*, vol. K, image 862.

21. Jonas Pettijohn to Stephen Riggs, 12 May 1865, Stephen R. Riggs and Family Papers.

22. For a list of all the fees involved in settling the estate, see *U.S., Wills and Probate Records, 1801–1925*, Minnesota, Nicollet Country, 306.

23. Jonas Pettijohn to Stephen Riggs, 12 May 1865, Stephen R. Riggs and Family Papers.

24. Jonas Pettijohn to Stephen Riggs, 26 Oct. 1863, Stephen R. Riggs and Family Papers.

25. Jonas Pettijohn to Stephen Riggs, 7 Mar. 1864, Stephen R. Riggs and Family Papers.

26. Jonas Pettijohn to Stephen Riggs, 15 May 1864, Stephen R. Riggs and Family Papers.

27. *U.S., Wills and Probate Records, 1801–1925*, Minnesota, Nicollet Country, 311.

28. Jonas Pettijohn to Stephen Riggs, 27 Mar. 1865, Stephen R. Riggs and Family Papers.

29. Jonas Pettijohn to Stephen Riggs, 28 Dec. 1863, Stephen R. Riggs and Family Papers.

30. Jonas Pettijohn to Stephen Riggs, 12 Jan. 1864, Stephen R. Riggs and Family Papers.

31. *U.S., Wills and Probate Records, 1801–1925*, Minnesota, Nicollet Country, 1266.

32. *U.S., Wills and Probate Records, 1801–1925*, Minnesota, Nicollet Country, 1265–1271. This file includes Riggs's petition, a copy of his guardian's bond, and guardian oath.

33. Jonas Pettijohn to Stephen Riggs, 7 Mar. 1864, Stephen R. Riggs and Family Papers.

34. Unfortunately, the letter detailing the sale of Thomas's land does not identify the author's name, though it does appear to match the writing of a man named S. Anderson—a prominent land profiteer—who sent numerous letters to Samuel Brown with schemes to obtain and sell Dakota scrip. N.A.

to Samuel Brown, 10 Mar. 1873, Joseph R. and Samuel J. Brown and Family Papers, Reel 8.

35. Jonas Pettijohn to Stephen Riggs, 30 Dec. 1863, Stephen R. Riggs and Family Papers.

36. In April 1864, Angelique wrote Riggs that "You may do what you please with the watch." Angelique Renville to Stephen Riggs, Apr. 1864, Stephen R. Riggs and Family Papers.

37. Daniel Renville to Stephen Riggs, 15 Feb. 1863, Stephen R. Riggs and Family Papers. This information is speculative. Louis Garcia translated this letter, which was written in Dakota, and found it to be particularly difficult to translate. His best guess was what I noted above, but Daniel's sentences could also have another meaning due to the difficult language used. A special thanks to Mr. Garcia for his invaluable work on this challenging letter.

38. Stephen Riggs to Thomas Williamson, 9 Apr. 1873, Stephen R. Riggs Papers, CWS.

39. Jonas Pettijohn to Stephen Riggs, 26 Oct. 1863, Stephen R. Riggs and Family Papers.

40. Jonas Pettijohn to Stephen Riggs, 7 Mar. 1864, Stephen R. Riggs and Family Papers.

41. Jonas Pettijohn to Stephen Riggs, 15 May 1864, Stephen R. Riggs and Family Papers.

42. Stephen Riggs to Thomas Williamson, 9 Feb. 1874, Stephen R. Riggs Papers, CWS.

43. https://www.investopedia.com/terms/q/quiet-title-action.asp, accessed 30 Dec. 2021.

44. According to Minnesota state statute, guardianships ended when "the minor arrives at full age." In addition, the "marriage of a female under guardianship as a minor, shall terminate such guardianship." *The Statutes at Large of the State of Minnesota, Comprising the General Statutes of 1866*, vol. 1 (Chicago: Callaghan and Company, 1873), 704, 708.

45. "Account for Angelique Renville with S. R. Riggs, guardian," Joseph R. and Samuel J. Brown and Family Papers, Reel 4.

46. *U.S., Wills and Probate Records, 1801–1925*, Minnesota, Nicollet Country, 575.

47. Stephen Riggs, "Home Notes," 26 June 1866, Stephen R. Riggs Papers, CWS.

48. Stephen Riggs, "Home Notes," 4 July 1866, Stephen R. Riggs Papers, CWS.

49. Mary Riggs to Lucy Spooner Drake, 29 Oct. 1865, Stephen R. Riggs Papers, CWS.

50. Mary Riggs to Stephen Riggs, 2 Aug. 1866, Stephen R. Riggs Papers, CWS.

51. Mary Riggs to Stephen Riggs, 2 Aug. 1866, Stephen R. Riggs Papers, CWS.

52. Mary Riggs to Stephen Riggs, 21 Sept. 1867, Stephen R. Riggs and Family Papers.

53. R. H. Bennet to Samel J. Brown, 13 Jan. 1870, Joseph R. and Samuel J. Brown and Family Papers, Reel 6.

54. See, *General Index to Deeds, Grantor v. 1–4 1853–1913*, image 253; and *General Index to Deeds*, vol. N, image 205.

55. Angelique Renville to E. St. Julien Cox, 6 Sept. 1869, Joseph R. and Samuel J. Brown and Family Papers, Reel 6.

56. *General Index to Deeds*, vol. N, image 205.

57. Angelique Renville to E. St. Julien Cox, 6 Sept. 1869, Joseph R. and Samuel J. Brown and Family Papers, Reel 6.

58. Ibid.

59. E. St. Julien Cox to Joseph Brown, 20 Mar. 1870, Joseph R. and Samuel J. Brown and Family Papers, Reel 6.

60. Angelique Crawford to E. St. Julien Cox, 20 Dec. 1870, Joseph R. and Samuel J. Brown and Family Papers, Reel 6.

61. E. St. Julien Cox to Samuel J. Brown, 31 Dec. 1870, Joseph R. and Samuel J. Brown and Family Papers, Reel 6.

62. E. St. Julien Cox to Samuel Brown, 13 Feb. 1871, Joseph R. and Samuel J. Brown and Family Papers, Reel 7.

63. E. St. Julien Cox to Joseph R. Brown, 20 Mar. 1870, Joseph R. and Samuel J. Brown and Family Papers, Reel 6.

64. *Charles Crawford and Angelique Crawford v. William H. Grant and Francis X. Brosseau*, 772 (Minnesota, Nicollet County District Court 1871). To find this case, see Nicollet County, Civil and Criminal Case Files, Judgement Books and Judgement Dockets, MNHS.

65. Deborah A. Rosen, "Women and Property across Colonial America: A Comparison of Legal Systems in New Mexico and New York," *The William and Mary Quarterly* 60, no. 2 (Apr. 2003): 365. See also, Micah A. Pawling, "A 'Labyrinth of Uncertainties': Penobscot River Islands, Land Assignments, and Indigenous Women Proprietors in Nineteenth-Century Maine," *American Indian Quarterly* 42, no. 4 (Fall 2018): 454–487.

66. The act stated: "All property owned by any married woman, at the time or previous to her marriage, shall continue to be her separate property after marriage." *General Laws of Minnesota for 1869*, chapter 56, 69. https://www.revisor.mn.gov/laws/1869/0/General+Laws/Chapter/56/pdf/, accessed 30 Dec. 2021.

67. *The General Statutes of the State of Minnesota*, 1866, chapter 69, 499. https://www.revisor.mn.gov/statutes/1866/, accessed 30 Dec. 2021.

68. E. St. Julien Cox to Joseph Brown, 20 Mar. 1870, Joseph R. and Samuel J. Brown and Family Papers, Reel 6.

69. *Charles Crawford and Angelique Crawford v. William H. Grant and Francis X. Brosseau*, 772 (Minnesota, Nicollet County District Court 1871).

70. Ibid.

71. Ibid.

72. All quotations from this case come from *Adele Buckholz and Emil Buck-*

holz v. William H. Grant, Francis X. Brosseau, and Abner C. Smith (State of Minnesota Supreme Court, 1870), William Henry Grant Papers, MNHS.

73. *Charles Crawford and Angelique Crawford v. William H. Grant and Francis X. Brosseau*, 772 (Minnesota, Nicollet County District Court 1871).

74. E. St. Julien Cox to Samuel Brown, 18 July 1871, Joseph R. and Samuel J. Brown and Family Papers, Reel 7.

75. Ibid.

76. E. St. Julien Cox to Samuel Brown, 30 Oct. 1871, Joseph R. and Samuel J. Brown and Family Papers, Reel 7.

77. Ibid.

78. Francis Brosseau to Samuel Brown, 2 June 1872, Joseph R. and Samuel J. Brown and Family Papers, Reel 8.

79. Francis Brosseau to Samuel Brown, 14 July 1872, Joseph R. and Samuel J. Brown and Family Papers, Reel 8.

80. Francis Brosseau to Samuel Brown, 2 July 1872, Joseph R. and Samuel J. Brown and Family Papers, Reel 8.

81. Francis Brosseau to Samuel Brown, 8 July 1872. Joseph R. and Samuel J. Brown and Family Papers, Reel 8.

82. E. St. Julien Cox to Samuel Brown, 3 Apr. 1872, Joseph R. and Samuel J. Brown and Family Papers, Reel 8.

83. Ibid.

84. *Charles Crawford and Angelique Crawford v. William H. Grant and Francis X. Brosseau*, 772 (Minnesota, Nicollet County District Court 1871).

85. Mary Riggs to Stephen Riggs, 20 July 1867, Stephen R. Riggs Papers, CWS.

86. Auditor's Office to Stephen Riggs, 2 Apr. 1869, Stephen R. Riggs and Family Papers.

87. Ibid.

88. *General Index to Deeds*, Grantee, Vol. 1–2, 1853–1881, image 561. https://www.familysearch.org/ark:/61903/3:1:3Q9M-C371-YRCZ?i=560&cat=447348, accessed 30 Dec. 2021.

89. *General Index to Deeds*, vol. N, image 430–31.

90. *General Index to Deeds*, Grantor, vol. 1–4, 1853–1913, image 255; and *General Index to Deeds*, vol. R, image 530.

91. Christian W. McMillen, "'The Red Man and the White Plague': Rethinking Race, Tuberculosis, and American Indians, ca. 1890–1950," *Bulletin of the History of Medicine* 82, no. 3 (Fall 2008): 610–611.

92. Riggs, *Mary and I*, 221.

93. Elizabeth James, "'Hardly a Family is Free From the Disease': Tuberculosis, Health Care, and Assimilation Policy on the Nez Perce Reservation, 1908–1942," *Oregon Historical Quarterly*, 112 no. 2 (Summer 2011): 144.

94. Meyer, *History of Santee Sioux*, p. 200.

95. ARCIA, p. 323.

96. Stephen Riggs to Selah Treat, 7 Jan. 1868, mss. 310, no. 82, ABCFM Papers; and John Renville to Stephen Riggs, [nd], mss. 309, no. 214, ABCFM Papers.

97. Catherine Tatidutawin to Jane Huggins Holtzclaw (translation by Alfred Riggs), 20 Mar. 1868, Alexander G. Huggins and Family Papers, MNHS.

98. John B. Renville to Stephen Riggs, [nd], mss. 309, no. 214, ABCFM Papers.

99. James, "'Hardly a Family is Free from the Disease'," p. 143.

100. Morris, "Angelique Renville Crawford."

101. All quotations from Martha's description of Angelique's death come from Morris, "Angelique Renville Crawford."

EPILOGUE

1. The title of this chapter references one of my favorite books, *Ties that Bind: The Story of an Afro-Cherokee Family in Slavery and Freedom*, by Tya Miles. Miles beautifully narrates the complexities and tensions that both separated and bound together an Afro-Cherokee family during the nineteenth century.

2. All quotations from Martha's description of Angelique's death come from Morris, "Angelique Renville Crawford."

3. *Missionary Herald* 77, no. 8 (Aug. 1881): 321.

4. *Word Carrier*, Sept.–Oct. 1890, p. 26.

5. Stephen Riggs to Anna Ackley, 26 June 1875, C. E. Van Norman Jr. Collection, CWS.

6. *Word Carrier*, 1 Oct. 1887, p. 3.

7. *Iapi Oaye*, 1 July 1879, p. 28; and *Iapi Oyate*, 1 Dec. 1882, p. 94.

8. "Theological Institute," 29–30 Sept. 1884, Santee Normal Training School, Santee Agency, Neb., 1885.

9. Stephen Riggs to Anna Ackley, 26 June 1875, C. E. Van Norman Jr. Collection, CWS.

10. Etta Crawford, for example, attended the Santee Normal Training School and then worked at the school after her graduation. Daniel Littlefield, Jr., and James W. Parins, *A Biobibliography of Native American Writers 1772–1924: A Supplement* (Metuchen, N.J.: Scarecrow Press, 1985), p. 12.

11. *Word Carrier*, 1 Sept. 1906, p. 18.

12. *Word Carrier*, 1 Sept. 1903, p. 19.

13. *Iapi Oaye: Vital Statistics, 1871–1879*, trans. Etta Perkins, p. 42, https://history.sd.gov/archives/docs/1871-1879.pdf, accessed 30 Dec. 2021.

14. *Iapi Oaye: Vital Statistics 1871–1879*, trans. Etta Perkins, p. 36,

15. *Iapi Oaye: Vital Statistics, 1880–1889*, trans. Etta Perkins, p. 10, https://history.sd.gov/archives/docs/1880-1889.pdf, accessed 30 Dec. 2021.

16. *Iapi Oaye*, 1 Mar. 1879, p. 12.

17. Stephen Riggs to Martha Riggs, 18–22 Mar. 1869, Stephen R. Riggs and Family Papers; and Riggs, *Mary and I*, p. 239.

18. *Annual Report of the ABCFM* (1872), p. 79.

19. Stephen Riggs to Annie Ackley, 4 Mar. 1872, C.E. Van Norman Jr. Collection, CWS.

20. Stephen Riggs to Anna Ackley, 22 Jan. 1872, folder 1, C.E. Van Norman Jr. Collection, CWS.

21. *Iapi Oyate*, 1 July 1879, p. 28.

22. Anna Jane Riggs Warner, *Our Martha* (Santee Normal Training School Press, nd.), p. 11.

23. Warner, *Our Martha*, p. 11.

24. For information on the Santee Normal Boarding School and the "Friends of the Indian Movement," see "Proceedings of the Fourteenth Annual Meeting of the Lake Mohonk Conference of the Friends of the Indian" (Lake Mohonk Conference, 1897), p. 64. The Riggs brothers often attended this national annual meeting.

25. Riggs, *Mary and I*, p. 261.

26. See Jennifer Graber, *The Gods of Indian Country: Religion and the Struggle for the American West* (New York: Oxford University Press, 2018).

27. Tom Holm, "Indian Lobbyists: Cherokee Opposition to the Allotment of Tribal Lands," *American Indian Quarterly* 5, no. 2 (May 1979): 115.

28. For more information about the second generation of Dakota missionaries, see Linda Clemmons, "'Substitute in this army of the Lord': Missionary Parents, Their Children, and the Conflicted Nature of Missionary Work," *South Dakota History* 51, no. 2 (Summer 2021): 166–95.

29. Moses Adams to Stephen Riggs, 10 Dec. 1868, Stephen R. Riggs and Family Papers.

30. Riggs, *Mary and I*, p. 406.

31. Ibid., p. 255.

32. Thomas Williamson, "Obituary of Miss Julia Lafromboise, 7 Nov. 1871, mss. 309, no. 255, ABCFM Papers.

33. Ibid.

34. Riggs, *Mary and I*, p. 255.

35. Ibid.

36. Riggs, *Mary and I*, p. 407.

37. Two letters reference Isabella's proposed "Triograph." See Stephen Riggs to Martha Riggs Morris, 13 Feb. 1880; and Stephen Riggs to Martha Riggs Morris, 25 Feb. 1880, Stephen R. Riggs and Family Papers. Her father, however, did not have much faith that his daughter would complete the book on time.

BIBLIOGRAPHY

PRIMARY SOURCES

Manuscript Collections

Ancestry.com

Digitized Probate Records: Joseph Renville, Agnes Renville, Joseph Renville, William Renville

The Center for Western Studies, Augustana University, Sioux Falls, SD (CWS)

Alfred L. Riggs Papers

Stephen R. Riggs Papers

Thomas L. Riggs Papers

C. E. Van Norman, Jr. Papers

FamilySearch.org

Digitized Nicollet County Probate and Land Records

Minnesota Historical Society, St. Paul, MN (MNHS)

ABCFM Papers, typescript

Alexander G. Huggins and Family Papers

Alfred Longley and Family Papers

Henry Hastings Sibley Papers, microfilm

James Hinds Papers

Joseph R. and Samuel J. Brown and Family Papers, microfilm

Lorenzo Lawrence Papers

Martin McLeod Papers

Minnesota Census Records

Moses N. Adams Papers

Pond Family Papers

Stephen R. Riggs and Family Papers, online digitized

Stephen R. Riggs Family Correspondence, Concerning Lac qui Parle Mission and other Matters, 1832–1869, typescript.

Thomas S. Williamson Papers

William Henry Grant Papers

Presbyterian Historical Society, Philadelphia, PA (PHS)

American Indian Correspondence: The Presbyterian Historical Society Collection of Missionaries' Letters, RG 224

John Poage Williamson Papers

Presbyterian Church in the U.S.A Dakota Mission Collection

Stephen Return Riggs Papers

South Dakota State Historical Society

Doane Robinson Collection, Samuel J. Brown correspondence

Wheaton College
ABCFM Papers, microfilm

Newspapers/Series
Annual Report of the American Board for Commissioners for Foreign Missions
Annual Report of the Commissioner of Indian Affairs
Dakota Tawaxitku Kin, or, The Dakota Friend
The Friends' Intelligencer United with the Friends' Journal
Iapi Oaye. The Word Carrier
The Journal (New Ulm, Minn.)
The Minnesota Pioneer
Minnesota Weekly Times
The Minnesotian
The Missionary Herald
The Saint Paul Press
Shakopee Weekly Argue
The St. Paul Daily Press
The St. Paul Press
St. Paul Weekly Minnesotian
Star Tribune
Winona Weekly Republican
The Word Carrier

State/Government Documents
Minnesota Territory and State Statutes
National Archives, Record Group 75
U.S. Department of the Interior, Bureau of Land Management. General Land Office Records, https://glorecords.blm.gov/

Printed Primary Sources
Anderson, Gary Clayton and Alan R. Woolworth, eds. *Through Dakota Eyes: Narrative Accounts of the Minnesota Indian War of 1862*. St. Paul: Minnesota Historical Society Press, 1988.
Barton, Winifred W. *John P. Williamson: A Brother to the Sioux*. New York: Fleming H. Revell Company, 1919.
Bray, Edmund and Martha Coleman Bray. *Joseph N. Nicollet on the Plains and Prairies*. St. Paul: Minnesota Historical Society Press, 1993.
Charles Crawford and Angelique Crawford v. William H. Grant and Francis X. Brosseau, 772 (Minnesota, Nicollet County District Court 1871), MNHS.
"Dakota Bibliography." *Minnesota Historical Collections* 3 (1870–1880): 37–42.
Day, George E. *The Theological Eclectic* vol. 1. Cincinnati: William Scott, 1864.
Deloria, Ella. *The Dakota Way of Life*. Ella Deloria Archive, http://zia.aisri.indiana.edu/deloria_archive/browse.php

———. *Speaking of Indians*. Lincoln: University of Nebraska Press, 1998.

Eastman, Charles. *From the Deep Woods to Civilization*. Lincoln: University of Nebraska Press, 1977.

———. *Indian Boyhood*. Lincoln: University of Nebraska Press, 1991.

———. *Old Indian Days*. Lincoln: University of Nebraska Press, 1991.

———. *The Soul of the Indian: An Interpretation*. Lincoln: University of Nebraska Press, 1980.

Hansen, James L., ed. "A Roll of Sioux Mixed-Bloods, 1855–56." *Minnesota Genealogical Journal* 7 (1984): 613.

———. "Two Early Lists of Mixed-Blood Sioux." *Minnesota Genealogical Journal* 6 (Nov. 1986): 523–30.

In the Court of Claims. The Sisseton and Wahpeton Bands of Sioux Indians vs. The United States. Original Petition. Washington D.C.: McGill and Wallace, 1901.

Isch, John. *The Dakota Trials: Including the Complete Transcripts and Explanatory Notes on the Military Commission Trials in Minnesota, 1862–1864*. New Ulm, Minn.: Brown County Historical Society, 2013.

Kappler, Charles J. *Indian Affairs. Laws and Treaties*. Washington: Government Printing Office, 1904.

Mayer, Frank Blackwell. *With Pen and Pencil on the Frontier in 1851*. St. Paul: Minnesota Historical Society Press, 1986.

McClure, Nancy. "The Story of Nancy McClure. Captivity Among the Sioux." *Minnesota Historical Society Collections* 6 (1894): 438–60.

McGuffey's Readers

Monjeau-Marz, Corinne L. *The Dakota Indian Internment at Fort Snelling, 1862–1864*. St. Paul, MN: Prairie Smoke Press, 2005.

"Names of the Condemned Dakota Men." *American Indian Quarterly* 28, no. 1–2 (Winter–Spring 2004): 175–83.

The Ohio Female College at College Hill, Hamilton Co., Ohio with the Plan, Reasons, and Encouragement for its Permanent Endowment as a First-Class Female Seminary. New York: Edward O. Jenkins, 1862.

Oneroad, Amos E. *Being Dakota: Tales and Traditions of the Sisseton and Wahpeton*. St. Paul: Minnesota Historical Society Press, 2005.

Perkins, Etta, trans. *Iapi Oaye: Vital Statistics, 1871–1879*. https://history.sd.gov/archives/docs/1871-1879.pdf.

———. *Iapi Oaye: Vital Statistics, 1880–1889*. https://history.sd.gov/archives/docs/1880-1889.pdf.

Pond, Samuel W. *The Dakota or Sioux in Minnesota as They Were in 1835*. St. Paul: Minnesota Historical Society Press, 1986.

Pond, Samuel. *Two Volunteer Missionaries among the Dakotas or The Story of the labors of Samuel W. and Gideon H. Pond*. Boston: Congregational Sunday School Publishing Society, 1893.

Renville, Gabriel. "A Sioux Narrative of the Outbreak in 1862, and of Sibley's

Expedition in 1863." *Minnesota Historical Society Collections* 10, no. 2 (1905): 595–618.

Riggs, Maida Leonard. *A Small Bit of Bread and Butter: Letters from Dakota Territory*. South Deerfield, Mass.: Ash Grove Press, 1996.

Riggs, Stephen R. "Biography of Men Connected with the Dakota Mission, 1835, 1860." Stephen R. Riggs and Family Papers.

———. *Dakota ABC Wowapi*. Santee Agency, NE: Santee Normal Training School Press, 1929.

———. *A Dakota-English Dictionary*. Washington: Government Printing Office, 1890.

———. "Dakota Portraits." *Minnesota History Bulletin* (Nov. 1918).

———. "The Dakota Mission." *Collections of the Minnesota Historical Society* 3 (1870–1880): 115–28.

———. *Mary and I: Forty Years with the Sioux*. Chicago: W.G. Holmes, 1880.

———. *Model First Reader: Wayawa Tokaheya*. Chicago: Sherwood and Co., 1873.

———. *Taȟ-Koo Wah-Kaŋ́; or, The Gospel among the Dakota*. Boston: Congregational Sabbath School and Publishing Company, 1869.

Riggs, Stephen and Martha Riggs. *A Tableau of the families, and single persons, connected with the American Board of Commissioners for Foreign Mission in the Dakota Mission, during the quarter of a century 1835–1860*. September 1861, MNHS.

"A Sioux Story of the War: Chief Big Eagle's Story of the Sioux Outbreak." *Collections of the Minnesota Historical Society* vol. 6 (1894): 382–400.

Sibley, Henry Hastings. "Sketch of John Other Day." *Collections of the Minnesota State Historical Society* 3 (1870–1880): 99–102.

Standing Bear, Luther. *My People the Sioux*. Boston: Houghton Mifflin, 1928.

The Thirteenth Annual Catalogue and Prospectus of the Ohio Female College, at College Hill, Hamilton Co., Ohio, for 1862. Cincinnati: Spiller and Brother, Book and Job Printer, 1862.

The War of the Rebellion: A Compilation of the Official Records of the Union and Confederate Armies, series 1, vol. 13. Washington: Government Printing Office, 1885.

Warner, Anna Jane Riggs. *Our Martha*. Santee Normal Training School Press, nd.

Whipple, Henry Benjamin. *Light and Shadows of a Long Episcopate*. New York: The Macmillan Company, 1902.

Zeman, Carrie Reber and Kathryn Zabelle Derounian-Stodola, eds. *Mary Butler Renville, Dispatches from the Dakota War: A Thrilling Narrative from Indian Captivity*. Lincoln: University of Nebraska Press, 2012.

SECONDARY SOURCES

Ackermann, Gertrude. "Joseph Renville of Lac qui Parle." *Minnesota History* 12, no. 3 (Sept. 1931): 231–46.

Adams, David Wallace and Crista DeLuzio, eds. *On the Borders of Love and Power: Families and Kinship in the Intercultural American Southwest.* Berkely, University of California Press, 2012.

Anderson, Gary Clayton. *Gabriel Renville: From the Dakota War to the Creation of the Sisseton-Wahpeton Reservation, 1825–1892.* Pierre: South Dakota Historical Society Press, 2018.

———. *Kinsmen of Another Kind: Dakota-White Relations in the Upper Mississippi Valley, 1650–1862.* St. Paul: Minnesota Historical Society Press, 1997.

———. *Massacre in Minnesota: The Dakota War of 1862, the Most Violent Ethnic Conflict in American History.* Norman: University of Oklahoma Press, 2019.

———. "The Removal of the Mdewakanton Dakota in 1837." *South Dakota History* 10, no. 4 (Fall 1980): 310–33.

Babcock, Willoughby M. "Major Lawrence Taliaferro, Indian Agent," *The Mississippi Valley Historical Review* 11, no. 3 (Dec. 1924): 358–75.

Barnard, Charles H. and John Jones. *Farm real estate values in the United States by counties, 1850–1982.* Washington, D.C.: U.S. Dept. of Agriculture, Economic Research Service, 1987.

Beatty, James K. "Interpreting the Shawnee Sun: Literacy and Cultural Persistence in Indian Country, 1833–1841." *Kansas History* 31, no. 4 (Winter 2008–2009): 243–59.

Bell, John. "The Sioux War Panorama and American Mythic History." *Theatre Journal* 48, no. 3 (Oct. 1996): 279–99.

Berg, Richard E. and James E. Myster. "Archaeological Remains of Two Mid-Century Dakota Homes Associated with the Riggs Hazelwood Mission Site." *The Minnesota Archaeologist* 65 (2006): 129–73.

Berg, Scott M. "Lincoln's Choice." *Quarterly Journal of Military History* 26, no. 2 (Winter 2014): 33.

Berger, Bethany Ruth. "After Pocahontas: Indian Woman and the Law, 1830 to 1834." *American Indian Law Review* 21, no. 1 (1997): 1–62.

Berkhofer, Robert F. Jr. *The White Man's Indian: Images of the American Indian From Columbus to Present.* New York: Alfred A. Knopf, 1978.

Berman, Cassandra. "Motherhood on a Mission: Missionaries, 'Heathens,' and the Maternal Ideal in the Early American Republic." *Early American Studies* 17, no. 4 (Fall 2019): 474–97.

Bieder, Robert E. "The Representations of Indian Bodies in Nineteenth-Century American Anthropology." *American Indian Quarterly* 20, no. 2 (Spring 1996): 165–79.

Black Thunder, Elijah et al. *Ehanna Woyakapi: History and Culture of the Sisseton-Wahpeton Sioux Tribe of South Dakota.* Sisseton-Wahpeton Tribe, 1975.

Blansett, Kent. *A Journey to Freedom: Richard Oakes, Alcatraz, and the Red Power Movement.* New Haven, Conn.: Yale University Press, 2018.

Brohough, Gustav O. "Sioux and Chippewa Half-breed Scrip and Its Application to the Minnesota Pine Lands." MA thesis, University of Wisconsin, 1906.

Burnham, Philip. *Song of Dewey Beard: Last Survivor of Little Bighorn.* Lincoln: University of Nebraska Press, 2018.

Bysiewicz, Shirley R. and Ruth Van de Mark. "The Legal Status of the Dakota Indian Woman." *American Indian Law Review* 3, no. 2 (1975): 255–312.

Carley, Kenneth. *The Dakota War of 1862*, 2nd ed. St. Paul: Minnesota Historical Society Press, 2001.

Carroll, Jane Lamm. *Daybreak Woman: An Anglo-Dakota Life*. St. Paul: Minnesota Historical Society Press, 2020.

———. "Naginowenah, Lucy Prescott, and the Wizard of Cereal Foods: Cultural Identity across Three Generations of an Anglo-Dakota Family." *Minnesota History* 63, no. 2 (Summer 2012): 58–68.

———. "'This Higgledy-Piggledy Assembly': The McLeods, an Anglo-Dakota Family in Early Minnesota." *Minnesota History* 60, no. 6 (Summer 2007): 218–33.

———. "'Who was Jane Lamont?': Anglo-Dakota Daughters on Early Minnesota." *Minnesota History* 59, no. 5 (Spring 2005): 184–96.

Carter, Sarah. *The Importance of Being Monogamous: Marriage and Nation Building in Western Canada to 1915*. University of Alberta Press, 2008.

Castañeda, Antonia. "Women of Color and the Rewriting of Western History: The Discourse, Politics, and Decolonization of History." *Pacific Historical Review* 61, no. 4 (Nov. 1992): 501–33.

Cavender Wilson, Angela. "The Role of Women in Eastern Dakota Society in the Early 1800s," Dakota Mission Culture Park Project, MNHS.

Child, Brenda. "The Boarding School as Metaphor." *Journal of American Indian Education* 57, no. 1 (Spring 2018): 37–57.

Chomsky, Carol. "The United States–Dakota War Trials: A Study in Military Injustice." *Stanford Law Review* 43, no. 1 (Jan. 1990), 13–98.

Clemmons, Linda. *Conflicted Mission: Faith, Disputes, and Deception on the Minnesota Frontier*. St. Paul: Minnesota Historical Society Press, 2014.

———. *Dakota in Exile: Untold Stories of Captives in the Aftermath of the U.S–Dakota War*. University of Iowa Press, 2019.

———. "'Substitute in this army of the Lord': Missionary Parents, Their Children, and the Conflicted Nature of Missionary Work." *South Dakota History* 51, no. 2 (Summer 2021): 166–95.

———. "We Find It a Difficult Work": Educating Dakota Children in Missionary Homes, 1835-1862." *American Indian Quarterly* 24, no. 4 (Autumn 2000): 570–600.

Clifton, James A. ed. *Being and Becoming Indian: Biographical Studies of North American Frontiers*. Waveland Press, Inc., 1989.

Clodfelter, Michael. *The Dakota War: The United States Army Versus the Sioux, 1862–1865* Jefferson, NC: McFarland, 1998.

Coleman, Michael C. "Not Race, but Grace: Presbyterian Missionaries and American Indians, 1837–1893." *The Journal of American History* 67, no. 1 (June 1980): 41–60.

Cook-Lynn, Elizabeth. "Life and Death in the Mainstream of American Indian Biography." *Wicazo Sa Review* 11, no. 2 (Autumn 1995): 91–93.

Coward, John M. *Indians Illustrated: The Image of Native Americans in the Pictorial Press*. Urbana: University of Illinois Press, 2016.

Creswell, R. J. *Among the Sioux: A Story of the Twin Cities and the Two Dakotas*. Minneapolis: The University Press, 1906.

Dahlin, Curtis A. *The Fort Sisseton Dakota Scouts and Their Camps in Eastern Dakota Territory*. Roseville, Minn., 2017.

Davis, Julie L. *Survival Schools: The American Indian Movement and Community Education in the Twin Cities*. Minneapolis: University of Minnesota Press, 2013.

Deer, Ada and Theda Perdue. *Making a Difference: My Fight for Native Rights and Social Justice*. Norman: University of Oklahoma Press, 2019.

DeMaillie, Raymond and Gilles Havard. "Writing the History of North America from Indian Country." *Journal de la Société des Américanistes* 105, no. 1 (2019): 13–40.

Denial, Catherine J. *Making Marriage: Husbands, Wives, and the American State in Dakota and Ojibwe Country*. St. Paul: Minnesota Historical Society Press, 2013.

———. "Pelagie Faribault's Island: Property, Kinship, and the Meaning of Marriage in Dakota Country." *Minnesota History* 62, no. 2 (Summer 2010): 48–59.

Dunlay, Thomas W. *Wolves for the Blue Soldiers: Indian Scouts and Auxiliaries with the United States Army, 1860–90*. Lincoln: University of Nebraska Press, 1987.

EagleWoman, Angelique A. "Re-Establishing the Sisseton-Wahpeton Oyate's Reservation Boundaries: Building a Legal Rationale from Current International Law." *American Indian Legal Review* 29, no. 2 (2005): 239–66.

Ehrlander, Mary F. *Walter Harper, Alaska Native Son*. Lincoln: University of Nebraska Press, 2018.

Ehrenhalt, Lizzie. "'The Most Satisfactory Proof': Revising an Anglo-Dakota Family History." *Minnesota History* 63, no. 4 (Winter 2012–2013): 144–55.

Estes, Nick. *Our History is Our Future: Standing Rock versus the Dakota Access Pipeline, and the Long Tradition of Indigenous Resistance*. New York: Verso, 2019.

Faimon, Mary Beth. "Ties that Bind: Remembering, Mourning, and Healing Historical Trauma." *American Indian Quarterly* 28, no. 1–2 (Winter–Spring 2004): 238–315.

Fear-Segal, Jacqueline. *White Man's Club: Schools, Race, and the Struggle of Indian Acculturation*. Lincoln: University of Nebraska Press, 2009.

Flynn, Sean J. *Without Reservation: Benjamin Reifel and American Indian Acculturation.* Pierre: South Dakota Historical Society Press, 2018.

Folwell, William Watts. *History of Minnesota* vol. 1. St. Paul: Minnesota Historical Society, 1922.

Foster, Thomas A., ed. *Women in Early America.* New York University Press, 2015.

Freeman, Victoria. "Attitudes Toward 'Miscegenation' in Canada, the United States, New Zealand, and Australia." *Native Studies Review* 16, no. 1 (2005): 196–221.

Gates, Charles M. "The Lac qui Parle Indian Mission." *Minnesota History* 16, no. 2 (June 1935): 133–51.

Geiger, Roger L., ed. *The American College in the Nineteenth Century.* Nashville, Tenn.: Vanderbilt University Press, 2000.

Gilman, Rhoda R. "Last Days of the Upper Mississippi Fur Trade." *Minnesota History*, 42, no. 4 (Winter 1970): 122–40.

Gordon-Reed, Annette. "Writing Early American Lives as Biography." *The William and Mary Quarterly*, 71, no. 4 (Oct. 2014): 491–516.

Graber, Jennifer. *The Gods of Indian Country: Religion and the Struggle for the American West.* New York: Oxford University Press, 2018.

Graves, Joseph L. Jr. *The Emperor's New Clothes: Biological Theories of Race at the Millennium.* New Brunswick, N.J.: Rutgers University Press, 2001.

Graybill, Andrew R. *The Red and The White: A Family Saga of The American West.* New York: W. W. Norton and Company, 2013.

Green, Rayna. "Native American Women." *Signs* 6, no. 2 (Winter 1980): 248–67.

Hämäläinen, Pekka. *Lakota America: A New History of Indigenous Power.* New Haven, Conn.: Yale University Press, 2019.

Hansen, Karen V, Grey Osterud, and Valerie Grim, "Land Was One of the Greatest Gifts": Women's Landownership in Dakota Indian, Immigrant Scandinavian, and African American Communities." *Great Plains Quarterly* 38, no. 3 (Summer 2018): 251–72.

Hassrick, Royal B. *The Sioux: Life and Customs of a Warrior Society.* Norman: University of Oklahoma Press, 1988.

Herbert, Maeve. "Explaining the Sioux Military Commission of 1862." *Columbia Human Rights Law Review* 40, no. 743 (2009): 743–98.

Higham, C. L. *Noble, Wretched and Redeemable: Protestant Missionaries to the Indians in Canada and the United States, 1820–1900.* Albuquerque: University of New Mexico Press, 2000.

Holm, Tom. "Indian Lobbyists: Cherokee Opposition to the Allotment of Tribal Lands." *American Indian Quarterly* 5, no. 2 (May 1979): 115–34.

Horsman, Reginald. *Race and Manifest Destiny: The Origins of American Racial Anglo-Saxonism.* Cambridge: Harvard University Press, 1981.

Hubbard, Lucius Frederick and William Pitt Murray, et al. *Minnesota In Three Centuries, 1655–1908: Early History* vol. 2. The Publishing Society of Minnesota, 1908.

Hyman, Colette A. *Dakota Women's Work: Creativity, Culture, and Exile.* St. Paul: Minnesota Historical Society Press, 2012.

Jacobs, Margaret. "The Eastmans and the Luhans: Interracial Marriage between White Women and Native American Men, 1875–1936." *Frontiers: A Journal of Women's Studies* 23, no. 3 (2002): 29–54.

———. "Entangled Histories: The Mormon Church and Indigenous Child Removal from 1850 to 2000." *Journal of Mormon History* 42, no. 2 (Apr. 2016): 27–60.

———. *A Generation Removed: The Fostering and Adoption of Indigenous Children in the Postwar World.* Lincoln: University of Nebraska Press, 2014.

———. "Getting out of a Rut: Decolonizing Western Women's History." *Pacific Historical Review* 79, no. 4 (Nov. 2010): 585–604.

———. *White Mother to a Dark Race: Settler Colonialism, Maternalism, and the Removal of Indigenous Children in the American West and Australia, 1880–1940.* Lincoln: University of Nebraska Press, 2009.

Jagodinsky, Katrina. "'In a Family Way': Guarding Indigenous Women's Children in Washington Territory." *American Indian Quarterly* 37, no. 1–2 (Winter–Spring 2013): 160–77.

———. "A Tale of Two Sisters: Family Histories from the Strait Salish Borderlands." *The Western Historical* Quarterly 47 (Spring 2016): 27–49.

James, Elizabeth. "'Hardly a Family is Free from the Disease': Tuberculosis, Health Care, and Assimilation Policy on the Nez Perce Reservation, 1908–1942." *Oregon Historical Quarterly*, 112, no. 2 (Summer 2011): 142–69.

Jobe, Margaret M. "Native Americans and the U.S. Census: A Brief Historical Survey." *Journal of Government Information* 30 (2004): 66–80.

Johnson, Jacqueline. *Western College for Women.* Mount Pleasant, S.C.: Arcadia Publishing.

Kane, Lucile M. "The Sioux Treaties and the Traders." *Minnesota History* 32, no. 2 (June 1951): 65–80.

Kidwell, Clara Sue. "Review: *The Encyclopedia of Native American Biography: Six Hundred Life Stories of Important People, from Powhatan to Wilma Mankiller.*" *The Journal of American History*, 84, no. 3 (Dec. 1997): 1026.

Kugel, Rebecca and Lucy Eldersveld Murphy, eds. *Native Women's History in Eastern North American Before 1900: A Guide to Researching and Writing.* Lincoln: University of Nebraska Press, 2007.

Lahti, Janne. "Colonized Labor: Apaches and Pawnees as Army Workers." *Western Historical Quarterly* 39, no. 3 (Autumn 2008): 261–81.

Lansing, Michael. "Plains Indian Women and Interracial Marriage in the Upper Missouri Trade, 1804–1868." *Western Historical Quarterly*, 31, no. 4 (Winter 2000): 413–33.

Lewandowski, Tadeusz. *Red Bird, Red Power: The Life and Legacy of Zitkala-Ša.* Norman: University of Oklahoma Press, 2016.

Littlefield, Daniel Jr. and James W. Parins. *A Biobibliography of Native*

American Writers 1772–1924: A Supplement. Metuchen, N.J.: The Scarecrow Press, Inc., 1985.

Lomawaima, K. Tsianina. *They Called it Prairie Light: The Story of Chilocco Indian School.* Lincoln: University of Nebraska Press, 1995.

Mangan, Patricia Hart. "Instantiating Vision at the Mount Holyoke Female Seminary." *Journal of Religious History* 40, no. 1 (Mar. 2016): 104–31.

Martínez, David. *Life of the Indigenous Mind: Vine Deloria Jr. and the Birth of the Red Power Movement.* Lincoln: University of Nebraska Press, 2019.

Meyer, Roy W. *History of the Santee Sioux: United States Indian Policy on Trial.* Lincoln: University of Nebraska Press, 1993.

McMillen, Christian W. "'The Red Man and the White Plague': Rethinking Race, Tuberculosis, and American Indians, ca. 1890–1950." *Bulletin of the History of Medicine* 82, no. 3 (Fall 2008): 608–45.

Millikan, William. "The Great Treasure of the Fort Snelling Prison Camp." *Minnesota History* 62, no. 1 (Spring 2010): 4–17.

Neylan, Susan. *The Heavens are Changing: Nineteenth-Century Protestant Missions and Tsimshian Christianity*. Montreal: McGill-Queen's Press, 2003.

Nichols, David A. "The Other Civil War: Lincoln and the Indians," *Minnesota History* 44, no. 1 (Spring 1974): 3–15.

Nute, Grace Lee. "Hudson's Bay Company Posts in the Minnesota Country." *Minnesota History* (1941): 270–89.

Pawling, Micah A. "A 'Labyrinth of Uncertainties': Penobscot River Islands, Land Assignments, and Indigenous Women Proprietors in Nineteenth-Century Maine." *American Indian Quarterly* 42, no. 4 (Fall 2018): 454–87.

Peacock, John. "An Account of the Dakota–US War as Sacred Text." *American Indian Culture and Research Journal* 37, no. 2 (2013): 185–206.

Perdue, Theda. *"Mixed Blood" Indians: Racial Construction in the Early South.* Athens: University of Georgia Press, 2005.

Peterson, Dawn. *Indians in the Family: Adoption and the Politics of Antebellum Expansion*. Cambridge: Harvard University Press, 2017.

Peyer, Bernd C. *The Tutor'd Mind: Indian Missionary-Writers in Antebellum America*. Amherst: University of Massachusetts Press, 1997.

Porterfield, Amanda. *Mary Lyon and the Mount Holyoke Missionaries.* New York: Oxford University Press, 1997.

Powers, William. *Sacred Language: The Nature of Supernatural Discourse in Lakota.* Norman: University of Oklahoma Press, 1986.

Price, Catherine. "Lakotas and Euroamericans: Contrasted Concepts of 'Chieftainship' and Decision-Making Authority." *Ethnohistory* 41, no. 3 (Summer 1994): 447–63.

Pruitt, Lisa Joy. *A Looking Glass for Ladies: American Protestant Women and the Orient in the Nineteenth Century*. Macon, Ga.: Mercer University Press, 2005.

Ramirez, Renya K. *Standing Up to Colonial Power: The Lives of Henry Roe and Elizabeth Bender Cloud.* Lincoln: University of Nebraska Press, 2018.

Ress, David. *The Half Breed Tracts in Early National America: Changing Concepts of Land and Place.* Palgrave, Macmillan, 2019.

Robinson, Doane. "A Comprehensive History of the Dakota or Sioux Indians." *South Dakota Historical Collections* vol. 2 (1904).

Rosen, Deborah A. "Women and Property across Colonial America: A Comparison of Legal Systems in New Mexico and New York." *The William and Mary Quarterly* 60, no. 2 (Apr. 2003): 355–81.

Routel, Colette. "Minnesota Bounties on Dakota Men During the U.S.-Dakota War." *William Mitchell Law Review* 40, no. 1 (2013): 1–77.

Sandefur, G. D., R.R. Rindfus, and B. Cohen, eds. *Changing Numbers, Changing Needs: American Indian Demography and Public Health.* Washington D.C.: National Academies Press, 1996, https://www.ncbi.nlm.nih.gov/books/NBK233091/#ddd00115.

Sarlos, Beatrice. "Noble Savage to Indian Fairy: An Analysis of 19th Century Schoolbook Illustrations of Native Americans." *Internationale Schulbuchforschung* 16, no. 4 (1994): 397–422.

Sheehan, Bernard W. *Seeds of Extinction: Jeffersonian Philanthropy and the American Indian.* Chapel Hill: The University of North Carolina Press, 1973.

Shoemaker, Nancy. "Native-American Women in History." *OAH Magazine of History* 9, no. 4 (Summer 1995): 10–14.

Smits, David. "'Squaw Men,' 'Half-Breeds,' and Amalgamators: Late Nineteenth-Century Anglo-American Attitudes Toward Indian-White Race-Mixing." *American Indian Culture and Research Journal* 15, no. 3 (1991): 29–61.

Spector, Janet D. *What This Awl Means: Feminist Archaeology at a Wahpeton Dakota Village*. St. Paul: Minnesota Historical Society Press, 1993.

Spence, Taylor. "Naming Violence in United States Colonialism." *Journal of Social History* 53, no. 1 (Fall 2019): 157–93.

Stanton, William. *The Leopard's Spots: Scientific Attitudes Toward Race in America 1815–59*. Chicago: The University of Chicago Press, 1960.

St-Onge, Nicole. "Familial Foes? French-Sioux Families and Plains Métis Brigades in the Nineteenth Century." *American Indian Quarterly* 39, no. 3 (Summer 2015): 302–37.

Sterling, Everett W. "Moses N. Adams: A Missionary as Indian Agent." *Minnesota History* 35, no. 4 (Dec. 1956): 167–77.

Strong, Pauline Turner and Barrike Van Winkle. "'Indian Blood': Reflections on the Reckoning and Refiguring of Native North American Identity." *Cultural Anthropology* 11, no. 4 (Nov. 1996): 547–76.

Sweet, Jameson. "Native Suffrage: Race, Citizenship, and Dakota Indians in the Upper Midwest." *Journal of the Early Republic* 39, no. 1 (Spring 2019): 99–109.

Sweet, Leonard I. "The Female Seminary Movement and Woman's Mission in Antebellum America." *Church History* 54, no. 1 (Mar. 1985): 41–55.

Takaki, Ronald T. *Iron Cages: Race and Culture in 19th-Century America.* New York: Alfred A. Knopf, 1979.

TallBear, Kimberly. "DNA, Blood, and Racializing the Tribe." *Wicazo Sa Review* 18, no. 1 (Spring 2003): 81–107.

Valandra, Edward. "The As-Told-To Native [Auto]biography: Whose Voice is Speaking?" *Wicazo Sa Review* 20, no. 2 (Autumn 2005): 103–19.

Vaughan, Alden T. *Roots of American Racism: Essays on the Colonial Experience.* New York: Oxford University Press, 1995.

Waggoner, Linda M. *Starring Red Wing! The Incredible Career of Lilian M. St. Cyr, the First Native American Film Star.* Lincoln: University of Nebraska Press, 2019.

Wahuta, Elissa. "I Will Write a Bestselling Native American Biography." *Black Warrior Review* 43, no. 1 (Fall–Winter 2016): 152–53.

Ware, Susan. "Writing Women's Lives: One Historian's Perspective." *The Journal of Interdisciplinary History* 40, no. 3 (Winter 2010): 413–35.

Waziyatawin. "*Colonial Calibrations*: The Expendability of Minnesota's Original People." *William Mitchell Law Review* 39, no. 2 (2013): 450–85.

———. *What Does Justice Look Like? The Struggle for Liberation in Dakota Homeland.* St. Paul, Minn.: Living Justice Press, 2008.

Waziyatawin Angela Wilson, ed. *In the Footsteps of Our Ancestors: The Dakota Commemorative Marches of the 21st Century.* St. Paul, Minn.: Living Justice Press, 2006.

Westerman, Gwen and Bruce White. *Mni Sota Makoce.* St. Paul: Minnesota Historical Society Press, 2012.

Whelan, Mary K. "Dakota Indian Economics and the Nineteenth-Century Fur Trade." *Ethnohistory* 40, no. 2 (Spring 1993): 246–76.

Willand, Jon. *Lac qui Parle and the Dakota Mission.* Madison, MN: Lac qui Parle Historical Society, 1964.

Williams, Carol, ed. *Indigenous Women and Work: From Labor to Activism.* Urbana: University of Illinois Press, 2012.

ACKNOWLEDGMENTS

Over the course of writing this book, I accumulated an extensive list of institutions and people I would like to thank. Illinois State University provided financial support through two awards: a Faculty Research Award and a Summer Faculty Fellowship. Many archives across the country provided access to their collections. I would specifically like to thank the librarians and staff at the Minnesota Historical Society Library in St. Paul, Minnesota; the Center for Western Studies at Augustana University in Sioux Falls, South Dakota; and Wheaton College in Wheaton, Illinois. Josh Layden from Milner Library at Illinois State University ordered many reels of microfilm for me. While I fortunately was able to visit archives after they reopened, I conducted much of my research for this book online during the long COVID-19 shutdown. A special thanks to all the archives with digitized census records, newspapers, and other primary sources that made my long-distance research possible.

Numerous colleagues assisted me with this project. I would specifically like to thank Kyle Ciani for talking me through numerous points during the research and writing process. Ross Kennedy, chair of the Illinois State University History Department, was especially supportive of my work. The critiques of anonymous readers helped me to improve and strengthen the overall book project. This book would not have happened without the support and guidance of the staff of the South Dakota Historical Society Press. Of course, any mistakes are entirely my own.

This book also benefitted immeasurably from the help of Mr. Louis Garcia, who translated several articles and letters for me from Dakota into English. Several historians graciously sent me various sources, especially Dr. Jameson Sweet, who shared his vast collection of Dakota language letters, documents, and land and probate records. Dr. Susanna Lee also sent me invaluable links to missionary articles. My fellow panel members at the SHEAR 2021 Conference—Jameson Sweet, Gwen Westerman, and John Legg—helped sharpen my arguments. Finally, I would like to thank my husband, Bill Jackson, my three children, Charlie, Sam, and Ellie, and my mother, Margaret Clemmons, for all for their love, patience, and support throughout this project.

INDEX